Praise for this book

Bringing together a chorus of therapeutic vo
Psychology provides a wealth of challenging id..., ...
critiques. If you had any doubts as to the continuing significance and
influence of Humanistic Psychology, prepare to have them allayed. An
important – even vital – book not only for Humanistic Psychology but for the
future direction of psychology as a whole.

> Professor Ernesto Spinelli, author, *Demystifying Therapy; Practising Existential Psychotherapy: The relational world*

At a time of dire worldwide economic and ecological crisis newly trained
counsellors and psychotherapists must respond sensitively to the claims
of widening cultural diversity, but at the same time keep their feet on the
ground in the face of the inflexibilities of state-approved therapy and its
daunting acronyms (EBP, NICE and IAPT etc.). Humanistic Psychology
emerged five decades ago in response to a rather different kind of crisis –
narrow academicism in behavioural psychology coupled with over-abstract
intellectualism in psychoanalysis. With greater pluralism and both a
relational and a contemplative turn these two traditions have responded
to the needs of our time. Can Humanistic Psychology similarly reach out
beyond its traditional, somewhat scattergun, oppositional stance and engage
with the mainstream? In short, can it provide a robust and reliable roadmap
for a new generation? This book is key in revitalizing an undervalued
tradition.

> Arthur Musgrave belongs to Western Valleys, a Member Group of the Independent Practitioners Network

With an all-star cast of authors, this book provides a thought-provoking
examination of the present state and future of Humanistic Psychology. It
raises important questions about what Humanistic Psychology still has to
offer society, what it should become, and what paths it needs to follow in the
future. The book touches on all the important topics that make Humanistic
Psychology unique, from creativity to Positive Psychology to psychotherapy,
to the important question of whether Humanistic Psychology needs to make
sure it never gets co-opted into the middle but always remains a rebel voice.
A profoundly important book.

> Arthur Bohart, Professor Emeritus, California State University Dominguez Hills, co-author of *How Clients Make Therapy Work: The process of active self-healing*

The Future of Humanistic Psychology

edited by

Richard House, David Kalisch & Jennifer Maidman

PCCS BOOKS
Ross-on-Wye

First published, 2013

PCCS BOOKS Ltd
2 Cropper Row
Alton Road
Ross-on-Wye
Herefordshire
HR9 5LA
UK
Tel +44 (0)1989 763900
www.pccs-books.co.uk

This collection © Richard House, David Kalisch and Jennifer Maidman, 2013

The individual chapters © the authors, 2013

All rights reserved.

No part of this publication may be reproduced, stored in a retrieval system, transmitted or utilised in any form by any means, electronic, mechanical, photocopying or recording or otherwise without permission in writing from the publishers.

The authors has asserted her right to be identified as the authors of this work in accordance with the Copyright, Designs and Patents Act 1988.

The Future of Humanistic Psychology

A CIP catalogue record for this book is available from the British Library

ISBN 978 1 906254 65 0

Cover designed in the UK by Old Dog Graphics
Printed in the UK by ImprintDigital, Exeter

Contents

Acknowledgements — vii

Foreword: ANDREW SAMUELS — ix

Editorial Introduction: JENNIFER MAIDMAN, DAVID KALISCH AND RICHARD HOUSE — xv

PART I: CONTEXTS

1. COLIN FELTHAM: The Past and Future of Humanistic Psychology — 3
2. LOUIS HOFFMAN, RUTH RICHARDS AND STEVEN PRITZKER: Creativity in the Evolution of Humanistic Psychology — 8
3. HARRIS L. FRIEDMAN: Reconciling Humanistic and Positive Psychology: Bridging the cultural rift — 17
4. STANLEY KRIPPNER AND DANIEL B. PITCHFORD: Future Opportunities for Humanistic Psychology — 23
5. LOIS HOLZMAN: The Development Community and Its Activist Psychology — 29
6. DEREK LAWTON AND SEAMUS NASH: The State of Humanistic Psychology: Where all monkeys are apes but not all apes are monkeys — 43
7. ANDY ROGERS: Absence and Presence – Carl Rogers in 2013 — 62

PART II: EXISTENTIAL, TRANSPERSONAL AND POSTMODERN PERSPECTIVES

8. KIRK J. SCHNEIDER: Humanistic Psychology's Chief Task: To reset psychology on its rightful existential-humanistic base — 73
9. HEWARD WILKINSON: Humanism, Tragedy, and Humanistic Psychotherapy's Potential as the Destiny of Psychotherapy — 77
10. JAMES T. HANSEN: The Future of Humanism: Cultivating the humanities impulse in mental health culture — 86

11.	CAROLINE BRAZIER: Creating Space: The future of Humanistic Psychology	93
12.	JOHN ROWAN: Directions for Humanistic Psychology	98
13.	ALEXANDRA CHALFONT: An Accidental Affiliation	101
14.	ROBIN SHOHET: On the Future of Humanistic Psychology: Possible avenues for exploration	107

PART III: FUTURE PROSPECTS

15.	NICK TOTTON: The Future of Humanistic Therapy	111
16.	WINDY DRYDEN: Humanistic Psychology: Possible ways forward	119
17.	DINA GLOUBERMAN: Humanistic Psychology: How it was and how it may be	125
18.	GAIE HOUSTON: The Future of Humanistic Psychology	131
19.	KEITH TUDOR: From Humanism to Humanistic Psychology and Back Again	136
20.	JILL HALL: Humanistic Psychology and the Evolution of Consciousness	149
21.	JOHN HERON: Humanism: The fourth wave	156

Editorial Conclusion: RICHARD HOUSE, DAVID KALISCH AND JENNIFER MAIDMAN	169
Afterword: MAUREEN O'HARA	177
Contributors	179
Index	187

Acknowledgements

The chapters in this book have been specially written for this volume, excepting the following which come from *Self & Society: International Journal for Humanistic Psychology:*

Chapter 1 first appeared in *Self & Society*, 40 (1), 2012, pp. 7–9

Chapter 2 first appeared in *Self & Society*, 40 (1), 2012, pp. 10–15

Chapter 3 first appeared in *Self & Society*, 40 (2), 2013, pp. 21–5

Chapter 4 – an earlier version of this chapter first appeared in *Self & Society*, 40 (3), 2013, pp. 37–9

Chapter 10 first appeared in *Self & Society*, 40 (1), 2012, pp. 21–5

Chapter 11 first appeared in *Self & Society*, 40 (3), 2013, pp. 34–6

Chapter 12 first appeared in *Self & Society*, 40 (3), 2013, pp. 40–1

Chapter 14 first appeared in *Self & Society*, 40 (1), 2012, pp. 30–1

Chapter 15 first appeared in *Self & Society*, 40 (1), 2012, pp. 16–20

Chapter 16 first appeared in *Self & Society*, 40 (1), 2012, pp. 26–9

Chapter 17 first appeared in *Self & Society*, 40 (2), 2013, pp. 18–20

Chapter 18 first appeared in *Self & Society*, 40 (2), 2013, pp. 26–30

Chapter 20 first appeared in *Self & Society*, 40 (4), 2013, pp. 53–7

Warm thanks to the authors, and to *Self & Society* journal, for permission to reproduce the above-listed chapters in this volume.

We dedicate this book to the founders of Humanistic Psychology.

Foreword

Andrew Samuels

Only in the therapy field could a celebratory book carry so many anxieties! But what's wrong with that? After reading the chapters of this book, I felt I had a pretty good idea of what was on people's minds, and this Foreword is both my digestion of those concerns and a critical discussion of them. What I write is informed by my personal history in connection with Humanistic Psychology and a set of parallel concerns in my own professional community (I am a Jungian analyst). I will return to these aspects later. Then there's a lifetime of involvement in the professional politics and 'cut and thrust' of theory-making in the psychological field. Finally, I developed a huge respect for the admixture of rigour and passion to be found in these pages, which I hope comes through in what follows.

First, let's look at the context that contributed to the content of the book as well as being the public space into which it enters. In the United States and Britain, with resonances in other Western countries, a full-scale war has broken out regarding emotional distress (and 'illness'): how we talk about it, whether we try to measure it or not, and – crucially – what we do about it. Behind this battle for ownership of the soul lies contemporary culture's profound ambivalence regarding psychotherapy and counselling. Many countries have now opted for what they believe to be a quick and effective form of therapy, cognitive behaviour therapy (CBT), which, proponents say, has been scientifically measured to have proven effects in relation to sufferers of anxiety and depression.

But if you read my last sentence again, you will see just below its surface the main grounds upon which the war is being fought. Are there really separate illnesses or diseases called 'anxiety' and 'depression'? No one in the field seriously believes that, hence the coinage 'co-morbidity'. And whether or not you can measure either the illness or the cure is such a hot topic that it will be keeping university philosophy of science departments busy for years. Is there such a thing as an 'effective' therapy? Don't people keep coming back?

Recently, a further front opened up in connection with the fifth version of the *Diagnostic and Statistical Manual of Mental Disorders* of the American Psychiatric Association (or *DSM-5*). Many established professional bodies are concerned that 'the psychiatrists' bible' adopts an over-easy pathologization of what are really ordinary – if difficult and painful – human experiences such as grief. Others have protested that *DSM-5* isn't scientific enough, failing to consider genetic determinants of mental illness. At the time of writing it seems that the DSM psychiatrists have seen off the opposition. What is your problem, they say, with taking a systematic approach to mental illness? How can that fail to help? The media agreed.

But will they actually win? The stock-in-trade of psychiatry remains drug treatments and, recently, a series of books and scholarly papers have appeared (notably Irving Kirsch's *The Emperor's New Drugs: Exploding the Antidepressant Myth*) that cast doubt on the reliability of the research that seems to support such treatments. Kirsch's point is that the methodology that underpins such research – randomized controlled trials (RCTs) – is liable to many kinds of distortion. For example, if a patient is given a placebo with a mild irritant in it, she/he will assume they have been given the actual drug being trialled (all drugs have side effects, don't they?) and Hey Presto! – they get better.

In Britain, there is great interest now in discussing the pros and cons of RCTs because they are used to ration therapy on the British National Health Service (NHS). Well-established approaches, such as humanistic, integrative, family systemic and psychodynamic, are vanishing from the NHS. Either CBT, or a watered-down version of it that I call 'state therapy', get the funding. This has led some to say that we should do RCTs of our own.

Others point to the fact that there is a huge amount of *non-RCT* evidence for the efficacy of psychotherapy and counselling. But the government agency that draws up guidelines for treatments on the NHS does not recognize the methodologies that underpin this research. At times, this National Institute for Health and Care Excellence (NICE) does seem to have been captured by the proponents of RCTs and – due to the way in which it has been researched via RCTs – CBT. The Department of Health claims that NICE is beyond its control, which has left many observers gobsmacked. Still others, notably my old friend John Rowan, say it is all pointless.

To say that nothing in this 'battle for the soul' is encouraging to the future prospects of Humanistic Psychology is to understate the position. But people and groups respond to challenges, and that is one way to understand the rationale and purpose of this book.

Humanistic Psychology has, traditionally, eschewed many of the features of other traditions within psychotherapy. It has not valorized theory. It has not sought to adopt a highly professional persona or set of personae. It has not attempted to align itself with the social 'now' and with the powerful. Maybe this went too far, and a humanistic therapist caricature can easily be imagined. But the key problem is how to fix the problems with the easy-going approach without getting into what Heraclitus called an *enantiodromia* – a total swing from one extreme position to the polar opposite. In this swing to do research, work out more theory and seek professional acceptance, Humanistic Psychology – to put it in a nutshell – wants the prizes it sees others as having, and adopts the tactics and tropes it understands – rightly or wrongly – these other groups as having adopted. Hence the 'purity' of the humanistic approaches might be lost. I actually think that this is a legitimate concern. Enantiodromias lead to totalizing outcomes.

But I am equally worried that adherence to an ideal of so-called 'pluralism' will be deployed to justify these innovations in the direction of greater acceptance, *aka* 'integration'. Pluralism does not simply mean 'the Many' or many new add-ons. Rather, pluralism, in all serious uses of the term, means *the relations between the One and the Many*. For Humanistic Psychology, that would mean not just reaching out to other ways of doing things, but, rather, holding the tension between there being One humanistic way of doing things and there being Many ways.

Most of the authors in the book do agree that Humanistic Psychology needs to change (or has changed for better or, more usually, for worse), but they don't want to lose the good bits. Baby and bathwater .... What I'd like to do here is signpost a number of areas within Humanistic Psychology, not all of them written about herein, to see how the changes that people desire might come about – but in a spirit of what Walter Bagehot (the 19th century British parliamentarian) called 'animated moderation' rather than fuelled by Anna Freud's 'identification with the aggressor'.

I've selected the following areas for what will have to be a few quite informal comments: (i) clinical ethos, (ii) diversity and equalities, (iii) aggression, lust and other difficult emotions, (iv) the past in the present (trauma and resilience), (v) the body, (vi) social responsibility and engagement including ecopsychology, and (vii) spirituality.

Clinical ethos. 'It's the relationship, stupid!' was recently seriously suggested as a slogan to advertize psychotherapy. Humanistic Psychology and psychotherapy can be seen as more than incidental precursors of what the pioneering relational psychoanalyst Stephen Mitchell called 'the relational turn' in psychotherapy. Naturally, as one who has become institutionally involved in relational psychoanalysis, I think that the psychoanalytic bit does offer some added value, especially when it comes to the algebraic intricacies of intersubjectivity. But the fact remains: unconditional positive regard (and, crucially, the perception of it by the client) and authentic relating have played an identifiable role in breaking the ground for these developments in psychoanalysis. Taking the field as a whole, I think it is reasonable to say that humanistic psychotherapists are *the* experts in the therapy relationship – and maybe in the therapeutic/working alliance as well. I must add that to achieve this, they have had to learn from relational psychoanalysis with regard to therapist self-disclosure, acknowledgement (of therapist mistakes) and enactments. It's a good example of cross-fertilization.

Diversity and equalities. I didn't find enough meaty attention in the book to questions of inclusivity and exclusivity in the field. It is not enough to say that 'we are not homophobic' or that Humanistic Psychology (like the Ritz Hotel) is open to all. Nor is it enough to claim that many humanistic trainings are in the vanguard when it comes to diversity and equalities. There is still a problem concerning who gets therapy and who gets to train as a therapist. What is needed is a raft of strategies and educational approaches applied systematically over time, making use of the expertise that already exists. Only then will we stop reading that 'the client was a 47-year-old Lesbian', or hearing a therapist say that she has immersed herself in the culture of a particular client and so understands where they are coming from.

Aggression, lust and other difficult emotions. For some, the positive and life-affirming nature of Humanistic Psychology is its strong point (and they can quite easily distinguish this from Positive Psychology). But for years now people have wondered whether the impression that humanistic therapists don't 'do' aggression is accurate. Do they always look on the bright side of life? I would argue (as would many, I think) that aggression, and even destructiveness, is a crucial part of self-actualization. As to sexual behaviour, my perception is that many aspects of what sexual minorities do tends to produce a moralistic response in a substantial number of humanistic practitioners (and probably other psychotherapists as well). For example, many are all at sea when confronted by promiscuity and infidelity in their clinical work, and tend to be rather conventional (and hence inadvertently condemning) in response.

The past in the present (trauma and resilience). The job is to allow for the influence of the past on the present without indulging in parent bashing and evading personal responsibility, isn't it? And, concerning trauma and abuse, to find ways to move forward, based on facilitating the client's resilient capacities. Terms like post-traumatic growth and adversity-activated development are still foreign to most psychoanalytically oriented practitioners. Yet they seem to be congruent with most of the core values of humanistic psychotherapy.

The body. This is a highly personal view, but I am no longer persuaded that to consider the body in its imaginary or imaginal sense (the 'subtle body') is a good-enough perspective for a clinician. The actual, sweaty, fleshy body is there, in the relationship, in the room, and those therapists that know how to touch the client's body, or how to set it in motion, have much to teach others. And closely allied to body is *imagination,* which means that one path for future evolution is to strengthen and enhance the relationships between humanistic psychotherapy and all the arts therapies. It's no accident that Natalie Rogers is such an influential figure in the creative arts therapies.

Social responsibility and engagement, including ecopsychology. Humanistic Psychology has been at the forefront of using 'therapy thinking' in social contexts and in contributing to deeper understandings of how it is that Western, capitalistic societies contribute to a suppression of human potential. More recently, developments in ecopsychology have emerged from within the humanistic (and other) traditions. These ideas are directly clinically relevant. Clients are irradiated with their negative experiences of living on a despoiled planet. However, the very term 'humanistic' might present some problems when the project of ecopsychology is specifically to go beyond human concerns to take in the non-human world of animals, plants, seas and earth. I don't think this problem should be finessed in too facile a manner.

Spirituality. There is a place within humanism for the spiritual, and, I would suggest, for a religious attitude. Spirituality is also about persons – Jung said 'the mysteries of life are always hidden between Two' and 'the soul is the very essence of relationship'. There's something I call 'social spirituality' as well. People come together in groups to achieve something in the social world, and a kind of spiritual dew descends on them, transforming what they do from being only a social movement into something concerned with the great spiritual-existential issues of meaning and purpose. Recent developments in transpersonal psychology are not only inspiring in themselves. Once again, we see how clinically vital they are. What brings two people (therapist and client) into such close psychological proximity that their hearts, minds and psyches inter-penetrate, thus helping the therapy along – if not their transpersonal connection?

I'll conclude the Foreword to this epic book by delivering on my promise to talk about my personal involvements, and bring in some parallels from the experiences of the Jungian community.

Back in the early 1970s, I was in training to be an encounter group conductor and a Jungian analyst – at the same time! I chose the Jungian route because of my intense personal need to bring my troubles to a protected setting where I was the only 'client'. But I kept up my interests in Humanistic Psychology and psychotherapy, as you can see from my biography in the book. In 2014, I am organizing (with others) a conference on the relationships between Jungian analysis and humanistic psychotherapy. We want to call it 'Beyond the two Carls', to use Brian Thorne's celebrated phrase. It's never too late to heal a split, I guess.

Jungians have struggled with professionalization. In the old days, you became a Jungian analyst if Jung agreed you were one. I think we have lost something with the growth of all the accoutrements of a profession such as rules and regulations about training. Nevertheless, Jungian psychology does resemble Humanistic Psychology in that there is more to it than the actual practice of therapy and analysis. Notably, there are the 'Jung Clubs' which are open to all, rather like the Association for Humanistic Psychology.

Jungians also have grievances that they have been overlooked in their prescience. For example, Jung saw that the mother was being neglected in Freudian psychoanalysis and so sought to rectify this – decades before Klein, Winnicott and object relations. We – the Jungians – don't know whether to go on complaining about this or not. Humanistic psychotherapists and psychologists have the same problem.

I'll return at the last to the book as a whole. Here is a field in ferment, assailed by self-doubt yet proud of past attainments. The editors and the contributors have produced what diplomats call a *tour d'horizon*, a survey that does not pretend to be neutral or cohesive, is not predictive or admonishing – yet will inspire discussion and debate for many years to come.

Editorial Introduction

Jennifer Maidman, David Kalisch and Richard House

Humanistic Psychology, like any cultural phenomenon, did not emerge from, or evolve in, a vacuum. It must be seen in its broader socio-historical context. It has been some 50 years since the humanistic 'brand' first entered the cultural mainstream in the United States, where it was widely hailed as a 'third force' to counterbalance the alleged reductionism of the behaviourists and the supposedly pessimistic outlook of psychoanalysis. Its optimistic ethos and emphasis on human potential, rather than upon deficiency, suited the 1960's *Zeitgeist* perfectly and, for a while at least, it went from strength to strength. Yet here we are in 2013 when, despite considerable propagation of humanistic *ideas* into the wider society, the humanistic approach, within both psychology and within the psychological therapies, seems to have a definite visibility problem. Has something gone wrong, or was this always the inevitable outcome for an approach whose common ground rested largely on shared values and attitudes, rather than on a single theoretical doctrine?

After the carnage and atrocities of the Second World War, there had been not only a widespread desire for a more equal society, but also a thirst for a deeper understanding of human nature. Humanistic psychologists such as Rollo May, Abraham Maslow, Carl Rogers and Eric Berne became virtual celebrities in their time, and the movement they founded began to recast psychology and therapy in more democratic terms, as something which could be 'all things to all people', and which no longer needed to be considered as lying purely in the realm of experts (e.g. Mair, 2011). To 'know oneself' was no longer to be the preserve of a few – anyone could have a go. This was indeed revolutionary stuff. You didn't have to be 'neurotic' or 'broken' to seek therapy, which came increasingly to be seen as more to do with self-discovery and healing society's problems from the inside out, rather than simply 'curing' an individual's psychological dis(-)ease. The emphasis was on autonomy, taking personal responsibility for oneself, and being fully alive in the moment. Carl Rogers went on to question whether 'professionals' were even needed any more in his seminal lecture on the helping professions, in which Rogers had a telling section entitled, 'Dare we do away with professionalism?' (Rogers, 1973; see also *Self & Society*, 2013b). Tellingly, his profound question still remains largely unanswered; and sadly, in our view, the pendulum seems in recent years to have swung back towards both the 'professionalization of helping' and a psychiatrically oriented, pathology-based model of human functioning. Therapy these days, at least in the mainstream, is once again for those who are seen as sick or deficient in some way. As we put it in the title of a recent theme issue of the *Self & Society* journal which we co-edit, 'Welcome to the paradigm war' (*Self & Society*, 2013a).

Still, back then Humanistic Psychology seemed, for a while at least, to be an unstoppable force which found common cause with other cultural movements of the time. Well-known therapists appeared on television, and popular therapy books such as Berne's *Games People Play* (1964 – over 5 million copies sold to date) and Janov's *The Primal Scream* (1970) became bestsellers, with the latter being read by tens of thousands of Americans, thereby bringing Arthur Janov great popular success. The sheer scale of the movement around that time, in the USA and beyond, is staggering by today's standards, with Rowan (2004) reporting that the fifth European Association for Humanistic Psychology (EAHP) Congress in Rome in 1981 attracted some 500 participants, and with the sixth Congress, held in Paris, attracting 800 participants – only to be trumped by the March 1985 quarter-century celebration in San Francisco, which attracted a mega-gathering over one thousand strong (Rowan, 2004, pp. 231–3).

John Rowan also describes a number of other extraordinary events in the history of Humanistic Psychology. For example, there was the conference held in Easton, Maryland State in 1979, at which some 120 leading government officials from virtually every government department assembled for three days to explore the implications of humanistic values and practices for social change. (Perhaps it's no coincidence that this occurred during the presidency of arguably one of the most progressive presidents of recent decades, Jimmy Carter.) According to then AHP President, Jean Houston (quoted in Rowan, 2004, p. 229), 'We in the AHP were asked by a number of key officials to continue to assist and consult with their departments ... The *Washington Post* featured a long editorial applauding the conference.'

During the heady late 1960s, then, therapists and 'alternative' psychiatrists, like R.D. Laing, Thomas Szasz and Arthur Janov, became as much the spokespeople of the 'counter-culture' as were the hippy poets, rock stars and novelists, and the new 'celebrity' political philosophers such as Herbert Marcuse, Jean-Paul Sartre and Noam Chomsky. These were the days when Ronnie Laing questioned the very foundations of mainstream psychiatric thinking (routinely attracting hissing whenever his name was mentioned at orthodox psychiatry conferences), took LSD, did 'the India thing', and wrote poetry, with his *Politics of Experience and The Bird of Paradise* (1967) becoming a cult classic; and when Art Janov helped John Lennon exorcise his inner demons and make an album about the experience: the 1970 release, John Lennon/Plastic Ono Band.

Many of us post-war 'baby boomers' were instinctively drawn to the values of the humanistic approaches (we use the plural advisedly), and perhaps above all by the belief that they offered a route to greater *authenticity* (cf. Jackson, 2013). The desire to be *real* (as opposed to 'phony', to use one of Fritz Perls' favourite words), resonated deeply with the rock and roll generation, tired of what many saw as their parents' generation's 'uptight' artifice and sexual repression. Humanistic Psychology seemed like a major step in the right direction, towards the kind of egalitarian, person-centred, forward-looking world which many longed for, but conveniently, without any of the totalitarian conformity of state communism – still a force to be reckoned with back then – or having to engage too much with the frustrations, compromises and general 'square-ness' of mainstream politics. In a word, rather like Dylan and the Rolling Stones, for a while at least, Humanistic Psychology was *cool*.

Some say that the 1960s ended, not on the 1st January 1970, but on the 8th December 1980, when John Lennon was shot in New York. One of the editors of this book (JM) was actually in a therapy group at Art Janov's Primal Institute in Los Angeles, California that very night. It was a large group, of perhaps 40 people, many of whom, despite not knowing Lennon personally, spent the evening screaming and crying out in inconsolable shock, horror and disbelief. How could this have happened? Lennon was the man who had sung 'Imagine all the people, living life in peace' to the whole world, and whose work had actually brought many of us to this 'therapeutic Mecca' in the first place. How could this figurehead of the 'peaceful revolution' be shot in cold blood by a crazed gunman? Didn't our *humanistic* philosophy say that people were basically good? – that the human organism could be trusted, if we allowed its inherent wisdom to prevail? Ten years earlier, on the Plastic Ono Band album, Lennon had sung 'The dream is over' – and now it seemed as if it really was.

With hindsight, there's something about the feelings which exploded in the primal group that night which seems emblematic of the bewilderment and shattering of hopes and dreams that the 'Woodstock generation' would encounter again and again as the 1980s unfolded, and ruthless Darwinian market forces, given free rein by Friedman- and Hayek-inspired Reaganomics and Thatcherism, raged pretty much unfettered across the planet. 'Self-actualization', the Holy Grail of the early humanistic movement, also began to manifest a darker, shadowy side: self-obsession and an insatiable appetite for 'stuff' (see, for example, Lasch, 1979; Wallach and Wallach, 1983; Furedi, 2004). The advertising industry, never slow to jump on a trend, also co-opted the humanistic message of authenticity and freedom. Authenticity now became something that could be attributed to a product – 'It's the *real* thing'; and as the Coke Generation 'taught the world to sing in perfect harmony', the message was clear: self-liberation could now be achieved through conspicuous consumption – 'because you're worth it!' At the same time, much mainstream 'therapy', humanistic or otherwise, seemed gradually to be moving away from (perhaps it had little choice?) a 'human potential' model, and increasingly towards ministering to the emotional and spiritual wounds of those who had fallen by the wayside in what had become, despite the smokescreen of 'touchy-feely' messages, a fiercely competitive and sometimes soul-destroying culture.

Editorial Introduction

It is probably no coincidence that US President Barack Obama seized on a line from the old Temptations song 'Yes we can!' as a campaign slogan when he first ran for President. The phrase perfectly encapsulates the ethos of his own generation, now middle aged, whose by now somewhat tarnished hopes and dreams he sought to re-awaken and re-connect with. As Obama realized, that generation remains to quite a large extent, if perhaps more by instinct than overt affiliation, a *humanistic* generation, whose core belief is an affirming, 'Yes we can – we *can* change the world one person at a time, starting with *me*!'; and who still, despite everything, want to believe that a just, progressive society is a real possibility. In terms of age, all three of us editors are part of that idealistic generation which now finds itself taking stock and asking – despite the inequality, the wars, the fundamentalism, the rampant capitalism, the terrorism, the political corruption, and the other ills which continue to plague the human race – to what extent might those of us who have been drawn to humanistic ideas have succeeded in sowing the seeds of the humanistic dream? And is that dream still valid in current cultural-historical circumstances, or do we need a new one (or, at the very least, a realistically updated one)?

This brings us to the book you now have in your hands, which broadly seeks to answer the question, 'Where are we now?' *Has* Humanistic Psychology fulfilled some, or any, of its early promise and potential? Has it floundered along the way, and turned into something that its founders, amongst others, might fail to recognize, were they alive today?

What does its current condition, and the trajectory of its development over the past half century, suggest about its future – if indeed it has one? What are its distinctive achievements, if any; and what might it have surrendered or compromised in the process of becoming more respectable, 'professional' and mainstream?

This new collection of essays, developed from a series first published in *Self & Society*, the quarterly journal of the Association for Humanistic Psychology in Britain, and augmented for this book by a number of newly written contributions, seeks to reflect on these and related questions. In keeping with the international flavour of both *Self & Society* and of Humanistic Psychology itself, we have contributions from some of the leading figures in the field from the USA and Aotearoa New Zealand as well as from the UK.

One of the great paradoxes of the trajectory of Humanistic Psychology, especially but not exclusively in the UK, is that whilst counselling and psychotherapy have without question enjoyed a boom period of increased social acceptance (so much so that it is indeed as if Philip Rieff's *The Triumph of the Therapeutic* had finally come to pass – Rieff, 1966), and within that social trend there is little doubt that many if not most counsellors and psychotherapists espouse at least *some* humanistic values and practices, nevertheless, affiliation to overtly 'humanistic' professional organizations is everywhere either at a standstill, or on the wane. Why is this? Is there perhaps a failure of 'branding'? Does it even matter when many adherents of both the psychodynamic and cognitive behaviour approaches embrace core Humanistic Psychology values, such as the centrality of the therapeutic relationship and Carl Rogers' 'core conditions' of empathy, congruence and unconditional positive regard? Perhaps we should all be happy, given that 'imitation is the sincerest form of flattery'! With the importance of the late Dan Stern's 'present moment in psychotherapy' recognized (*aka* 'the here and now', Stern, 2004; Owens, 2013), notions of 'embodied presence' and the 'embodied mind' fast becoming ubiquitous (e.g. Corrigall et al., 2006), and awareness commercially repackaged as 'mindfulness' (e.g. Bazzano, 2013), is it perhaps time to at least celebrate these successes of influence, and to reframe Humanistic Psychology as a revolutionary movement that is now being so comprehensively absorbed into the mainstream that it will soon no longer have anything distinctive to offer in terms of its own differentiated 'brand'?

Putting this in another way, and as some argue in this collection: was the term 'humanistic' *always* going to be too broad an umbrella-term for its constituent parts? And perhaps, thinking more widely, what are the characteristics of, and is there still a place for, humanistic values in a psychology field dominated to a large extent by 'audit-mindedness' (e.g. Power, 1997; King and Moutsou, 2010) and 'bang for buck' in the delivery of services that are increasingly standardized into protocol-driven and (supposedly) 'evidence-based' 'treatments' (e.g. Marzillier, 2004; Holmes et al., 2006; Elkins, 2007)?

Some of the writers in these pages imply that humanistic values are essentially little more than a relic of the hedonistic and overly optimistic 1960's mind-set. However, there is a strong counter-argument, also made in these pages, that on the contrary, humanistic values may represent the clearest expression thus far, within the field of psychology at least, of that great, liberalizing swathe of ideas and sensibility called 'humanism' (broadly defined), and that those values remain the strongest bulwark that we have against the triumph of technocratic scientism, soulless materialism, and fascism. But if the latter is true, then is humanism itself still sufficiently relevant in the world of postmodernity – and if not, what adaptations must it make to be so?

However, it would be short sighted to pursue these questions at the philosophical level alone, and not to question also the influence of, to use the Gestalt term, 'field conditions' nearer to home – namely, the political and socio-economic considerations which have shaped the current-day form of Humanistic Psychology. Internecine conflicts at the very heart of some humanistic institutions (though of course they are by no means unique to humanistic institutions!) continue to have a significant impact. When a significant contingent of nominally 'humanistic' practitioners are unsure if they wish to actually call themselves 'humanistic', is it any surprise that collective affiliation to the humanistic 'brand' is under threat, at least in the United Kingdom? And there are many other factors at work here, such as the adoption of the term 'integrative' as an obfuscator of difference, the accelerating trend towards non-modality-based professional bodies, the influence of some training schools promoting a 'we-cover-everything' approach as a sales pitch in a competitive market – and of course the increasingly pervasive distorting effect of regulators and bureaucrats who often seem to perceive the therapy field as chaotic and risky, rather than diverse and creative (Totton, 2011). These kinds of influences can all too easily lead to the triumph of the anodyne at the expense of the genuinely liberating, and to a conceptual vacuum that allows a dominant discourse – based around a kind of sanitized, bland, vaguely pseudo-medical formula which appeals to the lowest common denominators of managerialism and consumerism – to prevail.

This in turn brings us to the reason for publishing the current collection of essays under the banner, 'The Future of Humanistic Psychology'. As the current editors of *Self & Society* journal, about to enter its 41st year of uninterrupted publication, we all agreed that we wanted to encourage something of a re-launch of 'Humanistic Psychology' as an umbrella term, and to unashamedly celebrate its distinctive achievements whilst at the same time fully acknowledging its many and formidable challenges. There will always be tensions within any field. At the risk of over-simplification, there is currently in the UK considerable debate taking place between, on the one hand, those who feel that humanistic approaches need to be more pragmatic and do whatever is expedient in order to further their penetration into the mainstream, and on the other, those who feel that humanistic values, if authentically expressed, must always and necessarily embody a strong counter-cultural, even revolutionary quality. You will find these arguments, and a great deal more, discussed and dissected with passion and intelligence in the pages of this book.

The book itself is divided into three parts. The first part, 'Contexts', focuses primarily on instances of Humanistic Psychology in current practice, including areas where Humanistic Psychology interfaces (not always easily) with other approaches.

In Chapter 1, *Colin Feltham* provides something of a historical overview of Humanistic Psychology and then goes on to develop a typically 'critical-friendly' but compellingly pungent critique, before considering how we might play to our strengths more in moving forward. In Chapter 2, Saybrook University's *Louis Hoffman, Ruth Richards* and *Steven Pritzker* take us into a celebration and reminder of one of Humanistic Psychology's key and unique strengths, namely its focus on creativity.

Continuing the US-based focus, in Chapter 3, *Harris Friedman* reminds UK-based humanistic practitioners that in the USA, it is perhaps Positive Psychology rather than CBT that may be stealing not only Humanistic Psychology's thunder, but also some of its clothes. Harris helpfully outlines a possible pathway towards a fruitful reconciliation.

In Chapter 4, *Stan Krippner* and *Dan Pitchford*, again from Saybrook, explore how effective Humanistic Psychology continues to be – given its emphasis on going at the client's pace and developing the therapeutic relationship – in working with trauma, at a time when various protocol-based 'treatments' are gaining ground. They discuss how humanistic practitioners can promote their approach with confidence in this area of therapeutic work.

Then in Chapter 5 *Lois Holzman* from New York gives us a truly inspiring account of what she and her colleagues (including the late Fred Newman) have been able to achieve on the ground through treating great thinkers and theories as raw material to be played with and moulded into something Lois calls a 'psychology of becoming'.

In Chapter 6, *Derek Lawton* and *Seamus Nash* change the focus again, back to the internal politics of some of the main humanistic organizations in the UK; and it is indeed a concerning tale of intrigue and power plays that they have to tell. We are aware that this piece is somewhat contentious and polemical, but we have included it in the book as we feel that it documents a recent and important instance of how Humanistic Psychology can be impacted by the wider field in which it is situated. The chapter is also perhaps an instance of the kind of paradigm 'war' that Andrew Samuels refers to in his Foreword, and by which Humanistic Psychology is as impacted as any other therapy modality or approach.

Finally to round off Part I, in Chapter 7 *Andy Rogers* writes compellingly on the continuing importance and relevance of one of the seminal figures of Humanistic Psychology, Carl Rogers, whilst also pointing up the poignancy of the paradox whereby the movement that Rogers never intended to create has arguably encased his own quiet revolution in its own straitjacket.

Part II of the book is entitled 'Existential, Transpersonal and Postmodern Perspectives', and in Chapter 8, *Kirk Schneider* calls for Humanistic Psychology to urgently 'reset' itself on its 'rightful existential–humanistic base' in order that it might maintain its relevance and usefulness for those whom it can benefit.

Next, in Chapter 9, comes *Heward Wilkinson*, who sees humanistic psychotherapy as potentially the natural destiny of therapy, if it can come to terms with the implications of its own conceptual ingredients and fully integrate what Heward calls 'the tragic dimension'.

Chapter 10 is by prominent US-based therapist and academic *James T. Hansen*. Jim looks at the future of *humanism*, and ways in which the values and impulses we associate with Humanistic Psychology can be encouraged and cultivated in mainstream 'mental health' culture.

In Chapter 11, *Caroline Brazier's* piece looks-head on at the future of Humanistic Psychology and how we can go about 'creating the space' for alternatives such as the Buddhist and 'other-centred' models to move alongside the humanistic approach. Despite the differences, Caroline does indeed see considerable common ground.

Chapter 12 is by leading British humanistic theorist and practitioner, *John Rowan*, currently co-chair of the Association for Humanistic Psychology in Britain (AHPB) and one of the key figures of Humanistic Psychology in the UK since the 1970s. John looks at future directions for our field, and suggests that perhaps at the moment it is more important that we start asking the right questions rather than looking for easy answers.

Chapter 13 is by John's co-chair at the AHPB, *Alexandra Chalfont*. In her chapter, Alexandra looks at some 'accidental affiliates' of Humanistic Psychology (as she calls them) – viz. artist Kaspar David Friedrich, academic psychologist Jordan B. Peterson and writer Franz Kafka. In tracking developments in Humanistic Psychology and finding parallel motifs in her own life (e.g. around Esalen, and her involvement with *Self & Society* journal), Alexandra advocates the loosening of what she sees as Humanistic Psychology's unbalanced attachment to individualism; relaxing its sometimes wholesale antipathy to scientific method; and allowing itself to 'continue *becoming* in a vital, bold and experimental undertaking'.

To conclude Part II, in Chapter 14 we have *Robin Shohet* discussing some of his own personal areas of interest, which he sees as part of the wider context for the future evolution of Humanistic Psychology: viz. forgiveness, shock, the future of the planet and the 'non-dual', transpersonal dimension most often associated with Eastern, mystical philosophies such as Buddhism.

In Part III, we finally look in detail at the all-important 'Future Prospects' for Humanistic Psychology. In Chapter 15, *Nick Totton*, a much-respected and listened-to 'critical friend' of Humanistic Psychology, explores a number of key questions, including the autonomous status of humanistic therapy, possible bridge-building between humanistic and other modalities, and possible improvements to humanistic therapy at both clinical and theoretical levels. Will humanistic therapy, Totton asks, increasingly conform to the mainstream, or will it reassert its core values?

Then in Chapter 16 we have a welcome contribution from another 'critical friend' of Humanistic Psychology, the prolific *Windy Dryden*, who addresses four tasks, serious attention to which, Windy believes, would significantly strengthen Humanistic Psychology: viz. an inventory of its strengths and weaknesses; the publishing of up-to-date texts on Humanistic Psychology; considering whether to align, or not, with recent pluralistic developments in the field; and the pursuing of what Windy calls an 'engagement with reality'.

In Chapter 17, founder of Skyros *Dina Glouberman* then offers us 'a feel of what it was like at that time' to be involved in Humanistic Psychology's early heady days, as a prelude to exploring some possibilities for ways forward in the field. Humanistic Psychology has inspired Dina to become 'what I am, both personally and professionally', e.g. in her work on imagery, or Imagework; and she implores us that 'we will never never succeed if we simply box ourselves up in old categories and old diagnoses', and to always 'challenge our own limits, to go beyond what we think is true, to that which we don't yet know'.

Then in Chapter 18, much-respected elder of the British Humanistic Psychology and Gestalt therapy movements, *Gaie Houston*, argues for a kind of 'updating' of Humanistic Psychology, urging the importance of integrating neuroscience, anthropology, political science, and every other related discipline, into 'a co-operative endeavour towards creating the psychological conditions most conducive to community, creativity and sense of fulfilment'. Uneasy with how spirituality is sometimes privileged, Gaie wants education to be co-operative, learning- rather than teaching-focused, and to foreground the importance of groups of every size.

In Chapter 19, *Keith Tudor* reviews the origins of Humanistic Psychology, challenging the conventional view that it ('merely') represents a 'third force' in psychology. Keith argues for practitioners who identify as 'humanistic' returning to principles and theories of humanism that undergird diverse psychological and therapeutic practice – including working with unconscious as well as conscious material, with the dynamics of the psyche, and both cognitively and behaviourally. He provocatively concludes, 'As a third force, "Humanistic Psychology" is dead; long live humanism!'

In our penultimate Chapter 20, *Jill Hall* takes the conversation to the level of human consciousness evolution, arguing passionately that Humanistic Psychology needs to remember its roots if it is to play a central role, as new insecurities emerge amidst current cultural uncertainty and transitions. Jill argues against us being dragged backwards by the energy of contraction, and against giving way to fear of exclusion from controlling but limiting bodies – neither reacting nor capitulating to the disheartening backsliding which so often occurs within the underlying evolutionary expansion of human consciousness.

Finally, in Chapter 21, a key figure in the history and development of Humanistic Psychology in Britain, *John Heron*, looks deeply into what Humanistic Psychology would look like if it were an expression of what he characterizes as 'fourth-wave humanism'. For John, it would firmly put spirituality back where it belongs, 'in an enhanced, more rounded and grounded form at the very core of the human realm', thus manifesting as collegiality, and 'a collaborative regeneration of what it is to be a human being'. In such a realm, people 'co-operate to explore meaning, build relationship and manifest creativity through collaborative action inquiry into the integration and consummation of many areas of human development'. John goes on to outline a number of distinguishing features of such collegially applied spirituality, which he sees as 'encourag[ing] us to inquire together, imaginatively and creatively, about how to act together in a spirited way to flourish on and with our planet'.

We hope you enjoy reading the book as much as we've enjoyed putting it together. It can be read as either a breathless cover-to-cover read, or a 'source book' to be selectively dipped into, to suit readers' own particular interests. And having immersed yourself in such a rich and diverse collection of humanistically orientated material, perhaps you'll find yourself wondering – as we have – if the dream really is over? – or at least, whether it might have changed beyond all historical recognition. Whilst we have our own views on these issues (which we'll be exploring in our Editorial Conclusion), till then we naturally wish to leave it to you to decide!

References
Bazzano, M. (2013) 'In praise of stress induction: mindfulness revisited', *European Journal of Psychotherapy and Counselling*, 15 (2): 174–85.
Berne, E. (1964) *Games People Play: The Psychology of Human Relationships*, New York: Grove Press (latest edition, Penguin, 2010).
Corrigall, J., Payne, H. and Wilkinson, H. (eds) (2006) *About a Body: Working with the Embodied Mind in Psychotherapy*, London: Routledge.
Elkins, D.N. (2007) 'Empirically supported treatments: the deconstruction of a myth', *Journal of Humanistic Psychology*, 47 (4): 474–500.
Furedi, F. (2004) *Therapy Culture: Cultivating Vulnerability in an Uncertain Age*. London: Routledge.
Holmes, D., Murray, S.J. and Perron, A. (2006) 'Deconstructing the evidence-based discourse in health sciences: truth, power and fascism', *International Journal of Evidence-Based Healthcare*, 4: 180–6.
Jackson, C. (2013) 'Something more to say …', *Therapy Today*, 24 (5): 10–13.

Janov, A. (1970) *The Primal Scream – Primal Therapy: The Cure for Neurosis*, New York: G.P Putnam's (latest edition, Abacus, 1990).

King, L. and Moutsou, C. (eds) (2010) *Rethinking Audit Cultures: A Critical Look at Evidence-based Practice in Psychotherapy and Beyond*, Ross-on-Wye: PCCS Books.

Laing, R.D. (1967) *The Politics of Experience and The Bird of Paradise*, Harmondsworth: Penguin (latest edition, 1990).

Lasch, C. (1979) *The Culture of Narcissism*, New York: Norton.

Mair, K. (2011) 'The myth of therapist expertise', in R. House and N. Totton (eds) *Implausible Professions: Arguments for Pluralism and Autonomy in Psychotherapy and Counselling*, ext. 2nd edn. (pp. 101–13), Ross-on-Wye: PCCS Books; abridged from C. Feltham and W. Dryden (eds), *Psychotherapy and Its Discontents* (pp. 135–60), Buckingham: Open University Press, 1992.

Marzillier, J. (2004) 'The myth of evidence-based psychotherapy', *The Psychologist*, 17 (7): 392–5.

Owens, P. (2013) 'The humanistic scientist: an appreciation of the work of Daniel N. Stern', *Self & Society: International Journal for Humanistic Psychology*, 40 (3): 46–51.

Power, M. (1997) *The Audit Society: Rituals of Verification*, Oxford: Oxford University Press.

Rieff, P. (1966) *The Triumph of the Therapeutic: Uses of Faith after Freud*, London: Chatto & Windus.

Rogers, C. (1973) 'Some new challenges', *American Psychologist*, 28 (5): 373–87.

Rowan, J. (2004) 'Some history of humanistic psychology', *The Humanistic Psychologist*, 32 (Summer): 221–38.

Self & Society (2013a) Issue 40 (4): Special Theme Issue – 'Psychiatry, Big Pharma and the Nature of Distress: Welcome to the Paradigm War'.

Self & Society (2013b) Issue 41 (2): Special Theme Issue on 'Carl Rogers and the Helping Professions – 40 Years On'.

Stern, D.N. (2004) *The Present Moment in Psychotherapy and Everyday Life*, New York: W.W. Norton.

Totton, N. (2011) 'Not a tame lion: psychotherapy in a safety-obsessed culture', in L. Bondi, D. Carr, C. Clark. and C. Clegg (eds), *Towards Professional Wisdom* (pp. 233–46), Farnham: Ashgate.

Wallach, M.A. and Wallach, L. (1983) *Psychology's Sanction for Selfishness: The Error of Egotism in Theory and Therapy*, San Francisco: W.H. Freeman.

PART I

CONTEXTS

for feelings, the body, children and the environment. But I do not share the optimistic belief that (all? – most? – some?) human beings are deeply autonomous, self-actualizing and trustworthy. In my book *What's Wrong with Us? The Anthropathology Thesis* (2007) and in *Failure* (2012) in particular, I have outlined views about the ways in which I consider we are subject to entropic forces, negative evolutionary and genetic inclinations and capitalist threats. I think some practitioners of the humanistic therapies are perhaps stuck in a 1960's mind-set of naïveté and romantic optimism, and knee-jerk rejection of anything they think of as positivism and authoritarianism. If enough people trust their own organismic valuing process, primal or discharge away their inner distress, raise their children in a child-centred way, create local solidarity groups, meditate, dance, practise idiosyncratic spiritualties, eat the right things and recycle waste conscientiously, then all shall be well. Although I am obviously caricaturing here (and some, perhaps fairly, will think me cynical), there is some truth in the idea that most Humanistic Psychology/therapy is constituted by a simple set of optimistic values akin to religious faith, and is not characterized by much radical, rigorous critical thinking.

Probably, some of my opposition to Humanistic Psychology (and all things bright and beautiful) results from deep incurable pathologies of my own, as well as my ageing process. Not for nothing have I been attracted to writers like Schopenhauer, Camus, Cioran, Beckett and Houellebecq. Temperamentally I am somewhat more Freudian (pessimistic) than Rogerian. I have to some extent 'done my own thing' in life but I have also compromised extensively, and wrestled only half-successfully with relationships, work and peace of mind. But my opposition also comes from disappointment, ongoing observations and wide reading. Janov's primal therapy (which I had in the late 1970s) was not nearly as successful as he claimed. Transactional analysis did not remain simple and accessible for very long. Jackins' re-evaluation co-counselling did not really transform people or societies, and his biography casts serious doubts on him. Biographies about Krishnamurti too cast some doubts on his authenticity. My sons, raised in a positive, child-centred way, for all their good points, did not become anything like non-problematic, fully functioning adults.

A great deal of writing on evolutionary psychology and deep history renders the shallow account of all psychologies suspect. The Positive Psychology and mindfulness movements in CBT seem to have hijacked part of the Humanistic Psychology agenda. Every other person I meet in the counselling/therapy field claims to be on a spiritual journey and yet remains inarticulate about what they actually mean. People involved for many years in humanistic therapy (indeed, in all therapies) did not stand out as significantly different from others in terms of freedom from neuroses, vanity and folly. Petruska Clarkson killed herself.

But I have never entirely shaken off the influence of Krishnamurti's simple, sincere teaching, nor of primal therapy's focus on feelings. Years in academia exercised my head but not my feelings, my attention to detail but not to large, obvious human problems. My current 'position' is roughly, highly concisely, as follows.

1 | The Past and Future of Humanistic Psychology

Colin Feltham

In this first chapter, I declare my personal sympathy with aspects of Humanistic Psychology and state what I consider its strengths to be. I critique what I regard as its weaknesses – its lack of realism, lack of engagement with contemporary, harsh socio-economic realities, and some of its failures to live up to its promise. Humanistic Psychology may become a barely significant set of nostalgic theories and practices or yet find ways to bring its focus on birth, education, feelings and patriarchal civilization to a new readership and public.

I don't want to spend too long on any tedious, definitional preamble (that comes at the end of this piece!). Instead, let me recount briefly what some of my associations with Humanistic Psychology are. Born in 1950, I grew up within the late hippie era. In my searching, late-teenage years, academic psychology was disappointingly about anything except human experience, just as Anglo-American philosophy was far too analytical, and even much existentialist philosophy escaped my grasp. But pacifist protest, rock music and drugs were everywhere. I was loosely involved, or interested in, yoga, meditation, existentialism, Zen, Gandhi, Krishnamurti, Hermann Hesse, Timothy Leary, Alan Watts, the Continuum Concept, peace, primal therapy, primal integration and (later) Mahrer's experiential psychotherapy. But I never quite belonged to the light and the good, reading Thomas Hardy (especially *Jude the Obscure*), Kafka, Camus, Henry Miller and others with rather too much negative pleasure. I was also never a joiner as such, but a loner and an outsider.

I wonder if Humanistic Psychology, like all similar movements and disciplines, has had its heyday of impact and spike of optimism, which is now past and in decline. I realize that I am for many of the things Humanistic Psychology and therapy stand for, but I am also against some, or rather I am doubtful about many, of its explanations even while I may broadly support its aims. I still believe that ours is a damagingly patriarchal society that needs much more female influence and understanding of and respect

Human beings are evolved animals; many people still find this either unpalatable, or they do not really understand or accept it. In a nutshell, we humans retain all animals' need for food, and most of us also retain tendencies to be somewhat territorial, kin-protective and xenophobic, driven towards sex, with inflexible behavioural habits, and so on. The advent of complex human consciousness, symbolism and language led to something like a 'Fall'. For Ken Wilber this is a necessary dip, as it were, on the way to an awaited inevitable upward trend. For others, such as the primitivist-anarchist John Zerzan, our fall into agriculture, territoriality, patriarchy, symbolism, religion, etc. merely intensified via industry and technology in the last few thousand years, to the point where it remains an open question whether we will destroy ourselves. Layers of self- and other-deception have not been greatly overturned by the psychotherapies, in spite of this being one of psychotherapy's main foci and proudest claims. Many people remain in the grip of irrational religions and other dubious systems of thought; and this problem is compounded by political correctness and postmodernism which fetishize and promote 'difference' and tend to silence deep investigation and authentic dialogue. What is called 'capitalist realism' (the thick milieu of monetary illusion, economic inequalities, addictive consumerism, dehumanizing work and technologization of the mind) shows no real sign yet of being much modified or overturned. As individuals (all 7 billion of us) we are probably far less autonomous and free than we like to think, being shaped by ancient historical forces and continuing political and economic factors that are arguably too big and complex for most of us to truly grasp and change. Now we are faced with potentially catastrophic climate change and international economic threats that we may well fail to meet effectively.

All the psychotherapies promote a concentration on the individual and the view that he or she can make effective changes in self and society. But this is not borne out by observation. No counselling or psychotherapy training course genuinely addresses in any depth the evolutionary, genetic, socio-economic, environmental and entropic forces stacked against us. Indeed, our field is much happier moving in a hazy spiritual or transpersonal direction than tackling these 'real world' domains. I think it is true that some of the deeper humanistic therapies address aspects of human dysfunction untouched by others, but not necessarily with great understanding or success, more often slipping into romantic and esoteric practices. What I would like to see is much more willingness to address all such themes, along with identifying what, if anything, is durable and promising about Humanistic Psychology.

To my mind, recognition of the damage of patriarchy is one such theme, to include the dangers of suppressing bodily and emotional needs. Others include consolidation of research on childbirth, birth trauma and its long-term effects; the damage done by competitive mass education; the psychology of greed and violence; the notion of 'radical honesty' (put forward by Brad Blanton) that promotes the values of authenticity and parrhesia; wider experimentation in dialogue in the manner of David Bohm; the possibility that something like an 'anthropopathology-free' consciousness may be real and available to more than a handful of individuals like the Buddha, Jiddu

Krishnamurti and U.G. Krishnamurti, Eckhart Tolle et al. (all of whom may or may not have embodied such states). Humanistic Psychology still has some valuable proposals to bring to the table of research, practice and argument, but to do so it must be willing to think critically, to engage in interdisciplinary dialogue and to discard whatever is anachronistically redundant. And ultimately, do we need labels like 'Humanistic Psychology' any more than we need the labels of pathology?

One useful example of forward-moving psychology is Steven Pinker's recent book *The Better Angels of Our Nature* (2011), in which he demonstrates fairly convincingly that human violence of all kinds has declined significantly across the centuries, for diverse reasons. Pinker has some background in evolutionary psychology and uses statistics heavily in this book – factors which might alienate many Humanistic Psychology readers. Yet his message is extremely hopeful. It may take longer than we would like but we are becoming demonstrably more empathic and less violent as a species. Hopefully we will also gradually become less deceptive and greedy, and as much ashamed of these characteristics as we now are of violence against women and children, torture and capital punishment. Recent anti-capitalist protests focusing on bankers' excessive pay is one sign that deception and greed might be becoming significantly shameful.

Are there within the ranks of Humanistic Psychology people who can take on the challenge of research into radical human transformation? By this I refer to discoveries in the domain of freedom from anthropathology. Are there, as I intuit, links to be made between primal therapy and the kind of embodied 'mystical' states associated with Krishnamurti and others? I believe Janov, Reich and similar others took a wrong turn and came to premature conclusions about deep emotional and somatic access issues. I suspect that 'successful' deep primalling into an irreversibly innocent (pre-deceptive) state of human consciousness is currently a fortuitous reality granted only to a few gifted individuals, though I know that Tolle and some primal practitioners are much more optimistic about success in this area. Although I am sceptical about the claims of research on both meditation and primal phenomena, I think that here we potentially have Humanistic Psychology's equivalent of medicine's cancer research. Are these experiences real? Do they actually transform some people? Why do they fail with others? How can we learn from these questions? Can we put across such information in a way that scientists, politicians and the public cannot ignore?

As things stand, Humanistic Psychology and therapy no doubt have some sort of future, but probably not one that is massively influential. Those who have played an active part in its development and retain faith in its potency may well even regard it as thriving. On the pessimistic side I think we have to consider the possibility that it is now a relatively weak, minority-interest subject and practice sustained mainly by its committed or nostalgic elders and a handful of romantic enthusiasts. It has been eclipsed by the language-mesmerized intellectuals and the economically motivated technocrats and medicine men (e.g. proponents of postmodernist, social constructivist and Lacanian therapies, online therapy, CBT, psychopharmacology). Person-centred therapy and its tenets remain popular within some sections of the counselling world for mixed reasons: (1) because it appears to be 'easy' and 'nice' (my apologies at these observations, which I recognize as harsh but which I believe are necessary); and (2) because it appears to offer a form of attitudinal resistance to oppressive authoritarian trends and institutions.

I know this has been done before, but isn't there perhaps a need for a new humanistic (psychology) manifesto, spelling out values and aims for 2013 and beyond? The distinction between the confusing secular connotation of 'humanism' and Humanistic Psychology and psycho-practice might finally be made clear. The precise relationship between Humanistic Psychology and the human potential movement likewise, but also consideration of views on the human condition, human nature, trans/post-humanism and the multiplicity of (not only Western) relevant anthropologies, might be focused upon. Acceptance of Humanistic Psychology as a noble-enough ragbag of alternative lifestyles and modestly anti-establishment politics (if this is what it is) could be made explicit. Clarification of what still holds together the range of diverse therapies – Gestalt, Reichian, psychodrama, person-centred, Transactional Analysis, psychosynthesis, primal, existentialist, ecotherapy, etc. – under one identity could be a challenging task. It might also be accepted that in the irresistible mêlée of pluralism and entropy (what I think of as neophilia within *moribundity*), some parts of Humanistic Psychology are moribund, some thriving, and some transmuting, even perhaps joining past enemies in new enterprises.

We certainly need some pro-humanizing wedge between the dehumanizing and irrational forces shaping our collective future.

References
Feltham, C. (2007) *What's Wrong with Us? The Anthropathology Thesis,* Chichester: Wiley.
Feltham, C. (2012) *Failure,* Durham: Acumen.
Pinker, S. (2011) *The Better Angels of Our Nature,* London: Allen Lane.

2 | Creativity in the Evolution of Humanistic Psychology

Louis Hoffman, Ruth Richards and Steven Pritzker

… of the song-clouds my breath made
in cold air
a cloak has grown
white and,
where here a word
there another
froze, glittering,
stone-heavy.
A mask I had not meant
to wear, as if of frost,
covers my face.

(Levertov, 1987: 42)

Humanistic Psychology in recent years has too often focused on the same themes without bringing forth enough new perspectives, applications and voices. Creativity has two important roles in addressing this issue and advancing Humanistic Psychology. First, creativity is an important emergent theme in humanistic writing with relevancy for theory, research and practice. Second, it is important to creatively engage Humanistic Psychology to move beyond a re-telling of the same stories and themes. This chapter offers several practical suggestions for increasing creativity's presence and influence in Humanistic Psychology.

Humanistic Psychology emerged at a time when change was the *Zeitgeist*, offering a fresh voice and perspective on the human condition and psychological theory. Since its inception, the creative voices have too often grown into a chorus of familiar themes. If Humanistic Psychology is to retain its status as a force in psychology, it will be necessary to unfreeze its voice, shed its cloak, and find a new voice. This does not require a shedding of the basic principles and values of Humanistic Psychology. Rather, it advocates the need for new interpretations, experiences and applications of Humanistic Psychology that meet the needs and energy of contemporary times.

Creativity is essential to the renewal of Humanistic Psychology. Its very nature is change, adaptation and renewal. It is a vehicle for our higher human possibilities. We are advocating for Humanistic Psychology to embrace the study of creativity in general, but more importantly, to apply it within the humanistic paradigm for the purposes of human betterment and changing the world.

Creativity and Humanistic Psychology

Even today, many see human creativity as an extra. To some, it is not even worthy of serious study – it's a frill, a lark, an avocation for a rainy Sunday afternoon. Some think it is for a special few, or see it as largely about art (and perhaps science and leadership). It is common to hear phrases such as, 'I can't paint a picture; I am not creative!' For these people, they cannot do it, and that is the end of it. They have turned their back on their birthright (and ours).

In the future, we see all this changing dramatically. We see creativity, 'the originality of everyday life', becoming ever more obviously about ways of functioning more consciously and fully in all of life – or even as a way of life – relevant to personal change, social change, psychological and mental health, awareness, presence in the moment, a rich attention to our many options, and, for those so inclined, part of a spiritual path. It is 'natural' in Humanistic Psychology. This certainly resonates with Maslow's *self-actualizing creativity*.

Thematic analysis of a recent book, *Everyday Creativity and New Views of Human Nature* (Richards, 2007a) revealed twelve themes, typically process-related, that cut across the chapters: dynamic, conscious, healthy, non-defensive, open, integrating, observing actively, caring, collaborative, androgynous, developing, brave. Note also similarities to past writings about creativity by humanistic psychologists including Maslow, Rogers and May. Mike Arons and others have also addressed varied links between aspects of creative process and Humanistic Psychology (e.g. Arons and Richards, 2001; Arons, 2007; Combs and Krippner, 2007; Loye, 2007; Schneider, 2004).

An everyday creative product can be identified after Frank Barron (1969) in terms of only two criteria, originality and meaningfulness, and it can be applied broadly to individual lives at work and leisure. It is universally available, although often underdeveloped. It is less about what one does than how one does it. Hence, creative process again becomes key.

A highly creative participant in one study (Richards et al., 1988) was an automobile mechanic who devised his own tools. Many have probably known an uncreative car mechanic! One can be creative (or not) in how one teaches a class, organizes an office, landscapes their home, rears a child, or creates a special banquet on a tight budget. Creativity can literally save someone who is lost, starving, endangered, or otherwise at risk. But it is not just about survival or coping; it can also be about learning what one is surviving for.

Increasingly, for many in this field, interest is less in the creative product, described by these two criteria, than the creative process that leads to this rich ability to change, adapt, and move forward along a path of development, and even cultural evolution. Whenever a person is changing, shifting, flexibly adapting to their environment (or adapting it to themselves), improvising, or having a hunch or intuition, they are being 'everyday creative'. One becomes a mindful agent of the future, rather than an automaton, running through pre-set routines, habits and duties. One comes alive.

We also believe that we are not looking at only a cognitive skill or set of rules and procedures, but at complex holistic capabilities that engage all aspects of the person, including cognitive and affective functions, intentionality, conscious and unconscious, and at various points in the process different states or alterations in consciousness (see Richards, 2007a, 2011). It is also very much worth remembering that Maslow saw, ultimately, that self-actualizing in general, and self-actualizing creativity, were not all that different (Maslow, 1971).

It can even be asked whether creativity is good for those engaging in it. One finds increasingly more evidence of health benefits, including work on expressive writing (even including boosted immune function!) to a possible protective effect (or 'compensatory advantage') of high creativity in certain persons at risk for major psychiatric problems (Kinney and Richards, 2011; Richards et al., 1988). Highly creative people accept changes of aging more comfortably, and there are initial suggestions that people may actually live longer. One's ability to use mental imagery in creative healing creates a mind–body bridge that, for instance, can change patterns of local blood flow and other parameters. Uses of arts in cancer, HIV and coping with loss and trauma are just a few other examples (Richards, 2007a; Runco and Pritzker, 2011). These are complex topics, but we can see that we are dealing with powerful potentials of mind–body–spirit.

Why, then, are more people not emphasizing creativity, for instance, in schools? Remember, creativity is also about change, and the creator is a threat to the status quo. We are talking new values and new priorities. There is typically a resistance to the new, whether at work, at school, at home or internally, as one defends against the sorts of self-knowledge that can emerge when truly open to unconscious sources (Runco and Pritzker, 2011). It may be, in part, that unacknowledged fear of one's irrational mind, unconscious, or Shadow, may be one factor in pathologizing the highly creative person (Richards, 2011).

It is possible to work for a future that brings a new *definition* of normalcy, one that incorporates and cherishes the diversity of inspiration (and of many other things) and that accepts the sometimes odd-ball deviancy as part of the rich human range of possibility, rather than pathologizing it, or displacing a fear of one's depths on to certain vulnerable groups (certain psychiatric patients).

In fact, creativity and psychology have been intimately linked since Sigmund Freud, although the healthier implications emerged later with Humanistic Psychology. Freud proposed that creativity was the result of individuals' 'repression of instinctual libidinal energy' (Lemire, 1998: 109). Jung (archetypes), Kris (primary process), May (the daimonic) and other psychologists made significant contributions to the understanding of creativity in the early 20th century. Finally, in the 1950s and 1960s, humanistic psychologists brought a fresh perspective to the field by focusing on the individual in an idealistic positive fashion that was symbolic of the optimistic post-World War II American ethos.

Humanistic psychologists looked at creativity as a much more common human experience. For example, Abraham Maslow (1962) proposed that creativity was not limited to the traditional arts but could be a part of everyday life. He stated that almost everybody had the potential to be creative in their lives: '… we are dealing with a fundamental characteristic, inherent in human nature, a potentiality given to all or most human beings at birth, which most often is lost or buried or inhibited as the person gets enculturated' (p. 133). Maslow, based on his research, stated that the attributes of a creative individual include being able to be childlike at times, while at the same time having a strong ego that allows the integration of opposing ideas into unity. He discussed the importance of education in art, poetry and dancing, arguing that it could help students learn 'to accept and integrate the primary processes into conscious and preconscious life' (p. 136). Maslow's goal was to encourage the development of self-actualizing, flexible and spontaneous individuals who function in the world in a way that makes them psychologically and physically healthier, as well as attuned to higher needs in a culture. Loye (2007), in a key volume on the overlooked Darwin (regarding Darwin's views on pro-social and collaborative motives for humans), characterized humans as moving from defense to growth and caring (as per *Darwin's Descent of Man*) and on to a meta-motivational stage related to Maslow's (1971) self-actualizing individual.

Carl Rogers (1963), elaborating on Maslow's vision, proposed that a self-actualizing person would be a non-conformist with a strong sense of self who could make valuable contributions to society. Rogers suggested that this ability to continually evolve would provide the opportunity to develop leaders who would be 'likely to adapt and survive under changing environmental conditions …. He would be a fit vanguard of human evolution' (p. 23). Rogers' statement appears particularly prescient in view of our current environmental challenges.

Rollo May (1975) argued in *The Courage to Create* that we are living in an 'age of limbo' where constant change requires the courage to 'leap into the unknown' (p. 12). May proposed the theory that artistic creativity is an encounter in which the artist or writer engages subjectively with the objective world. The result is a unique expression that can influence the audience as well as the creator.

Prominent humanistic psychologists, including Rogers and May, along with others including Harvard's Gordon Allport and Henry Murray, attended the 1964 conference in Old Saybrook, Connecticut, now seen as the landmark event in the establishment of Humanistic Psychology as a field and a 'third force' in psychology (Taylor, 1994). Subsequently, several humanistic programs or institutions were established, including The Humanistic Psychology Institute in San Francisco (now called Saybrook University), and *Self and Society* journal, currently celebrating its 40th anniversary. May, whose books include the remarkable *Courage to Create* (1975), taught at Saybrook during the early years.

At Saybrook, today the spirit of Humanistic Psychology's connection to creativity continues to advance with new graduate programs. Saybrook was one of the first schools in the world to offer a Creativity Studies Certificate, a Masters in Psychology with a Specialization in Creativity Studies, and has just added a Doctorate in Psychology with a Specialization in Creativity Studies. The Creativity Studies curriculum is grounded in Humanistic Psychology, with a commitment to help develop healthy, self-actualizing students who in turn take their skills and intentions into the world to help others. Examples of unique emphases include, from Carl Rogers' daughter Natalie Rogers (2011), a rich program in expressive arts for personal and social change; from Stanley Krippner (Feinstein and Krippner, 2006), work in personal mythology and dreamwork (allowing conscious rewriting of unconscious personal and social scripts); and from Steven Pritzker (2007), work with creative expression and on the receiving end, with 'audience flow', whence we can help people become active creators in what might seem to be passive activity.

Saybrook's various programs are becoming popular with students, as seen in a recent article by a professor and ten students/alumni (Richards et al., 2011); as one sees, our students often want to change something significant in the world – or in themselves. They want to apply innovative approaches to clinical work, education, organizational development, self-improvement and more.

Although creativity can be used for 'evil', all else being equal, creative process can further one's openness, lack of defensiveness and general mental health. Indeed, creativity can change everything! Who we are. What we want in life. It can open doors to our higher potential. We hope, increasingly, at Saybrook and in general, to facilitate this journey.

Applying creativity in Humanistic Psychology

There are some notable examples of creativity in contemporary Humanistic Psychology. Kirk Schneider's existential-integrative psychology (Schneider, 2008; Schneider and Krug, 2009) provides a model for existential psychology to work with other psychological theories, including mainstream psychology, utilizing creativity through an integrative process. Schneider's model was praised by Wampold (2008), a leading therapy outcome researcher, who stated that 'an understanding of the principles of existential therapy is needed by all therapists, as it adds a perspective that might ... form the basis of all effective treatments' (p. 6). David Elkins (2009), in his book *Humanistic Psychology: A Clinical Manifesto*, took on some of the most important and controversial issues in contemporary psychology with a deeply humanistic voice. In particular, Elkins challenged attempts to narrowly regulate psychotherapy practice in ways antagonistic to Humanistic Psychology, while providing an important evidence-based defense of humanistic approaches to therapy. Mendelowitz (2008), in *Ethics and Lao Tzu: Intimations of Character*, embraced creativity on multiple levels. In his book, he integrated the arts into a story of his work with a client, who was herself an artist. The style as well as the content exudes creativity, while also speaking to the power of creativity to impact the human condition. While these represent important creative contributions to Humanistic Psychology, and show the potential to open possibilities in Western mental health, more applications are still needed.

Diversity, creativity and Humanistic Psychology

Great opportunities for creativity arise when one opens oneself up to that which is different. In a world that is becoming increasingly diverse, and increasingly international, opportunities for creativity are prominent. Even more, creativity is necessary in order to enter into dialogues that honor the history, traditions and values of cultures while advancing the collective wisdom and scholarship. Too often, as critiqued by Ren (2009), international dialogues quickly turn into attempts to impose one culture's values and approaches upon the other culture. It requires creativity, and a loosening of one's ideals, to engage in international dialogue in a manner that is respectful of differences and allows for something new to emerge.

As an illustration, beginning in 2007 a series of dialogues on existential psychology began in China (see Hoffman et al., 2009). Existential psychology emerged from a Western paradigm and, although it challenged much of the status quo of Western thought, it retained many Western values, such as individualism, that do not fit well with Chinese culture. In order to minimize the possibility of the imposition of Western values, several principles were utilized that encouraged a more creative approach:

1. Prioritizing relationship building as the foundation of dialogue.
2. The sharing of Western approaches to existential psychology was always accompanied by the encouragement of cultural critique, or critically thinking about how these ideas and approaches did not fit, or needed to be adapted, to be utilized in China in a culturally sensitive manner.
3. The conversations sought to identify *indigenous Chinese approaches to existential psychology*, which were understood as approaches to understanding human nature and change that shared many, but not all, of the values of existential psychology.
4. Encouraging dialogue between indigenous Chinese worldviews and approaches to psychology with the Western existential perspectives (see Yang and Hoffman, 2011).

Relational creativity becomes important here, where creative process is applied to interaction (see Richards, 2007b). These dialogues would not have achieved the success that has been attained without several applications of creativity. First, the relational foundation provided the safety for participants to share different perspectives and openly critique the Western approaches to existential psychology. This created the space for creative new expressions and applications of existential psychology to emerge. Second, being intentional in identifying and exposing differences and points of discomfort was necessary to begin exploring creative resolutions to the challenges of using an existential paradigm in Chinese culture.

Moats et al. (2011) provide a beautiful illustration of how growth and creativity can emerge from the natural tension of cross-cultural dialogue. These three authors participated in existential dialogues in China originally as students, and later as professionals. Their article reflects upon how their experiences in China dislodged them from their personal and professional comfort zones, often challenging deeply held beliefs. Partially because of the relationships they were developing, it was not easy to discard the sources of discomfort, leaving the necessity of finding creative resolutions to dealing with their discomfort. The result was a shift in their beliefs that has significantly impacted the way they apply and practice psychology.

As a second example, Cleare-Hoffman (2009) utilized an existential framework to explore the meaning of Junkanoo, a Bahamian festival. This festival originated with the African slaves brought to the Bahamas as a way of retaining aspects of their spiritual and cultural beliefs. Cleare-Hoffman illustrates that Junkanoo began as a celebration of freedom while the celebrants were still bound in slavery. This is a very different understanding of freedom compared to what is commonly held in many Western cultures. This, again, illustrates the potential for new, creative interpretations of foundational humanistic principles and values through engagement with diversity.

Conclusion

Creativity should be recognized as having an honored place in Humanistic Psychology. From its origins, Humanistic Psychology has been open to the humanities, literature and the arts. Many humanistic practitioners have long integrated the arts into the healing and change process. However, what is needed now is broader ways of understanding and applying creativity. Stated differently, there is a need for deeper engagement with creativity that will then permeate throughout Humanistic Psychology, across areas of endeavor and across cultures. These creative engagements have the potential to not only change Humanistic Psychology, but also to begin to transform the world.

References
Arons, M. (2007) 'Standing up for humanity: upright body, creative instability, and spiritual balance', in R. Richards (ed.), *Everyday Creativity and New Views of Human Nature: Psychological, Social, and Spiritual Perspectives* (pp. 175–93), Washington, DC: American Psychological Association.
Arons, M. and Richards, R. (2001) 'Two noble insurgencies: creativity and humanistic psychology', in K.J. Schneider, J.F.T. Bugental and J. F. Pierson (eds), *Handbook of Humanistic Psychology: Leading Edges in Theory, Research, and Practice* (pp. 127–42), Thousand Oaks, CA: Sage.

Barron, F. (1969) *Creative Person and Creative Process*, New York: Holt, Rinehart, and Winston.

Cleare-Hoffman, H.P. (2009) 'Junkanoo: A Bahamian cultural myth', in L. Hoffman, M. Yang, F.J. Kaklauskas and A. Chan (eds), *Existential Psychology East–West* (pp. 363–72), Colorado Springs, CO: University of the Rockies Press.

Combs, A. and Krippner, S. (2007) 'Structures of consciousness and creativity: opening the doors of perception', in R. Richards (ed.), *Everyday Creativity and New Views of Human Nature: Psychological, Social, and Spiritual Perspectives* (pp. 131–49), Washington, DC: American Psychological Association.

Elkins, D.N. (2009) *Humanistic Psychology: A Clinical Manifesto. A Critique of Clinical Psychology and the Need for Progressive Alternatives*, Colorado Springs, CO: University of the Rockies Press.

Feinstein, D. and Krippner, S. (2006) *The Mythic Path*, 3rd edn, Santa Rosa, CA: Energy Psychology Press.

Hoffman, L., Yang, M., Kaklauskas, F.J. and Chan, A. (eds) (2009) *Existential Psychology East–West*, Colorado Springs, CO: University of the Rockies Press.

Kinney, D. and Richards, R. (2011) 'Bipolar mood disorders', in M. Runco and S. Pritzker (eds), *Encyclopedia of Creativity* (pp. 140–8), 2nd edn, San Diego, CA: Academic Press.

Lemire, D. (1998) 'Individual psychology and innovation: the de-Freuding of creativity', *Journal of Individual Psychology*, 54 (1): 108–18.

Levertov, D. (1987) *Poems 1968–1972*, New York: New Directions Books.

Loye, D. (2007) *Darwin's Lost Theory*, Carmel, CA: Benjamin Franklin Press.

Maslow, A.H. (1962) 'Creativity in self-actualizing people', in A. Maslow (ed.), *Toward a Psychology of Being* (pp. 127–37), Princeton, NJ: D. Van Nostrand.

Maslow, A.H. (1971) *The Farther Reaches of Human Nature*, New York: Penguin.

May, R. (1975) *The Courage to Create*, New York: Norton.

Mendelowitz, E. (2008) *Ethics and Lao Tzu: Intimations of Character*, Colorado Springs, CO: University of the Rockies Press.

Moats, M., Claypool, T. and Saxon, E. (2011) 'Therapist development through international dialogue: students' perspectives on personal and professional life changing interactions in China', *The Humanistic Psychologist*, 39, 276–82.

Pritzker, S. (2007) 'Audience flow', in R. Richards (ed.), *Everyday Creativity and New Views of Human Nature: Psychological, Social, and Spiritual Perspectives* (pp. 109–29), Washington, DC: American Psychological Association.

Ren, Z. (2009) 'On being a volunteer at the Sichuan earthquake disaster area (translated version)', *Hong Kong Journal of Psychiatry*, 19 (3), 123–5.

Richards, R. (2007a) *Everyday Creativity and New Views of Human Nature: Psychological, Social, and Spiritual Perspectives* (pp. 168–75), Washington, DC: American Psychological Association.

Richards, R. (2007b) 'Relational creativity and healing potential: the power of Eastern thought in Western clinical settings', in J. Pappas, B. Smythe, and A. Baydala (eds), *Cultural Healing and Belief Systems* (pp. 286–308), Calgary, Alberta: Detselig Enterprises.

Richards, R. (2011) 'Everyday creativity', in M. Runco and S. Pritzker (eds), *Encyclopedia of Creativity*, 2nd edn (pp.683–8), San Diego, CA: Academic Press.

Richards, R., Kinney, D.K., Lunde, I. and Benet, M. (1988) 'Creativity in manic-depressives, cyclothymes, their normal relatives, and control subjects', *Journal of Abnormal Psychology*, 97, 281–8.

Richards, R., Kolva, J. Atkin, M., Cheatham, H., Crocker, R., Ockuly, M.D. et al. (2011) 'Creativity revalued: how professors, students, and an innovative university are turning the tide', *NeuroQuantology*, 9 (3), 468–93.

Rogers, C.R. (1963) 'The concept of the fully functioning person', *Psychotherapy: Theory, Research and Practice*, 1 (1), 17–26.
Rogers, N. (2011) *Creative Connection for Groups: Person-centered Expressive Arts for Healing and Social Change,* Palo Alto, CA: Science and Behavior Books.
Runco, M. and Pritzker, S. (2011) *Encyclopedia of Creativity,* 2nd edn, San Diego, CA: Academic Press.
Schneider, K.J. (2004) *Rediscovery of Awe: Splendor, Mystery, and the Fluid Center of Life,* St. Paul, MN: Paragon House.
Schneider, K.J. (ed.) (2008) *Existential-Integrative Psychotherapy: Guideposts to the Core of Practice,* New York: Routledge.
Schneider, K.J. and Krug, O.T. (2009) *Existential-Humanistic Psychology,* Washington, DC: American Psychological Association.
Taylor, E. (1994) 'Transpersonal psychology: its several virtues', in F. Wertz (ed.), *The Humanistic Movement: Recovering the Person in Psychology* (pp. 170–85), Lake Worth, FL: Gardner Press.
Wampold, B.E. (2008) 'Existential-integrative psychotherapy: coming of age [Review of *Existential-Integrative Psychotherapy: Guideposts to the Core of Practice*], *PsycCRITIQUES: Contemporary Psychology: APA Review of Books,* 53 (6), 4 February.
Yang, M. and Hoffman, L. (2011) 'Introduction to the special section on the First International Conference on Existential Psychology', *The Humanistic Psychologist,* 39, 236–9.

3 | Reconciling Humanistic and Positive Psychology: Bridging the cultural rift

Harris L. Friedman

Humanistic Psychology is often misportrayed as dying or dead, a claim that is especially egregious when made by positive psychologists, who minimize their debt to, as well as co-opt a narrow version of, Humanistic Psychology. This rift rests on a cultural divide that cuts broadly across many sectors of modern life. Through denigration of and distancing from Humanistic Psychology, Positive Psychology has gained considerable benefits siphoned from Humanistic Psychology. Consequently, a better future for Humanistic Psychology requires making explicit efforts to be more holistic, including valuing all methodologies, and emphasizing the importance of including both positive and negative phenomena within its purview. This could reclaim largely dormant aspects of Humanistic Psychology, undermining the efforts of Positive Psychology to assert itself as distinct, and perhaps facilitating an eventual reconciliation.

Dilthey's (1989) collection of essays, written shortly before his death in 1911, distinguished between natural and human sciences, with the former focused on material explanations while the latter focused on understanding humans and their unique lives within socio-historical contexts. Later, Snow (1959) bifurcated intellectual culture into two conflicting camps, the sciences and the humanities, a split which many others have attempted since to mend (e.g. Gould, 2003). What Snow identified as disparate cultures (i.e. the sciences seeking universal objective truths vs. the humanities seeking particularistic subjective understandings) has resulted in what some have called the paradigm wars. Opinion is divided as to whether these wars continue or have ended (e.g. Oakley, 1999).

Within psychology, Kimble (1984) applied this cultural delineation, bifurcating research and clinical psychology into scientific and humanistic cultures respectively. This approach to understanding rifts within psychology has been revisited a number of times (e.g. Nunez, Poole and Memon, 2003), including recently in relationship to divides within Positive Psychology (Bacon, 2005). Although some speculate that cultural reconciliation has finally percolated into psychology, which has been the last social science to resist acceptance of qualitative methods, the jury is still out (Willig and Stainton-Rogers, 2008).

The American Psychological Association, for example, is working hard to advance psychology as a science–technology–engineering–mathematics (STEM) discipline, which may bring enhanced benefits (e.g. status and money) for psychology departments (Kurtzman, 2011). Likewise, many psychology departments are even going to the extreme of renaming themselves to more closely identify with these STEM disciplines. These include the following major US universities: Dartmouth and Indiana (both now called the Departments of Psychological and Brain Sciences); Northern Kentucky, Ball State and Missouri (all three now called the Departments of Psychological Science); Duke (now called the Department of Psychology and Neuroscience); and Brown (now called the Department of Cognitive, Linguistic and Psychological Sciences) (Jaffe, 2011). Evidently much of psychology is attempting to disavow its humanistic aspects and be seen as a hard science.

One area in which this culture war manifests is in the rift between Humanistic and Positive Psychology. By definition through being labeled wars, such divides are not always peaceful. Seligman (2009), one of the co-founders of Positive Psychology, has frequently denigrated Humanistic Psychology for supposedly lacking 'mainstream, cumulative, and replicable scientific method' (p. xviii), which he claims to be foundational to Positive Psychology. He does, however, admit that both Humanistic and Positive Psychology share a common interest in what is positive (e.g. goodness and health), in contrast to the prevailing mainstream focus in psychology on the negative (e.g. evil and pathology). Positive Psychology has often asserted itself as being a distinct approach from its predecessor, Humanistic Psychology, by its embracing of quantitative research, while it evaluates Humanistic Psychology as unscientific for its frequent reliance on qualitative methods (Friedman, 2008).

In addition to the methodological divide, another major delineation between Humanistic and Positive Psychology rests on the former's emphasis on holism, including the negative, while the latter tends to exclude the negative, which creates an imbalance. Recently I illustrated this problem with the example of the largest applied psychology research study ever, viz. one training resiliency to literally every US soldier (Friedman and Robbins, 2012). In this paper, I argued that such emphasis only on the positive, while ignoring its potentially complementary shadow, could have a very negative backlash, such as resulting in resilient warfighters who could simultaneously be less likely to suffer from post-traumatic stress but more likely to commit atrocities. In a more general way, I argue that to be humanistic involves recognizing the holistic relationship between both positive and negative, and including both. In many other areas of psychology, this is becoming recognized, such as in the growing recognition of the importance of the understudied emotion of disgust, which is now being seen not just as a negative emotion to be avoided but, rather, one to be embraced as adaptive (Curtis, 2011). Likewise, I am increasingly interested in complex emotions central to humanistic thought, such as awe, which involves a rich intermixture of positive and negative affect (Bonner and Friedman, 2011).

Mruk (2008) provided a good way to delineate the complex rift characterizing the cultural divide separating Humanistic from Positive Psychology. Specifically, he delineated between what he called 'positivistic Positive Psychology' and 'Humanistic Positive Psychology'. He outlined their commonalities and differences, while denying that they are separate fields. With the increasing ascendency of Positive Psychology, claiming its superiority over Humanistic Psychology by supposedly restoring hard-science approaches to positive phenomena, there is both a threat and an opportunity for Humanistic Psychology. Although Humanistic Psychology usually identifies more with the humanities and the softer areas of the sciences, contrary to the tide of STEM disciplines on which Positive Psychology is rising, Humanistic Psychology does not have to exclude any approach to explaining and understanding any human experience and behavior, including both positive and negative. Humanistic Psychology thus has a strategic advantage over Positive Psychology, as it can both include and go beyond its rival.

To understand this rift, it needs to be appreciated as having developed from two complementary prejudices, paralleling Snow's (1959) two cultures. Positive Psychology seems to have become overly rigid, ignoring its shadow side (Friedman and Robbins, 2012), as well as becoming stuck in a naïve positivistic view of research favoring quantitative approaches, whilst hardly acknowledging the usefulness of qualitative approaches (Friedman, 2008). But Humanistic Psychology is also complicit in having veered in the opposite direction, often denigrating quantitative approaches whilst favoring qualitative approaches (Friedman, 2008). Seeing these opposites as complementary, I think they can perhaps best be viewed as cultural traps (see Bohanon, 1995; Friedman, 2009), which mirror the larger struggles in the culture wars. In regard to Humanistic Psychology, its rebellion against the established forces within the 1960's psychology of behaviorism and psychoanalysis led to an initially adaptive so-called 'third force' but, in accord with how cultural traps work, this stance became increasingly maladaptive. And this led to a lacuna in which the opposite emerged – namely, a Positive Psychology movement that disavows its connection with its progenitor, Humanistic Psychology. Such is the nature of revolutions, in the sense that they often revolve back to their starting-points, spurring counter-revolutions ad nauseum.

Lately, I have been addressing efforts to reconcile the split between Humanistic and Positive Psychology through emphasizing the importance of using mixed methods, which would not privilege any singular method (Friedman, 2008). To privilege either qualitative over quantitative, or vice versa, exemplifies what can be termed methodolotry, the elevation of a method to an object of worship (Friedman, 2002a), and I have noted in past work why it is important not to privilege any singular method (Friedman, 2003). Basically, I argue that there are two traps to avoid: namely, to elevate qualitative approaches, as has been prevalent in many areas of Humanistic Psychology, constitutes an error of romanticism, while to elevate quantitative approaches, as has been prevalent in Positive Psychology, constitutes an error of scientism (Friedman, 2002b, 2005). Quantitative and qualitative methods may be delineated in various way (e.g. grounded/abstract, hard/soft, hypothesis testing/speculative, fixed/flexible, objective/subjective, survey/case study, and value-free/political; Silverman, 2001), but I conclude that they cannot be valued as good or bad in any absolutist way. However, this contention can be debated (see Franco, Friedman and Arons, 2008).

That Humanistic Psychology is often depicted as dying, or even dead, ignores its continuing importance to psychology, science, and even humanity (Friedman, 2011). This misperception of its near or actual demise has recently been promoted by Positive Psychology, which has attempted to co-opt Humanistic Psychology, such as by disavowing its own origins within Humanistic Psychology and by accusing it of being anti-scientific. By this strategy, Positive Psychology has gained considerable benefits through attracting scholars and students under its banner, and has achieved many successes (e.g. through funding, media coverage, and publications) (Friedman, 2008).

Brent Robbins and I explored these dynamics within two special issues of *The Humanistic Psychologist* (Friedman and Robbins, 2008; Robbins and Friedman, 2009). We also responded to this need by chairing the Positive Psychology interest group of the American Psychological Association Division 32 (Society for Humanistic Psychology), as well as offering a symposium seeking rapprochement between leaders of both movements at a recent annual convention of the American Psychological Association.

Essentially, I consider it of paramount importance that Humanistic and Positive Psychology become reunited, as either will siphon off energy from the other, to the detriment of both. The future of Humanistic Psychology hinges on its ability to reclaim what Positive Psychology has co-opted, as well as to reclaim what it has itself abandoned by emphasizing one methodological stance to the detriment of others. The path I advocate to optimally move forward is for Humanistic Psychology to explicitly espouse *epistemological and methodological pluralism*, thus undermining any accusations of being anti-scientific, while building bridges with Positive Psychology, including advising that it not ignore the negative in pursuit of the positive. It is important to realize that if Humanistic Psychology were to remain primarily wedded to only one method, namely qualitative, it would short shrift its potential to make many important contributions. Humanistic Psychology also needs to actively showcase its numerous successes in having influenced many areas within psychology, including in its seminal relatedness to Positive Psychology. That it has been relatively ignored, or even denigrated, by many key forums within contemporary psychology (e.g. in undergraduate textbooks) requires overt challenge against its being further marginalized. For example, one area of science that could benefit from a more humanistic perspective is neurobiology, which unfortunately is often approached in solely reductionist ways (e.g. equating mind with brain) that minimizes the role of the human as a whole, including human experience. Humanistic psychologists can demonstrate the importance of understanding consciousness from holistic perspectives that go beyond hard-science neurobiological reductionism, an area I have recently been pursuing (e.g. Krippner and Friedman, 2010). It is also important that Humanistic Psychology demonstrate its broader impact on science in general, as well as on how it benefits humanity and many of its social institutions. In these regards, Humanistic Psychology has a great future, but only if past cultural traps are circumvented, starting with resisting its co-option by, and working toward reconciling with, Positive Psychology.

References
Bacon, S. (2005) 'Positive psychology's two cultures', *Review of General Psychology*, 9 (2), 181–92.
Bohanon, P. (1995) *How Culture Works*, New York: Free Press.
Bonner, E. and Friedman, H.L. (2011) 'A conceptual clarification of the experience of awe: an interpretative phenomenological analysis', *The Humanistic Psychologist*, 39, 222–35.
Curtis, V. (2011) 'Why disgust matters', *Philosophical Transactions of the Royal Society: Biological Sciences*, 366 (1583), 3478–90.
Dilthey, W. (1989) *Selected Works, Vol. 1: Introduction to the Human Sciences* (eds, R.A. Makkreel and F. Rodi), Princeton, NJ: Princeton University Press.
Franco, Z., Friedman, H.L. and Arons, M. (2008) 'Are qualitative methods always best for humanistic psychology research? A conversation on the epistemological divide between humanistic and positive psychology', *The Humanistic Psychologist*, 36, 159–203.
Friedman, H.L. (2002a) 'Psychological nescience in a post-modern context', *American Psychologist*, 57, 462–3.
Friedman, H.L. (2002b) 'Transpersonal psychology as a scientific field', *International Journal of Transpersonal Studies*, 21, 175–87.
Friedman, H.L. (2003) 'Methodolotry and graphicacy', *American Psychologist*, 58, 817–18.
Friedman, H.L. (2005) 'Problems of romanticism in transpersonal psychology: a case study of Aikido', *The Humanistic Psychologist*, 33, 3–24.
Friedman, H.L. (2008) 'Humanistic and positive psychology: the methodological and epistemological divide', *The Humanistic Psychologist*, 36, 113–26.
Friedman, H.L. (2009) 'Xenophilia as a cultural trap: bridging the gap between transpersonal psychology and religious/spiritual traditions', *International Journal of Transpersonal Studies*, 28, 107–11.
Friedman, H.L. (2011) 'It's premature to write the obituary for humanistic psychology', *Journal of Humanistic Psychology*, 51 (4), 424–7.
Friedman, H.L. and Robbins, B. (eds) (2008) Special issue on positive psychology, *The Humanistic Psychologist*, 36 (2).
Friedman, H.L. and Robbins, B. (2012) 'The negative shadow cast by positive psychology: contrasting views and implications of humanistic and positive psychology on resiliency', *The Humanistic Psychologist*, 40, 1–16.
Gould, S. (2003) *The Hedgehog, the Fox, and the Magister's Pox: Mending the Gap between Science and the Humanities*, New York: Harmony.
Jaffe, E. (2011) 'Identity shift: US psychology departments change their names to reflect the field. The new labels spell out what psychological scientists actually do', *Observer*, 24(7). Retrieved from http://www.psychologicalscience.org/index.php/publications/observer/2011/september-11/identity-shift.html
Kimble, G. (1984) 'The scientific review of mental health practice', *American Psychologist*, 39 (8), 833–9.
Krippner, S. and Friedman, H.L. (eds) (2010) *Mysterious Minds: The Neurobiology of Psychics, Mediums, and Other Extraordinary People*, Santa Barbara, CA: Praeger.
Kurtzman, H. (2011) 'A year of progress: APA works to advance psychology as a STEM discipline: initiatives in 2011 encompass federal advocacy, public education, multi-

disciplinary training, treatment guidelines and K-12 education', *Psychological Science Agenda,* December. Retrieved from http://www.apa.org/science/about/psa/2011/12/stem-discipline.aspx

Mruk, C. (2008) 'Self-esteem, humanistic positive psychology and positivistic positive psychology', *The Humanistic Psychologist,* 36 (2), 143–58.

Nunez, N., Poole, D. and Memon, A. (2003) 'Psychology's two cultures revisited: implications for the integration of science with practice', *Scientific Review of Mental Health Practice,* 2 (1), 8–19.

Oakley, A. (1999) 'Paradigm wars: some thoughts on a personal and public trajectory', *International Journal of Social Research Methodology,* 2 (3), 247–54.

Robbins, B.N. and Friedman, H.L. (eds) (2009) Special issue on methodological pluralism, *The Humanistic Psychologist,* 370 (1).

Seligman, M. (2009) 'Foreword', in S. Lopez (ed.), *The Encyclopedia of Positive Psychology* (pp. xviii–ixx), Malden, MA: Wiley-Blackwell.

Silverman, D. (2001) *Interpreting Qualitative Data: Methods for Analyzing Talk, Text, and Interaction,* 2nd edn, London: Sage.

Snow, C.P. (1959) *The Two Cultures,* London: Cambridge University Press.

Willig, C. and Stainton-Rogers, W. (eds) (2008) *The Sage Handbook of Qualitative Research in Psychology,* London: Sage.

4 | Future Opportunities for Humanistic Psychology

Stanley Krippner and Daniel B. Pitchford

People do not adapt to trauma easily. It is common for men and women to undergo potentially traumatizing events; however, some of these become traumatizing events that lead to traumatic experiences. Post-traumatic stress disorder (PTSD) results not from events but from experiences, the way someone gives meaning to an event. This attribution of meaning is a core concept of Humanistic and existential psychology and psychotherapy, which are undervalued resources in the treatment of PTSD (Greening, 1997). Humanistic and existential perspectives on dealing with PTSD can be practiced on their own or as a supplement to cognitive-behavior therapy, group therapy, or any of the other mainstream approaches to alleviating suffering and helping clients turn post-traumatic stress into post-traumatic strength.

The field of psychology is making an impact in contemporary society. Psychologists write blogs and books. Psychologists are interviewed in the media, and many of these interviews are transformed into videos and other media made widely available by advances in technology. Humanistic psychologists in particular have unique insights to offer, and ought to make the most of these opportunities.

One of the areas in which humanistic psychologists can make an impact is bioethics, where they can provide responses to such questions as: 'What role can psychologists play in alerting people to the factors that have put the planet and its inhabitants at risk?', 'What are the motives that compel some individuals to commit murder in school settings, and to kill civilians while serving overseas on military duty?', and 'How can psychologists help traumatized people who are coping with the aftermath of an event that not only was life-threatening, but that radically challenged their prevailing worldview?'

In focusing on this last question, we know that there are many ways to treat post-traumatic stress disorder (see Krippner, Pitchford and Davies, 2012). Many of these treatments interweave and overlap with one another, and many have had high success rates in reducing or extinguishing stress-related symptoms. Sometimes a combination of treatment approaches produces especially positive results, where 'meaning and connectedness to lived experiences can emerge' (Pitchford, 2009: 441). Each case of PTSD is different, and an integrated approach will often provide something of value for those people who try it.

People are an 'expression' of social, cultural, and individual 'reflections that capture the most personal of experiences' (Pitchford, 2009: 445). However, individually, human beings do not adapt easily to trauma, given too that 'trauma' is dependent upon the individual in what makes a potentially traumatizing event a traumatic experience. A significant change mechanism for trauma to take form, then, is the brokenness of the soul – encountered through its shattering from a loss of meaning, purpose and identity (Greening and Vallejos, 2013), and from its loss of safety due to the disruption of a person's world experiences and beliefs (Pitchford, 2009).

Contrary to popular stereotype, early human beings rarely engaged in long-term warfare or other forms of deadly assault. As a result, a number of biological defenses that could have fostered resilience and rapid recovery did not have an opportunity to develop. Early humans may have been attacked by wild animals or beset by natural disasters, but these traumata were rarely accompanied by guilt, shame, or other emotions that elicit withdrawal, suspicion and suicide among today's combat veterans and survivors of rape and bullying.

The term 'treatment approaches' for PTSD refers to systematic programs designed to eliminate or reduce those problematic symptoms and unpleasant experiences associated with a person's post-traumatic stress. Usually, a qualified person administers these programs to an individual or a group, but some programs are self-administered. They are 'therapeutic' because they have been designed to promote healing. The word 'therapeutic' is, in fact, derived from the Greek term for a group of professional servants, *therapeutae*. Hence, therapists are specially trained 'servants', and therapeutic programs serve people who are in need of help. Almost all psychotherapists are psychologists, counselors, psychiatrists or social workers who have undergone extensive training in order to serve their clients.

Most of these treatment approaches fall under the category of 'psychological therapy' or 'psychotherapy'. The goals of such programs include increasing self-understanding and self-acceptance, and learning how to change behaviors and beliefs that are harmful because they block the PTSD survivor's enjoyment of life. Often, this can take form through encountering fundamental issues, such as guilt (e.g. survivor's guilt), inviting the transformation of emotional pain and personal loss (e.g. loss of innocence, the end of a relationship) through the confrontation and development of purpose and meaning (especially with regard to shame and guilt-associated experiences). This is not an easy journey, and requires a mature, willing, courageous therapist to walk alongside the suffering individual. The therapy often becomes vulnerable through the nakedness of viewing the core areas of self changed by trauma, often bringing the individual to grieve separation from former meanings and ways of relating to self (and self-identity). The courage to act also rests upon the trauma survivor, as the *will* to make a choice may not appear so freely available and may seem risky to face (unsure of the outcome) and provoke unwanted feelings (e.g. anxiety). This is a paradoxical point that may be the most freeing moment from the binding chains upon the soul. It can be freeing because in facing the anxieties and horrors of the trauma, moments are created for 'new opportunities to occur and provide tools for engaging life and future encounters' (Pitchford, 2009: 446). Such parts of the journey require time for rituals of 'goodbye', but with openness of re-emergence of the 'new' person. This is often a spiritual process, where the metaphorical demon that suffocates the individual's soul via the trauma(ta) is vanquished and the person, through his or her courage to face the dark, is thus freed.

This freeing, however, often occurs beyond mainstream therapy's understandings of healing – that is, therapeutic programs that are not primarily based on conventional psychological principles. They range from acupuncture to art, from MDMA[1] to massage. The word 'therapy' refers to the remediation or healing of a psychological, physical or spiritual disorder. There are physical therapists, occupational therapists and speech therapists. In addition, there are spiritual counselors who have been trained to treat spiritual, religious or existential crises, including the loss of one's faith.

Some people with PTSD have a religious crisis because a trusted pastor or priest took sexual advantage of them. Some people have spiritual crises because they are plagued with guilt after a good friend is killed in a highway accident when they were driving the car. Others have existential crises because their very existence has lost meaning due to the inadvertent killing of civilians during a combat operation. Despite how the trauma may affect individuals, which is equally important as the very nature of the trauma(ta) dictate(s) the responses and expressions in experience, the overarching 'goal' is to support individuals to reconnect to self and soul, and unveil the choices they have control over. This goal is meant to empower them in demonstrating how they might decide 'to act on those choices and potentially transform their lives' (Pitchford, 2009: 446).

An epidemic of trauma

The future of Humanistic Psychology is closely linked to the epidemic of traumatic stress reactions. The US military has invested millions of dollars in suicide prevention programs, only to see the rate increase year after year. US combat veterans take their own lives five times more often than their civilian peers. At least 20 percent of the men and women returning from duty in Iraq and Afghanistan develop PTSD; half of them never seek help, and half

---

1. MDMA (3,4-methylenedioxy-methamphetamine), popularly known as ecstasy. MAPS (Multidisciplinary Association for Psychedelic Studies) is conducting research into treating post-traumatic stress with MDMA-assisted psychotherapy. See http://www.maps.org/research/mdma

of those who do, drop out after the first one or two sessions (Paulson and Krippner, 2010). Relatively few are directed to a humanistic psychotherapist, one who would do more than prescribe medication and focus on symptom reduction. By virtue of their training and orientation, humanistic psychologists could help veterans face their existential crises and focus on developing post-traumatic strengths (Greening, 1997).

When a tsunami hit Asia, the media interviewed local members of the Christian and Muslim clergy. When asked why God or Allah allowed such a tragedy to occur, the typical response was, 'We don't know the reason, but we must trust the Divine, who is all-powerful'. Some survivors found consolation in this response, but others did not. Nor, on other occasions, were they satisfied with similar palliatives when children were killed in the wars overwhelming Iraq, Afghanistan and Pakistan.

In contemporary society, trauma is everywhere. Civilian deaths in recent wars have outnumbered those of combatants. Girls and women are mutilated or killed for alleged religious transgressions. Ethnic and tribal rivalries trigger random murders, and innocent people are caught in the cross-fire of interminable drug wars. It is naïve to think that an infusion of Humanistic Psychology could stop the escalation of trauma, but at least this goal could be put on the agenda of humanistic psychologists and the groups with which they have influence.

Psychotherapy has addressed the sequelae of trauma since its beginning. For decades, research studies have failed to demonstrate its effectiveness appropriately. However, more recent data not only support the proposal that psychotherapy works, but indicate that each of the major schools of psychotherapy work equally well. A recent comparison of half a dozen interventions for US combat veterans with PTSD found that each alleviated suffering, and in comparable proportion. Furthermore, medication without therapy was less effective than therapy without medication. When an antidepressant was used without therapy, its effect upon patients varied little from that upon those given only a placebo (Benish et al., 2008).

Historically, humanistic psychotherapy was not evaluated for a very simple reason: not enough data were available for comparisons to be made. As a result, humanistic psychotherapy is out of the loop when funding is available to study treatments for PTSD. Sadly, humanistic psychotherapy is not the only intervention that has failed to receive attention from funding agencies; so, too, has rational emotive behavior therapy, expressive arts therapy and hypnotically facilitated psychotherapy, not to mention such self-regulation regimens as biofeedback, neurofeedback and Yoga.

When one looks carefully at the nature of PTSD, it is apparent that humanistic psychotherapy is an overlooked asset in restoration and healing. Potentially traumatizing events occur all the time. For some people, genetics and early life experiences make these events actually become traumatic. The traumatic experience does not always lead to PTSD, but when it does, those persons' worldviews and senses of self are assaulted. Their personal myths about, and relationship to, existence are shattered – myths which have served as means for deeper discovery of self and reality, providing opportunities to view the hidden internal capabilities not otherwise known, and shape the present moment, meaning and understanding of the world. Recurring nightmares and flashbacks attempt to replay the traumatic experience (or experiences) until it makes sense. Hyper-arousal tries to protect PTSD survivors against further assault, and emotional numbing buffers the feelings of guilt, shame, fear, depression and anxiety. Social activities are avoided, work opportunities are ignored, and poor concentration prevents mindful, joyous living: a survivor who is barely surviving has not completed the journey to wholeness.

From the point of view of humanistic psychologists, the 'disorder' in PTSD rests not only in the survivor but in the society – a social order that sends its youth into unnecessary combat, does not protect ethnic or sexual minorities against discrimination and ridicule, and fails to provide a safety net when people are struck by natural or human disasters. Neither conventional religion nor conventional psychotherapy dares listen to the trauma survivors who question the notion of a compassionate God, a benevolent government or a benign universe. Yet these are exactly the questions that humanistic, existential and transpersonal psychotherapists are uniquely equipped to confront.

Sarah's story

Sarah came from a small American town, one in which good deeds and honest relationships were not only valued, but very real. Filled with excitement and anticipation, she entered a university in a neighboring state. She was eager to learn and spent long hours in the library. One night walking home, she was intercepted by a bulky figure that put a knife to her throat and warned her not to struggle. When the rape ended and the figure disappeared, Sarah was left helpless in a timeless space of pain, revulsion and fear. She felt that the wound had penetrated the depths of her soul, for she could not cry, nor summon up a voice appropriate enough to tell others of the horror.

Sarah's grades plummeted, she lost interest in her friends, and she cancelled a trip back home. She would not venture outside at night, and when she was able to sleep, the husky figure assaulted her over and over again in her dreams. Sarah's inherent mythology was that the world was a safe place, with the university being a protective abode, and that people were basically good at heart. These myths had been blown apart and there was nothing to take their place. Eventually, she summoned the courage to talk to a university chaplain and a physician. Both listened sympathetically. The chaplain told her to pray, and the doctor put her on medication.

Both of these measures gave palliative relief but did not strike at the core of Sarah's existential and spiritual struggles. Fortunately, her university had a long-standing women's support group and Sarah became a regular member. It was in this group that she felt listened to, respected, understood and supported. Other women shared similar stories, and Sarah slowly began to put her life back together. When she shared her new personal mythology with her family, they found it somewhat cynical. But Sarah had substituted realism for naïveté, spirituality for religion, and practical action for repetitive rumination. She had several counseling sessions with a social worker who was an advisor to the women's group, and found ways to reduce her nightmares through keeping a journal and illustrating it with images of the traumatic experience. She had found post-traumatic strengths that produced positive meaning from the trauma, imbuing her with empathy and courage that she never realized she possessed.

In today's tattered world, there are many Sarah's. Humanistic Psychology offers countless methods of support, including establishing support groups, model communities, and psychotherapeutic services that will help those who are alienated, marginalized and disempowered by trauma to explore within their selves, as well as search beyond. This union of the personal and the transpersonal, the introspective and the communal, the acknowledgment of chaos accompanied by the determination to create meaning, have the potential to actualize the vision that Humanistic Psychology can share with Earth and its inhabitants.

References

Benish, S., Imel, Z. and Wampold, B. (2008) 'The relative efficacy of bona fide psychotherapies for treating post-traumatic stress disorders: a meta-analysis of direct comparisons', *Clinical Psychology Review*, 28, 746–58.

Greening, T. (1997) 'Posttraumatic stress disorder: an existential-humanistic perspective', in S. Krippner and S.M. Powers (eds), *Broken Images, Broken Selves: Dissociative Narratives in Clinical Practice* (pp. 125–35), Washington, DC: Brunner/Mazel.

Greening, T. and Vallejos, L. (2013) *Existential Shattering*, Unpublished paper presented at APA Division 32 conference, Santa Barbara, CA.

Krippner, S., Pitchford, D.B. and Davies, J. (2012) *Posttraumatic Stress Disorder*, Santa Barbara, CA: ABC-CLIO.

Paulson, D.S. and Krippner, S. (2010) *Haunted by Combat: Understanding PTSD in War Veterans*, New York: Roman and Littlefield.

Pitchford, D.B. (2009) 'Existentialism of Rollo May: an influence on trauma treatment', *Journal of Humanistic Psychology*, 49 (4), 441–61.

5 | The Development Community and Its Activist Psychology

Lois Holzman

I don't have much use for labels, categories or academic disciplines, except as entities to disrupt by playing and creating with them. So, by way of introducing myself, let me use a big label: I'm a radically humanistic, practical-critical, postmodern Marxist developmentalist. I'm a community organizer working to involve the masses in a global conceptual revolution, a researcher and scholar located outside the university. I work/play to bring together people and things and ideas – often ones (such as those with which I just described myself) that have been kept apart by ideology, politics, or societal and cultural norms and traditions. That's when it's the most difficult, most fun and most gratifying. Great thinkers, great ideas and great movements need to be brought together and played with, in my experience, to be useful to people. In the following pages, I will share some of what my colleagues and I have brought together in creating *a psychology of becoming*, and what I see as its role in the emergence of an international progressive movement for the re-initiation of human development through performance and play. This new psychology and performance activism movement will be located within the changing dynamics within both the Humanistic and the critical psychology arenas in the USA, of which they have been a part.

The psychology of becoming and performance activism have their roots in the upheavals of the 1960s. Among the millions who were radicalized then was Fred Newman, a New York City working-class man who got his education when public universities in New York were free. He received a Ph.D. in philosophy of science and the foundations of mathematics from Stanford University in 1965 and for a few years taught philosophy at several colleges and universities. Newman resonated with the ways that the cultural movements of the time were challenging the Western glorification of individual self-interest, and was excited by the grassroots communal experiments to transform daily life going on at the time. He felt the need to confront America's failure to honestly deal with its legacy of slavery and racism, as its African-American population remained poor and shut out of America's prosperity.

Believing that profound social change would not come from the university campus, Newman stopped teaching philosophy and left academia. With a handful of student followers, he set up community organizing collectives in working class neighborhoods of New York City. Soon after, they became involved in welfare rights organizing. During the late 1970s two main organizing thrusts were developed: organizing in the poorest, mostly African-American communities of New York City to activate and empower people politically; and engaging the subjectivity of community organizing and the mass psychology of contemporary capitalism. Over four decades the number and variety of projects led by Newman grew exponentially to encompass culture, health, mental health, education and politics.

Two guiding principles were there at the start and remain to this day: first, to be independently funded and supported, and not take money or be constrained by government or other traditional funding sources. This involved reaching out to ordinary Americans for financial support and participation, initially by stopping them on street corners and knocking on the doors of their homes. What has evolved is a new kind of partnership between wealthy Americans and the poor. Second, there was the creation of new kinds of institutions that in their very design and activity challenge the foundations of their traditional 'counterparts'. Some examples: a labor union for welfare recipients who did not labor and, therefore, were at no point of production; a school for children that denied the individuated, knowledge-seeking model of learning that is the bedrock of schooling, East and West; therapy centers with an approach to emotional help that denies the individualism and medical model of mainstream psychotherapy; a 'university' that is free, open to everyone who wants to participate, and has no grades or degrees; a national network of talent shows for youth that denies the conception of talent; electoral political campaigns that are not concerned with winning and political parties that exist to transform political culture – including the possibility of doing away with political parties as the mode of citizen participation.

Today, the organizations that comprise what is now called the 'development community' are the All Stars Project and its youth development programs, university-style development school (UX) and political theatre (Castillo Theatre); the East Side Institute for Group and Short Term Psychotherapy; the Social Therapy Group in NYC and social therapy affiliates in other cities; www.independentvoting.org; and the biennial Performing the World conferences. These organizations have national and international reach, with the direct participation of tens of thousands who impact on hundreds of thousands. Along with their varied foci is a shared methodology that involves people of all ages in the ongoing collective activity of creating new kinds of environments where they can be active performers of their lives. This methodology 'practically-critically' engages the institution of psychology and its impact on people's daily lives (Holzman, 2009; Newman and Holzman, 1996/2006).

From the beginning, it was clear to us that mainstream psychology – with its individualistic focus, claim to objectivity, emulation and imitation of the physical and natural sciences, and, overall, dualistically divided worldview –

was a powerful impediment to ongoing social development and social activism. Along with many, many others at the time, we believed that the personal and political were intimately connected, and put this belief into practice in a new and radical therapy – social therapy. Created by Fred Newman, social therapeutic methodology initially stemmed not from the tradition of Humanistic Psychology, but rather from two other sources: analytic philosophy, philosophy of science and the foundations of mathematics, the area of Newman's doctoral studies; and Marxism, the area Newman began to study seriously when he left university teaching to become a community and political activist. What I added to this was a critical psychology perspective, initially stemming from socio-cultural, cultural-historical activity theory (CHAT) and Vygotskian theory. Before I was aware that there existed a critical psychology critique of Humanistic Psychology as based in and fostering individualism, I considered humanistic approaches to be a form of critical psychology in that they were designed as alternatives to both behaviorism and psychoanalysis (and, to varying degrees, the 'inside–outside' dichotomy which mainstream psychology embraces and perpetuates). Decades later, having been a player in the postmodern turn that a sizable portion of the Humanistic Psychology division of the American Psychological Association took in the 1990s, I still think so. I hope the following brief history of critical psychology in the USA helps illustrate the humanism of Newman's and my work.

Critical psychologies

In the USA, critical psychology, officially designated, is almost non-existent. There are no university departments and only a handful of courses devoted to critical psychology. Dennis Fox and Isaac Prilleltensky, authors of the first American college text on critical psychology (*Critical Psychology: An Introduction*, which first appeared in 1997, and was revised in 2009 by the two original authors and Stephanie Austin), characterize the field as an alternative to mainstream psychology, especially its practices toward the oppressed and vulnerable, and advocate for fundamental changes to existing social structures, with the goal of materializing greater social justice and human wellbeing (Fox et al., 2009: 3–5).

In addition to what is formally termed critical psychology, however, there are dozens of approaches that critique and challenge, in theory and/or practice, the foundations of mainstream psychology. What follows is a summary of these approaches as identity-based, ideology-based and epistemology-based.

Identity-based critical psychology
Here we find psychologies that are critical of how mainstream psychological theory and/or method exclude, ignore or misrepresent vast groupings of people by virtue of psychology's unquestioned allegiance to white, European males as normative. In the USA these psychologies stem from the political movements of the 1960s, including the Black Power movement, La Raza (Latino power), women's liberation and gay liberation. Black, feminist and

gay psychologies were developed (primarily by African Americans, women, and lesbians and gay men, respectively) with psychological conceptions, practices and research agendas specific to what were thought to be the unique characteristics, needs and societal restrictions of each grouping. Black psychologists and feminist psychologists successfully organized themselves and formed professional associations in 1968; for lesbian and gay psychologists, the road was a longer one.

The Association of Black Psychologists (ABPSI) was founded 'to have a positive impact upon the mental health of the national Black community by means of planning, programs, services, training, and advocacy' (ABPSI, n.d.). Still in existence today, the organization has chosen African identity as their mission and the heart of their alternative psychology (termed African psychology) (ibid.). Most Black psychologists working on issues of race, class and ethnicity, however, work within the mainstream, and many are part of the American Psychological Association's (APA) Society for the Psychological Study of Ethnic Minority Issues, established in 1986.

Feminist psychology arguably stems from Karen Horney's work in the 1920s and 1930s critiquing Freud, but contemporary American feminist psychology began with Weisstein's essay, 'Psychology Constructs the Female' – again, in 1968 – and the founding a year later of the Association for Women in Psychology (AWP) during the annual APA convention. In response to the continuing challenges of feminist psychologists within its ranks, a Psychology of Women division within the APA was established in 1973. Since then, most psychology of women issues have been subsumed within the division. The AWP continues with a more activist agenda that links identity politics and identity psychology (AWP, n.d.).

In the 1960s, gay activists in the USA directly confronted governmental and institutional discrimination and police violence targeting homosexuals. The famed 1969 Stonewall riots in NYC's Greenwich Village marked the spark of the gay liberation movement in the USA. For gay activists and their allies, challenging the ways that psychiatry and psychology institutionally oppressed gay people was next on the agenda. The American Psychiatric Association included homosexuality as a mental disorder in its first *Diagnostic and Statistical Manual of Mental Disorders*, published in 1952. From the late 1960s, gay activists, as well as gay psychiatrists within the professional association, aggressively pressured the establishment, and the diagnosis was removed from the manual in 1973. The APA established the Society for the Psychological Study of Lesbian and Gay Issues in 1985, now called the Society for the Psychological Study of Lesbian, Gay, Bisexual and Transgender Issues (SPSLGBTI, n.d.). In the ensuing decades, the depathologizing of homosexuality has yet to be completed, and there is still struggle within the professions of psychiatry, psychology and mental health concerning support for specific legal issues such as gay marriage and gay parenting.

Ideology-based critical psychology
While fully supporting the empowerment and liberation of the above-mentioned identity groups, the critique of the ideology-based psychologies

is from a political-ideological position rather than from a particular identity position. All anti-capitalist ideologies fall into this category. While Marxism is the most prominent, others of note, although little discussed in the USA, are Marxist-feminist critique, postcolonial critique and liberation psychology. The anti-capitalist ideological critique of psychology that has arisen in the USA is centered on how psychology supports the status quo by socializing its citizens to a capitalist ideology through dichotomizing the individual and society, with the result being that individuals become asocial and ahistorical entities. The resulting practices can be devastating, because 'Following this ideological reasoning, solutions for human predicaments are to be found almost exclusively with the self, leaving the social order conveniently unaffected' (Prilleltensky, 1994: 34–5).

My bookshelves are filled with critiques of psychology, nearly all of which make the same point as Prilleltensky does. It is worth noting the nearly complete absence of Marx in these writings. Aside from British psychologist Ian Parker, perhaps the most prolific Marxist ideologically based critical psychologist, we find little reference to (let alone discussion of) Marxism in the works of other well-known ideologically based critics, such as Cushman (1996), Richardson, Fowers and Guignon (1999), Sampson (1993) and Sloan (2000).

Epistemology-based critical psychology

To the extent that the approaches already described include a critique of psychology's methodology, they do so in the service of their identity or ideology critique. In contrast, epistemology-based critiques take mainstream psychology's methodology straight on and offer alternative methodologies for how to understand, study and support human life.

At the core of epistemology-based critiques is mainstream scientific psychology's exclusion of the (inter)subjectivity of human life – a mistake stemming from when psychology adopted and adapted the scientific mindset of the early 20th century, and promoted itself as an endeavor no different in kind from the natural and physical sciences. Psychology devised ways to relate to human beings as if we were no different from the fish in the sea and stars in the sky, and continues to do so with increasing technological sophistication (Danziger, 1990, 1997; Newman and Holzman, 1996/2006). Because, however, human beings have access to our subjectivity, are self-reflecting and self-reflexive, use language, make meaning and sense of our world, a psychology whose knowledge-seeking excludes both the study of these characteristics and the incorporation of these characteristics into its methodology is not a human science at all.

There are many alternative methodologies that are inherently critical of mainstream psychology's epistemology. Some, such as phenomenological and hermeneutic psychology, study human experience interpretively. Devised from the works of the early 20th century German philosophers Heidegger and Husserl, the two approaches in psychology are best known through the works of Gadamer (1976), Levinas (1998), Merleau-Ponty (1962) and Ricoeur (1996). As developed in the USA, Humanistic Psychology has incorporated the seminal ideas from these European scholars in its theoretical and empirical research.

More recent epistemology-based critical psychology includes approaches that fall under the headings of social constructionism and postmodern psychology. It is noteworthy that in the USA the group that was open to social constructionist and postmodern theory and practice, and helped to place them on a broad stage during the 1990s, was the Humanistic Psychology division of the APA, primarily through the efforts of Ken Gergen (1994, 2001, 2006).

What is common to these approaches is the exploration of the very nature of knowledge and how it is generated. There is a focus on language as the meaning-making tool through which human beings construct knowledge and understanding. Meaning making is understood as a relational or social process that occurs between people, rather than within or by an individual. As Lock and Strong state in their recent volume tracing the historical roots of social constructionism, '[Social constructionism] provides a more adequate framework than the dominant tradition for conceptualizing and then exploring the meaning-saturated reality of being human. Our meaningful reality is much "messier" than the Cartesian heritage has had us believe, and much more mysterious' (Lock and Strong, 2010: 353; see also Lock and Strong, 2012).

Another target of these epistemological critiques is psychology's presumption of objectivity and truth. Alternative subjectivist accountings of truth are put forth. For example, social constructionists search for forms of dialogue alternative to objectivist-based debate and criticism (McNamee and Gergen, 1992, 1999), narrativists work to expose the 'storiness' of our lives and help people create their own (and, most often, better) stories (McLeod, 1997; Monk et al., 1997; Rosen and Kuehlwein, 1996; White and Epston, 1990), and collaborative therapists emphasize the dynamic and co-constructed nature of meaning (e.g. Anderson, 1997; Paré and Larner, 2004; Strong and Paré, 2004).

Another group of psychologists critical of the epistemology of mainstream psychology are those within the socio-cultural and cultural-historical activity theory (CHAT) traditions, who draw their inspiration from Soviet activity theory and the writings of Lev Vygotsky (1978, 1987, 1993, 1994, 1997) and Mikhail Bakhtin (1981, 1986). The critique of mainstream psychology is that it relates to human beings not only as isolated from each other, but as isolated from culture and human history. For developers of socio-cultural and CHAT approaches, what it means to develop, learn and live is to engage in human activity so as to become a member of a culture. Similar to the social constructionists and postmodernists, human life is understood as a social-cultural-historical phenomenon, with language (conversation, dialogue) playing a key role in how human beings come to understand and act upon the world.

Where these two epistemological critical psychologies diverge is in their view of human language-making and -using ability. For most socio-cultural and CHAT psychologists, language is understood and empirically studied as a cultural mediator, and so the emphasis in their work is not so much on how meaning is made, but rather on how meaning is appropriated from the culture and the role that language plays as a 'psychological tool' in acculturation (e.g.

Cole, 1996; John-Steiner, 1985; Kozulin, 2001; Rogoff, 2003; Wertsch, 1991). As will be discussed next, the psychology of becoming/social therapeutics is another direction that has emerged as a CHAT perspective that focuses not so much on the use of tools for cultural appropriation, but on the making of tools for the transforming of culture.

Activating postmodernism and postmodernizing activity theory

As a player in the CHAT and postmodern psychology arenas, I see both of them as simultaneously critical and humanistic. Each is rooted in deep concerns and unhappiness with the current state of the world's people and the seemingly intractable poverty, inequality and the failure of the dominant institutions to promote the general welfare. Each implicates the institution of psychology in the mess we are in. Each has evolved a critique of mainstream psychology's core conceptions, and put forth alternative conceptions and practices which have at their core the understanding of human beings as social and cultural (and, to a lesser extent, as historical). Both, it seems to me, are potentially psychologies of becoming. Newman's and my work and the activities of the development community are, methodologically, a synthesis of CHAT and postmodern psychology, fusing postmodern psychology's philosophical critique of psychology with Vygotsky's dialectical method and his understanding of development, learning and play to yield a performatory process ontology (Holzman, 2006).

Our synthesis begins with Marx. His early philosophical writings speak to the fundamentality of human beings as social and active in creating themselves and the world simultaneously (his dialectical methodology): (1) 'As society itself produces man as man, so it is produced by him. Activity and mind are social in their content as well as in their origin: they are social activity and social mind' (Marx, 1967: 129); (2) 'The coincidence of the changing of circumstances and of human activity or self-changing can be conceived and rationally understood only as revolutionary practice' (Marx, 1974: 121). Revolutionary practice is not so much the organizing toward a specific goal, as it is a new conception of method that involves a unity of human beings and the world we have created/are re-creating.

Bringing this Marxist conception into psychology, Vygotsky posited a new conception of method, one that prefigured postmodernism in capturing the always emergent, or 'becoming-ness', of human beings:

> The search for method becomes one of the most important problems of the entire enterprise of understanding the uniquely human forms of psychological activity. In this case, the method is simultaneously prerequisite and product, the tool and the result of the study.
> (Vygotsky, 1978: 65)

Tool-and-result points the way out of the objective–subjective and theory–practice dichotomies that permeate psychology and social movements. Tool use is a main focus of CHAT researchers, who are primarily concerned with the relation between culture and cognition and how children appropriate the culture they are part of. But Vygotsky's tool-and-result suggests that we human beings are not only tool users, but that we are also collective creators of new tool-and-results (we create culture). To the extent that contemporary human beings can become world historic or revolutionary, they must exercise this power (Newman and Holzman, 1993, 2003).

Vygotsky showed how little children learn and develop through tool-and-result activity. Describing play, he said; 'It is as though a child is a head taller than he is. Play is a leading factor in development' (Vygotsky, 1978: 102). He is telling us that in play, we are who we are *and* who we are becoming *at the same time*. Vygotsky noted that children learn by playing with the adults and older children around them, creating performances of learning. Looking at the organizing work we and our colleagues were doing in therapeutics, youth organizing, theatre building, and independent politics, Newman and I came to realize that human development happens, not just with children, but with people of all ages, when we relate to people as 'a head taller' – that is, as who they are becoming. Just as a baby and mother perform conversation before the baby speaks correctly, school-age children can perform reading or math or science before they know how, and adults can learn how to run their world by performing power (Holzman, 1999, 2009; Newman and Holzman, 1993).

We all have the capacity to play as children do, to do what we do not yet know how to do, to be who we are and other than who we are at the same time. The babbling baby, the actor on the stage, the student in a school play, the researcher singing her data, and all of us – are capable of creating new performances of ourselves continuously, if we choose to. In this way, performance is a new ontology, a new understanding of how development happens – through the social-cultural activity of people together creating new possibilities and new options for how to be in, relate to, understand and change the world, which, of course, includes ourselves.

Mainstream psychology is designed as the study of product – the isolated individual at different points in time. It is incapable of seeing, let alone understanding, process. In this way, mainstream psychology contributes mightily to alienation, i.e. relating to the products of production severed from their producers and from the process of their production, that is, as commodities. This way of relating is not limited to cars, loaves of bread and computers. It is, rather, the normal way of seeing and relating to everything in contemporary Western culture. People relate to their lives, their relationships, their feelings, their culture, and so on, as things, torn away from the process of their creation and from their creators. While such 'thingification' is a major factor in people's emotional and learning problems, therapists and educators vary widely in the extent to which they engage alienation in practice, and almost none speak about it theoretically or methodologically.

Performing sociality

If we are commodified and alienated individuals, then transformative social change needs to entail the de-commodification and de-alienation of 'human products' through a positive and constructive process of *producing sociality*. The synthesis of Vygotsky's cultural-historical contributions with postmodern psychology's challenge to the philosophical-psychological conceptions of self, truth, reality and identity yields a method to de-commodify and de-alienate, through a deconstruction–reconstruction of the ontology of modernist psychology in which human beings are understood to be only who we are. The performatory process ontology relates to human beings as both who we are and who we are becoming. And who we are becoming are creators of tools (-and-results) that can continuously transform mundane specific life practices (including those that produce alienation) into new forms of life. Creating these new kinds of tools is the *becoming activity* of creating/giving expression to our sociality.

For Newman, me and the development community, the human capacity to perform – that is, to be both 'who we are' and 'who we are becoming/who we are not' at the very same time – is the source of development (Newman, 1996; Newman and Holzman, 1997). Performance is the activity by which human beings transform and continuously reshape the unity that is *us-and-our environment*. The potential of this activity perspective on performance has been noted by Neimeyer:

> The ironic but liberating insight that the basic 'reality' of human beings is that they are 'pretenders' lies at the heart of [the] performative approach to social therapy .... This non-essentializing stance undermines the totalizing identification of self with any given role, and gives impetus to activity-based initiatives that prompt communities of persons to transcend the limiting scripts they are offered by dominant social institutions.
> (Neimeyer, 2000:195)

This non-essentializing activity calls into question the subjectivist accountings of truth (many truths, all with a small 't') offered by some postmodernists. The social therapeutic methodology rejects truth (in both its upper- and lower-case forms) *in favor of activity*. The ontological shift to activity transforms discourse (in particular, therapeutic discourse) from an epistemological appeal to either an objective, outer Truth/Reality or subjective, inner truths and realities – to an activistic, self-reflexive engagement of the creating of the discourse itself (what is/is becoming). The shift involves relating to therapeutic discourse as performance, and to clients as an ensemble of performers who are, with the therapist's help, staging a new therapeutic conversation (a therapy play) each session. Performing therapy exposes the fictional nature of 'the truth' of our everyday language, our everyday psychology and our everyday stories, and allows people to experience themselves as the collective creators of their emotional growth (Holzman and Mendez, 2003; Newman, 1999).

In the current economic, political and cultural climate, human beings are socialized as commodified and alienated individuals. Mainstream psychology relates to them as such, that is, as *who we* are, not as simultaneously *who we are and who we are becoming*. Transforming the current economic, political and cultural climate involves de-commodifying and de-alienating its human 'products'. Neither negative nor destructive, it is the positive and constructive process of producing sociality by the continuous transformation of mundane specific life practices into new forms of life.

This postmodern understanding of activity dissolves the dualist gap between self and world, between thought and language, between who we are and who we are becoming, between theory and practice, in such a way that we can approach human beings as activists and activity-ists, as tool makers, meaning makers and culture makers, rather than as knowers and perceivers. Further, it actualizes the postmodern critique of modernist psychology's isolated individual through a new ontology – group activity. As a process ontology, a social-relational ontology, group activity raises a new set of questions and challenges for postmodernists, activity theorists, critical psychologists and humanists. For the unit of study and transformation becomes the social unit creating itself.

This shift in focus from the individual to the relationship or group exposes a problematic assumption of psychology – namely, if it is individuals who perceive, read, problem solve, experience emotional distress or disorder, and so on, then the instruction, learning, teaching, treatment or therapy must be individuated. While group work in general and group therapy in particular might at first appear to be challenges and counter examples, typically the group is understood to be a context for individuals to learn and/or get help. In contrast, the process ontology of group activity suggests that individuals need to be organized as social units in order to carry out the tasks of learning and developing, not unlike countless other human endeavors in which people become organized as social units to get a specific job done (Holzman and Newman, 2004).

We are faced with the question, 'What does all this look like in practice?' Some years ago, a group of scholars (Danish critical psychologists) published a review of three of our (Newman and Holzman) books in which they commented that it might well be that one has to experience our work in order to understand it (Nissen et al., 1999). I suspect they meant that critically (i.e. negatively) and, yet, I think they make a critical (i.e. methodological) point – descriptions and maps are not identical to what they describe or map, but all too often the two are confused. Technology has freed us, to some extent, of having to use words to describe what happens in a given situation or environment. I say, 'to some extent' because it is even more seductive to mistake video images for 'what *actually* happened', despite the fact that the camera also represents and has a point of view. With that caveat, I invite you to view some videos of the ways the performance process ontology is manifest differently in the various projects of the development community.[1] I also now provide a few words of description (with the same caveat).

---

1. Dozens of videos can be found at East Side Institute on Vimeo – vimeo.com/esinstitute and All Stars Project, on YouTube – http://www.youtube.com/user/AllStarsProject, as well as on the organizations' websites (eastsideinstitute.org and allstars.org).

Social therapy groups conducted in centers for social therapy in the USA are comprised of 10–25 people, a mix of women and men of varying ages, ethnicities, sexual orientations, class backgrounds and economic status, professions and 'presenting problems'. Such heterogeneous groups are designed to challenge people's notion of a fixed identity (e.g. based on gender, ethnicity, diagnostic label, or 'That's the kind of person I am'). By virtue of this diversity, such groups have more varied 'material' with which the group can work. Those from other countries who have trained in social therapy have created practices in a structure and manner that is coherent with their specific cultural environments, different in varying ways from those in the USA.

Clients who come together to form a social therapy group are given the task to create their group as an environment in which they can get help. This *group activity* is a collective, practical challenge to the assumption that the way people get therapeutic help is to relate to themselves and be related to by others as individuals, complete with problems and with inner selves. This is not to say that people don't come to social therapy individuated and wanting help to feel better or to change. They come to social therapy as they might to any therapy, relating to feelings as individuated and private, something that contributes to people feeling isolated and alone with the 'possession' of their feelings. They look to the therapist for some advice, solution, interpretation, or explanation. The social therapist works with the group (rather than the individuated selves that comprise the group) to organize itself to discover a method of relating to emotional talk relationally rather than individualistically, and as activistic rather than as representational (Newman and Gergen, 1999; Newman and Holzman, 1999). The focus of the social therapeutic group process is, 'How can we talk so that our talking helps build the group?' Speaking as truth telling, reality representing, inner thought and feeling revealing are challenged, as people attempt to converse in new ways and to create something new out of their initial individuated, problem-oriented presentations of self. In this process, people come to appreciate what (and that) they can create, and simultaneously to realize the limitations of trying to learn and grow individually. Group members, at different moments, realize that *growth comes from participating in the process of building the groups in which one functions* (Holzman and Mendez, 2003; Holzman and Newman, 2004, 2012).

In the programs of the All Stars Project, performing and pretending activities, both on and off the theatrical stage, engage youth (and, more recently, adults) who are typically from low-income, Black, Latino and immigrant families with two priority developmental issues: (1) to help them become more worldly and cosmopolitan, i.e. to perform their way from the margins into the mainstream of American society; and (2) to have them experience, over and over again, their capacity to grow, i.e. to create an active understanding *that* they can create endless performances for navigating life's complex mix of scripted (institutional) and unscripted (non-institutional) situations. All Stars programs are voluntary. Participants are reached through multiple methods of grassroots outreach – door-knocking in housing projects, posting and handing out flyers in neighborhoods, subways and outside of schools, and making presentations at schools and churches. There is also significant neighborhood word of mouth.

When young people come to an All Stars Project program, they participate in creating ensemble performances in which they are taken seriously and given the chance to perform as community citizens (Newman and Fulani, 2011). They are helped to do so by the staff and middle-class and affluent adults, often business professionals and performing artists who are also volunteers, who perform 'a head taller' along with them. All Stars Project programs intervene on the impact that these young people's life circumstances have on their capacity to see possibilities and to act on them. Growing up in poverty more often than not creates hopelessness, a narrow choice of identities and, not infrequently, anger – ways of being that in turn have negative consequences on so many aspects of people's lives. The work to re-initiate development as the capacity to see possibilities and to act on them is a new form of social activism based in a psychology of becoming.

Whether rich or poor or in between, all people need to have the opportunity to participate in qualitatively transforming themselves – and the world. In my experience, performing – with and as 'other' – is the humanistic imperative of our day.

References

Anderson, H. (1997) *Conversation, Language and Possibilities: A Postmodern Approach to Therapy*, New York: Basic Books.
ABPSI (n.d.) Association of Black Psychologists: history. Retrieved 10 May 2013 from http://www.abpsi.org/about_history.html
AWP (n.d.) Association for Women in Psychology: objectives. Retrieved 10 May 2013 from http://www.awpsych.org/index.php?option=com_content&view=article&id=51&Itemid=65&limitstart=1
Bakhtin, M.M. (1981) *The Dialogic Imagination: Four Essays*, Austin, TX: University of Texas Press.
Bakhtin, M.M. (1986) *Speech Genres and Other Late Essays*, Austin, TX: University of Texas Press.
Cole, M. (1996) *Cultural Psychology: A Once and Future Discipline*, Cambridge, MA: Harvard University Press.
Cushman, P. (1996). *Constructing the Self, Constructing America: A Cultural History of Psychotherapy*, New York: De Capo Press.
Danziger, K. (1990) *Constructing the Subject: Historical Origins of Psychological Research*, New York: Cambridge University Press.
Danziger, K. (1997) *Naming the Mind: How Psychology Found Its Language*, London: Sage.
Fox, D. and Prilleltensky, I. (1997) *Critical Psychology: An Introduction*, London: Sage.
Fox, D., Prilleltensky, I. and Austin, S. (2009) *Critical Psychology: An Introduction*, 2nd edn, London: Sage.
Gadamer, H.-G. (1976) *Philosophical Hermeneutics*, Berkeley, CA: University of California Press.
Gergen, K.J. (1994) *Realities and Relationships: Soundings in Social Construction*, Cambridge, MA: Harvard University Press.
Gergen, K.J. (2001) *Social Construction in Context*, London: Sage.
Gergen, K.J. (2006) *Therapeutic Realities: Collaboration, Oppression and Relational Flow*, Chagrin Falls, OH: Taos Institute Publications.

Holzman, L. (ed.) (1999) *Performing Psychology: A Postmodern Culture of the Mind*, New York: Routledge.
Holzman, L. (2006) 'Activating postmodernism', *Theory and Psychology*, 16 (1), 109–23.
Holzman, L. (2009) *Vygotsky at Work and Play*, London and New York: Routledge.
Holzman, L. and Mendez, R. (2003) *Psychological Investigations: A Clinician's Guide to Social Therapy*, New York: Brunner-Routledge.
Holzman, L. and Newman, F., with Strong, T. (2004) 'Power, authority and pointless activity: the developmental discourse of social therapy', in T. Strong and D. Paré (eds), *Furthering Talk: Advances in Discursive Therapies* (pp. 73–86), New York: Kluwer Academic.
Holzman, L. and Newman, F. (2012) 'Activity and performance (and their discourses) in social therapeutic practice', in A. Lock and T. Strong (eds), *Discursive Perspectives in Therapeutic Practice* (pp. 184–95), Oxford: Oxford University Press.
John-Steiner, V. (1985) *Notebooks of the Mind. Explorations of Thinking*, Albuquerque, NM: University of New Mexico Press (2nd edn, 1997).
Kozulin, A. (2001) *Psychological Tools: A Sociocultural Approach to Education*, Cambridge, MA: Harvard University Press.
Levinas, E. (1998) *Otherwise than Being*, Pittsburg, PA: Duquesne University Press.
Lock. A. and Strong, T. (2010) *Social Constructionism: Sources and Stirring in Theory and Practice*, New York: Cambridge University Press.
Lock, A. and Strong, T. (2012) *Discursive Perspectives in Therapeutic Practice*, Oxford: Oxford University Press.
Marx, K. (1967) 'Economic and philosophical manuscripts', in E. Fromm (ed.), *Marx's Concept of Man* (pp. 90–196), New York: Frederick Ungar Publishing Co.
Marx, K. (1974) 'Theses on Feuerbach', in K. Marx and F. Engels, *The German Ideology* (pp. 121–3), New York: International Publishers.
Marx, K. and Engels, F. (1974) *The German Ideology*, New York: International Publishers.
McLeod, J. (1997) *Narrative and Psychotherapy*, London: Sage.
McNamee, S. and Gergen, K.J. (eds) (1992) *Therapy as Social Construction*, London: Sage.
McNamee, S. and Gergen, K.J. (eds) (1999) *Relational Responsibility: Resources for Sustainable Dialogue*, Thousand Oaks, CA: Sage.
Merleau-Ponty, M. (1962) *Phenomenology of Perception*, London: Routledge & Kegan Paul.
Monk, G., Winslade, J., Crocket, K. and Epston, D. (eds) (1997) *Narrative Therapy in Practice: The Archaeology of Hope*, San Francisco: Jossey-Bass.
Neimeyer, R.A. (2000) 'Performing psychotherapy: reflections on postmodern practice', in L. Holzman and J. Morss (eds), *Postmodern Psychologies, Societal Practice and Political Life* (pp. 190–201), New York: Routledge.
Newman, F. (1996). *Performance of a Lifetime: A Practical-philosophical Guide to the Joyous Life*, New York: Castillo.
Newman, F. (1999) 'A therapeutic deconstruction of the illusion of self', in L. Holzman (ed.), *Performing Psychology: A Postmodern Culture of the Mind* (pp. 111–32), New York: Routledge.
Newman, F. and Fulani, L. (2011) *Solving the Education Crisis in America: A Special Report. 'Let's Pretend'*, New York: All Stars Project, Inc. Retrieved 7 June 2013 from http://www.allstars.org/content/lets-pretend
Newman, F. and Gergen, K. (1999) 'Diagnosis: the human cost of the rage to order', in L. Holzman (ed.), *Performing Psychology: A Postmodern Culture of the Mind* (pp. 73–86), New York: Routledge.
Newman, F. and Holzman, L. (1993) *Lev Vygotsky: Revolutionary Scientist*, London: Routledge.

Newman, F. and Holzman, L. (1997) *The End of Knowing: A New Developmental Way of Learning*, London: Routledge.

Newman, F. and Holzman, L. (1999) 'Beyond narrative to performed conversation ('In the beginning' comes much later)', *Journal of Constructivist Psychology*, 12 (1), 23–40.

Newman, F. and Holzman, L. (2003) 'All power to the developing!', *Annual Review of Critical Psychology*, 3, 8–23.

Newman, F. and Holzman, L. (2006) *Unscientific Psychology: A Cultural-performatory Approach to Understanding Human Life*, Lincoln, NE: iUniverse Inc. (originally published Westport, CT: Praeger, 1996)

Nissen, M., Axel, E. and Jensen, T.B. (1999) 'The abstract zone of proximal conditions', *Theory and Psychology*, 9 (3), 417–26.

Paré, D.A. and Larner, G. (eds) (2004) *Collaborative Practice in Psychology and Therapy*, New York: Haworth Clinical Practice Press.

Prilleltensky, I. (1994) *The Morals and Politics of Psychology: Psychological Discourse and the Status Quo*, Albany, NY: State University of New York Press.

Richardson, F.C., Fowers, B.J. and Guignon, C.B. (eds) (1999) *Re-envisioning Psychology: Moral Dimensions of Theory and Practice*, San Francisco: Jossey-Bass.

Ricoeur, P. (1996) *The Hermeneutics of Action*, London: Sage.

Rogoff, B. (2003) *The Cultural Nature of Human Development*, New York: Oxford University Press.

Rosen, H. and Kuehlwein, K.T. (eds) (1996) *Constructing Realities: Meaning-making Perspectives for Psychotherapists*, San Francisco: Jossey-Bass.

Sampson, E.E. (1993) *Celebrating the Other*, Hemel Hempstead: Harvester Wheatsheaf.

Sloan, T. (ed.) (2000) *Critical Psychology: Voices for Change*, London: Macmillan.

SPSLGBTI (n.d.) Society for the Psychological Study of Lesbian, Gay, Bisexual and Transgender Issues. About Division 44. Retrieved 10 May 2013 from http://www.apadivision44.org/about

Strong, T. and Paré, D.A. (eds) (2004) *Furthering Talk: Advances in Discursive Therapies*, New York: Kluwer Academic.

Vygotsky, L.S. (1978) *Mind in Society*, Cambridge, MA: Harvard University Press.

Vygotsky, L.S. (1987) *The Collected Works of L.S. Vygotsky, Volume 1*, New York: Plenum.

Vygotsky, L.S. (1993) *The Collected Works of L.S. Vygotsky, Volume 2*, New York: Plenum.

Vygotsky, L.S. (1994) 'The problem of the environment', in R. van der Veer and J. Valsiner (eds), *The Vygotsky Reader* (pp. 338–54), Oxford: Blackwell.

Vygotsky, L.S. (1997) 'The historical meaning of the crisis in psychology: a methodological investigation', in *The Collected Works of L.S. Vygotsky, Volume 3* (pp. 233–343), New York: Plenum.

Weisstein, N. (1968) ' Psychology Constructs the Female.' Available from http://www.uic.edu/orgs/cwluherstory/CWLUArchive/psych.html

Wertsch, J.V. (1991) *Voices of the Mind: A Sociocultural Approach to Mediated Action*, Cambridge, MA: Harvard University Press.

White, M. and Epston, D. (1990) *Narrative Means to Therapeutic Ends*, New York: W.W. Norton.

6 | The State of Humanistic Psychology: Where all monkeys are apes but not all apes are monkeys

Derek Lawton and Seamus Nash

I Introduction

This is a shortened version of a larger work on the professional identity of Humanistic Psychology in Britain. This version focuses on how the identity and integrity of Humanistic Psychology may be vulnerable to internal and external exploitation, and how the ethos of the tradition remains in danger of being subsumed within a broad-based 'integrative' identity, which has little identification with, or adherence to, the fundamental tenets of Humanistic Psychology.

The chapter offers an informed, first-hand testimony of how humanistic psychotherapy has been represented with regards to professional developments within the section/college structure of the UK Council for Psychotherapy (UKCP) in ways at odds with the humanistic tradition as held by the UK Association of Humanistic Psychology Practitioners (UKAHPP). In raising awareness of what has transpired in the name of Humanistic Psychology, the authors would support the emergence of an open debate in the hope that a solution might be reached whereby both 'humanistic' and 'integrative' perspectives can co-exist, without either being reduced to the terms and values of the other.

II 'Humanistic' – A philosophical identity: The integrative question

Statutory regulation and the 'Skills for Health' initiative
The UK Association for Humanistic Psychology Practitioners (UKAHPP) was a founder member of the UK Standing Conference for Psychotherapy (later known as the UKCP). Established in the late 1980s, the UKCP would go on to accredit training organizations and establish a register of psychotherapists, although individual registrants would not gain member status until 2010 (see also Rowan, 2013).

The UKCP adopted an organizational structure known as 'sections' (later known as 'colleges'). However, a number of training organizations found it difficult to fit into the section structure: some were 'integrative' in nature, drawing on theory and practice informed by more than one psychotherapy modality, while others did not meet the rigorous training standards set by their section of choice. Eventually, these 'homeless' organizations were welcomed into the Humanistic Section, and thus the Humanistic and Integrative Section (or 'HIPS') was born. The flagship statement of HIPS read:

> This Section includes different psychotherapies which approach the individual as a whole person, including body, feelings, mind and spirit ... Organizations in this Section practise approaches compatible with the following: Humanistic Psychotherapy, Existential Psychotherapy, Transpersonal/Psycho-spiritual Psychotherapy, and Integrative Therapy.
> (UKCP, 2007)

At the UKCP Extraordinary General Meeting on 3 November 2007, it was announced that the Department of Health (DH) had set out a specific modality training list for psychotherapy, which included psychoanalytical/psychodynamic, cognitive behavioural and family/systemic modalities. There was an outcry at the exclusion of *Humanistic and Integrative Psychotherapy* from this list.

In accordance with the UK Government's White Paper *Trust, Assurance and Safety: The Regulation of Healthcare Professionals in the 21st Century* (DH, 2007) and additional provision for secondary legislation under Section 60 of the Health Act (Health Act, 1999), on 13 December 2007 the Health Professions Council (HPC, 2008), a regulator set up by the last Labour Government, announced its intention to investigate and make recommendations to the Secretary of State for Health on the statutory regulation of counsellors and psychotherapists. The HPC (2008) remit is to:

1. Maintain and publish a public register of properly qualified members of the professions
2. Approve and uphold high standards of education and training, and continuing good practice
3. Investigate complaints and take appropriate action
4. Work in partnership with the public, and a range of other groups, including professional bodies
5. Promote awareness and understanding of the aims of the Council

However, unlike other professions previously regulated under the HPC (such as psychology), psychotherapy and counselling had not applied to be regulated; instead, the government had instructed the HPC to commence proceedings for statutory regulation on an unsolicited basis.

In July 2008 the HPC set up a Professional Liaison Group as a consultative body working with representatives from the UK Council for Psychotherapy

(UKCP), the British Association for Counselling and Psychotherapy (BACP), the British Psychoanalytic Council (BPC), and the British Association for Behavioural and Cognitive Psychotherapies (BABCP), as well as representatives of service users, trainers and other professions. The liaison group was charged with considering:

1. The structure of the register
2. Professional titles
3. Standards of proficiency
4. Standards of education and training
5. Post-registration standards
6. Grand-parenting arrangements

On 14 December 2007, a campaign was launched within UKCP/HIPS which put forward the case for 'Integrative' as the title of choice to represent HIPS psychotherapists in the process of statutory regulation, stating that the term 'Humanistic' should be dropped, as it was insufficiently robust to stand up to parliamentary scrutiny, and could easily be used in discriminatory ways to smear and discredit HIPS, with some describing it as comprising 'cranky hippies from the 1960s'. The HIPS Executive Group which was responsible for co-ordinating section business did not authorize this campaign.

On 28 February 2008, a letter from a leading 'integrative' campaigner and ex-member of the HIPS Executive was published in *The Times* newspaper, stating that '... there are at least four recognised modalities of psychotherapy: CBT, psychodynamic, family/systemic and integrative' (*The Times*, 2008). There was no mention of 'humanistic'.

Whether by accident or design, it now seemed that internal and external forces were determined to exclude, or at least marginalize, Humanistic Psychology as a political player in the field of psychotherapy.

Also in 2008, the Department of Health launched the Skills for Health (SfH) initiative, and set out to establish research-based occupational standards for counselling and psychotherapy on a modality basis, again limiting the range to psychoanalytical/psychodynamic, cognitive behavioural and family/systemic, and stating, to the astonishment of many, that 'most other modalities are variants of these, or post-basic specialisms'.

Tensions between those who proclaimed 'integrative' as the unifying identity, and those who wished to preserve the identity of the humanistic tradition, were addressed at a section meeting held at the UKCP 2008 Annual General Meeting. The 'integrative' lobby took the initiative and put forward three proposals:

1. That the HIP Section elect a task force immediately to address the issue of statutory regulation
2. That the HIP Section agree to collectively discuss the possibility of the title 'Integrative' being used for the purpose of statutory regulation in order to gain a place on the parliamentary agenda

3. That the HIP Section involve the task force for statutory regulation with the process of producing a document that could represent the training standards of an integrative theoretical framework, core competencies and principles of professional practice which represented the HIPS member organizations effectively

(UKCP: HIPS, 2008a)

A tense discussion ensued and a position, though not unanimous, was reached: 'it was decided that for the purpose of our approach to the government that we would use "Humanistic Integrative" or "Integrative Humanistic" [no 'and'] and our statement would be written to reflect this' (UKCP: HIPS, 2008a).

With regards to Skills for Health, nominations for a modality working group were put forward:

The purpose of the group will be to write the National Occupational Standards for Humanistic and (hopefully) Integrative psychotherapy that reflect the interpretation of research based evidence. Once in the group, members act on behalf of the tradition of the modality, not their member organisation, or to the HIP Section.

(UKCP: HIPS, 2008c)

In an effort to unite the HIP Section within a single title, whilst attempting to legitimize an integrative modality, the Integrative Humanistic Psychotherapy (IHP) task force, or 'political group', as it would become known, put forward numerous papers for statutory regulation and Skills for Health purposes. These papers offered a plausible argument for an integrative perspective, had the IHP lobby wished to establish a new and separate integrative section within the UKCP, but this was not the case. Not everyone agreed with the IHP worldview, and those who opposed it ran the risk of something akin to character assassination. The 'political group' did not want to establish 'Integrative' as a stand-alone modality. Consequently, in an effort to attain validity for Skills for Health purposes, the group claimed humanistic research as a sub-component as evidence of an integrative modality, which it claimed could 'safely hold and protect' all psychotherapy approaches represented by the HIP Section.

The Department of Health was clear about the terms of reference for joining the Modality Expert Reference Working Group, in that participants were invited as modality specialists, not organizational representatives. Despite this, the IHP political group launched a co-ordinated strategy to gain influence and win over the Expert Reference Group.

In response to an 11 March 2008 e-petition seeking independent chartered professional status for psychotherapy, the Prime Minister's website (Prime Minister's Office, 2008a) stated:

We wish to avoid an increase in different types, or modalities, of psychotherapy. All models share some basic function, and Skills for Health consulted on the competencies of these models earlier this year. Our view of a comprehensive mental health programme is that it should provide three main modalities. These are psychoanalytical or psychodynamic, cognitive behavioural therapy and family or systemic psychotherapy. Most other modalities are variants of these or post-basic specialisms.

An HPC representative on the SfH Strategy Committee reported that the Prime Minister's website statement was a mistake, that a Humanistic and Integrative modality was always one of the four modalities originally discussed, and that an error had been made by a junior official who was 'not fully in the know'. The representative also said that the matter of omission by the Department of Health would be rectified. On 7 May 2008 a follow-up statement appeared on the Prime Minister's website (Prime Minister's Office, 2008b):

> We are aware that some people have interpreted this as implying that final decisions about the scope of psychotherapy regulation have now been taken. This is not the case. We are also aware that there is an ongoing debate about the precise number of modalities which should be included within the scope of regulated practice in future and that there is an argument for more than three modalities to be included. Final decisions about the precise scope of practice to be regulated have yet to be taken. This will be done in consultation with the stakeholders, including the professional bodies.

The IHP political group presented a modality statement to Skills for Health (UKCP: HIPS, 2008b). An additional statement (UKCP: HIPS, 2008c) was sent to Peter Fonagy, chair of the Strategy Reference Group for SfH, which proclaimed:

> Integrative Humanistic Psychotherapy (IHP) as an umbrella term for a group of approaches that have developed within the Humanistic/Existential philosophical tradition over a period of more than seventy years ... with a scholarly and research-based tradition ... which ... has given rise to ... specific principles for psychotherapy practice and research.

The statement implied that any affiliation to Humanistic Psychology included an integrative perspective, and that all integrative psychotherapists are humanistic, which is not the case, and thus the diversity within the HIP Section had been compromised. The notion of 'third force' psychology as a legitimate alternative to psychoanalytic and CBT perspectives was being misrepresented. Evidence indicating that psychotherapy is beneficial not because of the therapist's philosophical allegiance, but due to common factors unique to the therapist and client, was construed to mean that there are as many styles of psychotherapy as there are psychotherapists, and therefore all psychotherapists are integrative.

Concern was expressed about the meaning of the term 'integrative'. Some seemed to use the term to pull together different theories, which is inadequate for modality purposes, as it makes it difficult to scrutinize evidence with any consistency. Drawing on the work of Norcross and Goldfried (2005), which was often quoted by the integrative IHP lobby as a supporting reference, four definitions are identified:

> a. *Assimilative Integration:* 'A firm grounding in one system [or philosophy] of psychotherapy but with a willingness to incorporate or assimilate, in a

considered fashion, perspective or practices from other schools' (Messer, 1992: 151, cited in Norcross and Goldfried, 2005).

b. *Theoretical Integration:* 'Two or more therapies are integrated in the hope that the result will be better than the constituent therapies alone' (Norcross, 2005: 8).

c. *Common Factors:* 'Seek to determine the core ingredients that different therapies share in common' (Norcross, 2005: 9).

d. *Technical Eclecticism:* 'The best treatment for the person and the problem ... guided primarily by data on what has worked best for others' (Norcross, 2005: 8).

If the integrative political group were claiming that IHP fits the first definition (assimilation) and if 'humanistic' is the philosophical grounding within the HIP Section, then 'integrative' is a redundant modality title. On this basis it would make sense for the UKCP-HIP Section/College to rally around humanistic psychotherapy as the unifying title and identity.

The second definition (theoretical integration) could be seen as a basis for establishing a new modality – but it would not offer IHP much legitimacy in the short term. Like the last two psychotherapist-specific definitions, they do not meet the inclusion criteria for modality purposes:

1. Evidence of effectiveness by a minimum of two randomized controlled trials
2. Evidence of a manualized conceptualization of the modality

Skills for Health took the view that those psychotherapy approaches which could not be ascribed to the philosophical underpinning of one of the four specified modalities were too difficult to evaluate, and assumed that they were either eclectic, sat outside the field of psychotherapy or, as the Department of Health had previously stated, were 'variants of these, or post-basic specialisms'.

The fundamental error of the IHP lobby is what philosopher Gilbert Ryle (1949) termed a 'category mistake', which is the error of ascribing to something of one category a feature attributable only to another category. Therefore, to ascribe 'humanistic' to 'integrative' is a misrepresentation of the 'humanistic' category. This is a philosophical crux of the debate which, up to the present, has not been openly addressed.

The British Association for the Person-Centred Approach (BAPCA) aimed to pressurize the government to accept the person-centred approach as a viable modality in its own right. The initial modality working title was 'Humanistic – Person-Centred – Experiential', but like 'integrative', 'person-centred' and its sub-variants could not be accepted as a psychotherapy modality in its own right. Although some within the person-centred community have attempted to distance their approach from Humanistic Psychology (and, for that matter, all other professional affiliations), the person-centred approach was highly influential in establishing Humanistic Psychology as the 'third force' in psychology, and person-centred psychotherapy has since become well established as a humanistic approach. Rogers (1965) affirmed his allegiance to Humanistic Psychology, which is also reflected in his statement about: '… our contribution as Humanistic Psychologists with a Person-Centered philosophy …' (Rogers, 1980: 205).

The Skills for Health Expert Reference Group (ERG; see Fonagy, 2010), headed by Professor Robert Elliott, explained that IHP was not an existing modality and, as a consequence, could not claim to represent the majority of humanistic and integrative approaches in the UK. The ERG also emphasized that IHP had no established research standing to evidence its efficacy or effectiveness; and although a solid body of evidence exists in support of humanistic and integrative independently of one another, IHP could not piggyback on this evidence to legitimize a new modality. As there was no reference to IHP in any integrative literature, it was clearly something new. It cannot be assumed that by simply bolting together two or more approaches, the philosophical integrity of those approaches will be preserved without encountering issues of compatibility. The assertion that 'IHP represents more than 5,000 psychotherapists and students in training' seems to have been nothing more than wishful thinking, fashioned by those who had coined the term in an effort to re-write the psychotherapy lexicon to further an alternative ideology, whilst compromising the identity and tradition of Humanistic Psychology.

There is, however, compelling evidence that humanistic psychotherapy has a robust research tradition, and that humanistic practice built on empathy, acceptance, collaboration and a genuine therapeutic relationship 'support[s] the humanistic assumption that clients are the principle drivers of therapeutic change' (Cooper, 2008: 162). Thus, 'Meta-analyses of humanistic therapies, as a whole, support the hypotheses that they are efficacious and effective forms of therapy, with a large average pre-post effect size of 0.99, reducing down to 0.89 when compared against wait-list or no-therapy controls' (Elliott, Greenberg et al., 2004, cited in Cooper, 2008: 162).

The final version of the National Occupational Standards (Fonagy, 2010) was approved for publication in June 2010, and sits alongside the *Professional Occupational Standards for Psychotherapists and Psychotherapeutic Counsellors* developed by the UKCP (UKCP, 2010) in anticipation of the statutory regulation of psychotherapy via the Health Professions Council. Ironically, the term 'humanistic', claimed by many to be redundant, cranky and unacceptable to government departments, was eventually agreed by senior clinicians and academics as the unifying title for the fourth modality.

III Professional renaissance and promised reformation

Meanwhile, following a lengthy process, changes to the UKCP Byelaws – version 9 and UKCP Standing Orders – version 3 (UKCP, 2009a) had been agreed, and were to take effect on 5 December 2009. These constitutional changes would herald the transformation of UKCP sections into colleges; and the enfranchisement of *registrants*, who became *individual members* with full voting rights. It was a bold step for the 84 training organizations to now share power with some 6,500 registrants.

The UKCP 2009 election for a new chair marked the beginning of UKCP reforms, and for the first time, all members (organization and individual) would be eligible to vote.

The UKCP 2009 chair election

The activities of the HIPS political group re-emerge with the advent of the 2009 UKCP election for a new chair. On the assumption that statutory regulation through the Health Professions Council was part of the fabric of the UKCP, the HIPS political group openly challenged the legitimacy of one of the proposed candidates to stand for election as UKCP chair. Professor Andrew Samuels included in his manifesto proposals to make it possible for UKCP members who did not favour regulation via HPC to enter into 'principled non-compliance' (later referred to as Alternative Professional Accountability). Samuels made his strong opposition to HPC completely clear. He also stated that he wished to start a conversation within the profession, and between the profession and the government, to determine a more appropriate route for psychotherapy regulation, a position for which he had canvassed with the Alliance for Counselling and Psychotherapy.

On 27 September 2009, and without any consultation with the appointed executive, the HIPS political group assumed executive power over the functioning of the section with regards to any political matters associated with professional regulation. The group issued a 12-page briefing statement to the wider UKCP membership, entitled 'The Future in Your Hands' (UKCP: HIPS, 2009a). The bulk of the document was self-congratulatory, proclaiming the successes of the political group and their associates. The document also warned members that their professional interest would be greatly impaired as a consequence of Andrew Samuels being elected UKCP chair: 'To elect a chair who is associated with the leadership of the "Alliance for Counselling and Psychotherapy Against State Regulation" ... would undermine the UKCP's central aims, purpose and function for the last twenty years' (UKCP: HIPS, 2009a).

Contrary to what was written, the political group was not speaking on behalf of the HIP Section; it had no authority from the HIPS Executive to act in this manner. This was a clear illustration of the exercise of power to advance a single position at the exclusion of any other position. By accident or design, the political group would often adopt tactics akin to what Antonio Gramsci referred to as 'hegemony' – the organization of consent, without the overt use of physical force, through the continued dissemination of information as if it were fact.

The UKAHPP and the Institute of Psychosynthesis formally lodged complaints with the UKCP, emphasizing that the political group was acting without authority as fifth columnists, and that the personal attack against Andrew Samuels was unacceptable.

The political group also stated that Andrew Samuels 'refers to himself as being above the law as he is a Jungian analyst rather than a "bog-standard psychotherapist"...'. Samuels took exception, and insisted on a retraction. On 29 September 2009 the political group recognized that the statement 'could be taken to mean that he is intending to do something against the law'. However the retraction only provided the political group with the opportunity to distribute their 12-page document to a wider audience, albeit without the offending statement, but with additional quotations from Samuels' website, presented out of context, suggesting that he could not be trusted to represent the interests of the UKCP's diverse membership. In effect, this was not really an apology, nor a retraction.

The political group appealed for support to the HIP Section delegates at their meeting on 20 October 2009 and, surprisingly, the following resolution was carried:

> That we move toward to express [sic] confidence in the action taken by the political group in issuing the statement entitled 'The Future in Your Hands'.
> – For: 16; Against: 1; Abstentions: 1.
>
> (UKCP: HIPS, 2009b)

With renewed vigour and a re-affirmed mandate, the political group seemed confident in executing their next plan. On 21 October 2009, a member of the group approached the President of the International Association of Analytic Psychology (IAAP) requesting a reference, and any other information concerning Andrew Samuels' standing for the chair of the UKCP. This request was signed off as 'UKCP Fellow, External Affairs Officer, Humanistic and Integrative Section'; there is no evidence to indicate that references were requested for other candidates. The person who signed the letter was not a member of the HIPS Executive, and no one was ever appointed 'External Affairs Officer'. The IAAP President assumed it was a legitimate reference request, and contacted Samuels about the election. As a consequence, the significance and severity of the situation emerged and Samuels lodged a complaint with the UKCP, with possible legal implications.

It has been reported that at its meeting in September 2009, the UKCP Board of Trustees was advised that it was legitimate for it to express a view about the imminent election for UKCP chair. It has also been reported that outside normal session, it was agreed that each college would do its best to persuade its members not to vote for Samuels, and that care should be taken not to go too far in this unusual project which, though legal, carried a risk of backfiring – which in the event is what happened.

On 9 November 2009, the UKCP election result announced that Andrew Samuels had won with 66 per cent of the votes cast, equating to 31 per cent of eligible voters. On the same day, the following statement was issued by the HIPS political group:

> The HIPS political group during the teleconference on November 9th formally and unanimously took the decision to stand down in their capacity as representing the political interests of the section with immediate effect from this date. Our achievable work being done we would like to thank the section as a whole for all their support.
>
> (UKCP: HIPS, 2009c)

Although the political group had been dissolved, its members continued to influence decision making within HIPS and the UKCP; and a new professional interest group, 'Integrity', was also set up, with the advancement of statutory regulation through the HPC being one of its objectives.

In order to move on and take up his role as UKCP chair, Samuels reached an amicable agreement about the unsolicited reference request. But the matter had not gone away, and on the 27 January 2010 the following resolution was put forward and carried:

> Xxx is reimbursed for the legal costs incurred in clearing Xxx's name as a consequence of working on behalf of HIPS. – For: 13; Against: 0; Abstentions: 2
> (UKCP: HIPC, 2010a)

In accordance with the section's Expenses Policy and Guidelines, the section Finance Committee reported that it had declined payment of these costs, as it could not be determined whether they were legitimate expenses incurred as a direct result of discharging duties authorized by and on behalf of the section. In addition, no formal claim with receipts had been lodged. Any subsequent developments regarding these costs would be referred to the UKCP (UKCP: HIPC, 2010b).

The UKCP 2009 constitution

The transformation of the HIP section to a college and the election of officers were not easy to implement. The transition required more than a change of name, but to some this was as far as they were willing to go. At first there was optimism. A working group was established to formulate a college constitution. Its main challenge was to ensure that both individual and organizational member interests were accommodated. A draft constitution was drawn up, and anxieties about organizational members sharing power with individual members ran high. Some advocated the retention of the old section structure with token individual member representation; others were not so generous – 'What if they make the wrong decisions?' Other models and frameworks were considered, but nothing could be agreed. In an effort to restore some integrity, the original constitution working group suggested that any pre-election constitution (including their own) would be an imposition, and the best that could be offered was a transitional arrangement to allow for the election of a college executive, which could formulate a constitution with a mandate from the membership. It was proposed that:

> The above group will meet together to fine tune and agree the transitional constitution and to implement it. – For: 17; Against: 0; Abstentions: 0.
> (UKCP: HIPC, 2011)

Although this resolution was carried, further dispute over the meaning of the word 'implement' would unfold – the majority of delegates conformed to the then chair and vice-chair's position that it does not mean 'to make something happen'. Repeating sentiments expressed at the 4 October 2011 HIPC delegates meeting, the UKCP vice-chair questioned the validity of the

UKCP democratic process. He went on to say that he was not able to find a single reference as to how college officers should be selected, never mind elected, and that there is no necessity to hasten the process of developing a way in which members of the college can participate and contribute to the work of the college. Thus, in the absence of any clarity he was suggesting that it was up to the colleges (dominated by organizational member interests) to determine the future, to do what they want, when they want, and without any redress.

The case for college elections
The rights of individual and organizational members as stakeholders of the charity are enshrined in the UKCP 2009 constitution, which came into effect on 5 December 2009:

- 'Members of the charity prior to the effective date, and individuals existing on the charity register as of the effective date, are members of the charity' (UKCP Articles of Association 2.1b).

- The UKCP defines colleges as 'a forum for the coming together of Organisational and Individual Members under the umbrella name of the College reflecting shared modality interests' (UKCP Standing Orders 7), including a vested interest in the development of the college(s) with which they have affiliation. A college is an umbrella/container for members with shared modality beliefs and values to come together, with equal status.

- The UKCP Byelaws and Standing Orders also set out requirements for colleges, including the election/appointment of executive officers in the capacity of: 'Chair, Vice Chair, Treasurer, Council Representative' (UKCP Standing Orders 7).

- The structure and appointment of offices to Colleges, Faculties, Board of Trustees and Psychotherapy Council is governed by the UKCP Byelaws Part 2, Structure 10–15 (pp. 3–6). The voting rights of 'organizational members' and 'individual members' in respect of the structures stated is covered in Byelaws 7 and 15. 'Full Individual Members ... and Full Organisational Members ... shall each be eligible to vote' (UKCP Byelaws 7.1); 'voting in elections ... will be on the basis of one full member one vote' (UKCP Byelaws 15.1).

- The UKCP Byelaws also state that 'a Quality Review of each UKCP College will periodically be conducted in accordance with the appropriate quality review procedure' (UKCP Byelaws 10.9), and that the 'UKCP will investigate any allegation that a College is not complying with the regulations as set out in the Articles and Byelaws' (UKCP Byelaws 11.1).

The above rationale is supported by Monk-Steel (2010), former UKCP Registrar, in a briefing to UKCP members on constitutional change:

> On 5 December 2009, the constitution of UKCP changed ... The next step is for individual members of UKCP to be enabled to vote for the chairs and officers of their respective colleges ... I believe a maximum of 12 months should be allowed by the board of trustees to implement individual members' democratic rights.
>
> (Monk-Steel, 2010: 37)

Andrew Samuels decided to stand down as UKCP chair at the beginning of 2012 and a new election was scheduled. Much concern was expressed when the HIPC chair used the HIPC logo to nominate a candidate from the Council for Psychoanalysis and Jungian Analysis College (CPJAC), one of three nominations; the other two were from the HIPC College. Meanwhile, following a lengthy debate within HIPC and consultation with UKCP, during which time the HIPC chair had opposed a college election, proclaiming they were college chair until May 2012, a decision was reached that an election would be held without further delay.

The HIPC Executive convened in an attempt to draw up an election schedule and protocols, but the HIPC chair was reluctant to relinquish power, and, with the co-operation of the vice chair, kept a firm hold on every aspect of the election process. An unrealistic election schedule was drawn up and constantly changed throughout the campaigning period: candidates were forbidden from communicating with the membership, except for two website statements; voting did not commence until a week after campaigning was closed; and in the absence of nominations for vice-chair, the out-going HIPC chair, Tree Staunton, automatically assumed this office post elections. The UKCP was aware of these concerns, but was unwilling to intervene in college affairs unless a formal complaint was lodged. The election returned Heward Wilkinson as chair for what would be his third term. As no nominations were received for treasurer, the post was filled via the HIPC delegates meeting. To date, there is no evidence available to suggest that any provision has been put in place to reform the HIPC delegates meeting as a training organizations' monopoly.

Janet Weisz (2010), chair of the Colleges and Faculties Committee (CFS) and chair of the Council for Psychoanalysis and Jungian Analysis (and UKCP chair as from January 2012), states:

> Under the new constitution, UKCP registrants became individual members, and with that gained voting rights. However, at present, colleges still operate on the delegate structure and do not mirror the changes to UKCP's voting structure. One of the CFS's tasks is to consult through colleges on what, if any, changes or additions colleges need to put in place in light of these changes, and to look at resource and other implications.
>
> (Weisz, 2010: 36)

It seemed that there was something being played out between the interests of organizational members and individual members that could not be resolved to the overall benefit of the profession. The 2009 constitution and the additional levy on individual member subscriptions to finance colleges are evidence of change, yet the old training organization structure holds strong.

However, organizational members have been challenged by the UKCP provision for direct membership: a provision which seemed to have a life of its own, as no one can evidence its legitimacy under the 2009 constitution. Direct membership is a threat to the membership size and revenue of organizational members, as it is assumed that individual members are no longer required to hold membership with a training or accrediting organization.

In 2009 a decision was reached to discontinue the practice of organizational members collecting UKCP registrant fees. There was also debate about facilitating member mobility between organizational members, but no record of any agreement to implement direct membership as a class of membership can be provided by the UKCP. It has been suggested that a clause in a UKCP transition document forms the basis for direct membership:

6.3 Phase 3 – 2012/2015 given HPC Statutory Regulation

Post statutory regulation some colleges may transition to faculties or merge as the needs of the post-regulation climate emerge.

Cyclical review procedures for individuals and organisations that synchronise with HPC where useful and possible will be introduced.

UKCP will be rolling out a cyclical individual re-accreditation process that mirrors the HPC frequency but pays attention to the ingredients that we consider will be the hallmark of a UKCP accredited psychotherapist. We want it to be minimalist in bureaucratic overhead and sensitive to psychotherapeutic values.

We imagine that the re-accreditation process will be delivered by our organisational members (both training and accrediting and accrediting only). Organisational members may choose to offer this as a service to practitioners, evaluating their portfolio of practice and reflection and validating it for accreditation.

(UKCP, 2009b)

As this provision was made with Health Professions Council regulation in mind, which in the event did not come about, the clause is somewhat redundant, and it would be rather underhand to sneak in under the radar a provision that does not really have the best interest of individual or organizational members at heart. The UKCP has strongly urged individual members to find an appropriate professional home with a member organization that provides continued professional development and evidence of a member's 'good professional standing'. The colleges do not have the facility to accommodate direct members, and as consequence have put out to tender the task of re-accreditation to organizational members. Although the UKCP has discouraged the practice, the number of direct members is increasing. Whether this increase has something to do with individual members being dissatisfied with their training organization or not, the option of direct membership is an attractive proposition in the current economic climate, and for no other reason could lead to a further increase. The UKCP Byelaws, approved at the 4 July 2009 EGM, state:

> 10.1 Colleges shall be established by the Charity on the basis of a degree of commonality of underpinning philosophy and/or practice. The proposed College shall have a mechanism whereby individual registrants can be accredited and reaccredited through an Organisational Member.
> (UKCP, 2009a)

If direct membership was intended in the manner in which it has unfolded, and if clause 6.3 of the UKCP transition document (UKCP, 2009b) dated 9 June 2009 is the rationale for direct membership, then surely it would have been included in the revised UKCP (2009a) Byelaws and presented at the 4 July 2009 EGM?

A change of direction

On 16 February 2011 the newly formed coalition government issued a command paper entitled *Enabling Excellence: Autonomy and Accountability for Healthcare Workers, and Social Care Workers* (DH, 2011), which set out the government's strategy for reforming the regulation of UK health workers, including psychotherapists. It signified a change in direction, away from the statutory regulation of counsellors and psychotherapists by the Health Professions Council. Instead, it laid the foundations for individual health-related professional bodies, including potentially those in the field of counselling and psychotherapy, to be accredited en-bloc, and on a voluntary basis, by the Council for Healthcare Regulatory Excellence (CHRE), soon to become the Professional Standards Authority (PSA) under a new Assured Voluntary Register scheme (AVR).

The scheme was rolled out for consultation in 2011, with the UKCP, BACP and UKAHPP all participating. The first wave of accreditation applications commenced in 2012 involving a small, medium and large-sized organization. BACP was chosen as the large organization. This has unfortunately allowed BACP to take a 'market lead' in offering professionals the PSA/AVR kite mark ahead of the 'competition'. It would have been more equitable had all organizations within the psychological therapies field been processed together in the same wave to create a level playing field; and despite BACP having a large membership, it is unlikely that the number of accredited members it will place on a PSA-approved register will be in excess of those on the current UKCP register.

The re-emergence of the integrative question

In December 2012 the Board of the UK Association for Humanistic Psychology Practitioners (UKAHPP) received from the UKCP: Humanistic and Integrative College (HIPC), draft 1 of a document entitled 'Are We All Humanistic Psychotherapists Now?'(UKCP: HIPC, 2012). At first glance, the document seems to put forward a theoretical case for humanistic and integrative psychotherapists to rally under a unifying public identity based on the term 'humanistic'. However, on closer inspection this does not seem to be the case. Instead, the document draws attention to the divisions with the humanistic and integrative community and drawing on an old IHP briefing statement (UKCP: HIPS, 2008c) rejected by the Skills for Health Expert Reference Group, it sets out to promote 'integrative' as the unifying title.

In ascribing attributes associated with personal style to philosophical modality, the document makes some sweeping statements about psychotherapy. It asserts that 'it's well established that Integration ... is what mature practitioners of all modalities tend toward as they emerge from the apprenticeship phase of training', implying that any therapist who maintains allegiance to an established psychotherapeutic approach has not matured, and is therefore of a lesser order.

The document also claims that a profoundly client-centred psychotherapist may also invoke transferential process understanding and/or assumptions in a manner akin to CBT, without contradicting or compromising the central premise of the client-centred approach. It goes on to say that it is extremely arguable that all psychotherapies do this. Though Rogers (1951) has acknowledged the likely existence of transferential phenomena, he has been very clear that consciousness-raising about such phenomena is not a preoccupation of client-centred psychotherapy. On the contrary, the unsolicited imposition of meaning formulated by the therapist about the client from a psychoanalytic or cognitive-behavioural perspective is not consistent with client-centred psychotherapy (Brodley, 1986; Rogers, 1951, 1959, 1987; Shlien, 1984).

As a justification for an 'integrative' identity, the document goes on to claim that the humanistic vision is 'too broad and too narrow to easily serve as a basis for identity, and consequently our identity has always been less assured than that of the other major meta-modalities'. This is not a justifiable reason to assimilate Humanistic Psychology within an integrative identity, or for those integrative practitioners with a humanistic allegiance to abandon 'Humanistic Psychology' and nail their colours to an integrative mast. As a descriptive identity, 'integrative' offers little understanding of what is being integrated: philosophies, theories, approaches, skills/interventions, or what? Also, integrative approaches are not unique to the humanistic modality. HIPC does not hold a monopoly on the term 'integrative', yet no other UKCP college incorporates 'integrative' as part of their title. The issuing of this document affirms that there is a faction with minimum allegiance that inhabits Humanistic Psychology, and is more than willing to subvert the humanistic tradition within an identity that has little standing, and has been rejected in the field as a title conducive for modality purposes.

IV Conclusion

This chapter has raised issues about the professionalization of psychotherapy and its place within statutory NHS provision. Some have argued that psychotherapy, particularly the humanistic variety, has no place in today's NHS, as the medical model compromises our understanding of the human condition with an alien culture. Others, whilst acknowledging these cultural difficulties, also recognize that there are practitioners within the NHS who are not willing to surrender their humanistic integrity to alien values, and do not wish to limit accessibility to psychological wellbeing services to the voluntary sector and those who can afford to pay private sector fees. Perhaps both positions hold some truth?

Rogers (1973/1980) expressed his concerns about the professionalization of the helping professions through certification and licensing as 'they fail in their aims ... freezing the profession in a past image ... discourage innovation ... build up a rigid bureaucracy ...', which becomes no substitute for sound 'judgement' or 'quality', and goes on to emphasize: 'there are as many certified charlatans and exploiters of people as there are uncertified' (Rogers, 1973/1980: 244).

In his capacity as Professor Carl Rogers Ph.D., he certainly demonstrated his ability and willingness to conform to professional and academic requirements in the advancement of a career in psychology. In 1947, as President of the American Psychological Association, albeit with reservations, Rogers helped to introduce the American Board of Examiners in Professional Psychology. He was wrestling with some important considerations – not proposing the abandonment of academic and professional rigour in favour of a free-for-all. Rogers clearly knew that to flourish and advance as a practitioner, psychotherapists and counsellors have to demonstrate integrity and commitment to the therapeutic endeavour, by attending to some pre-determined expectations of what constitutes quality and a 'good-enough' practitioner. With the development of client-centred psychotherapy and the application of the person-centred approach, Rogers' concerns were three-fold: first, the professionalization of the helping professions as already outlined; second, protecting the philosophical integrity of the person-centred approach from external imposition and standardization, contrary to the central premise of the approach – but without declaring person-centred therapy a no-go zone, beyond external scrutiny; and third, attending to the quality of the psychotherapy practice.

Sadly, Rogers (1973/1980: 247) did not have an answer to this dilemma and hoped that 'there was some more creative method of bringing together those who need help and those who are truly excellent in offering helping relationships'. Until then, perhaps the best our professional bodies can do is to acknowledge that therapists are faced with a professional as well as a personal challenge and provide a multidimensional approach to quality and regulation, whilst keeping in check those who would assume the authority to dictate what is best for the whole profession by rolling out imposed 'one-size-fits-all' solutions.

'Humanistic' is an umbrella term for a collection of traditional and integrative psychotherapy approaches which draw on Humanistic Psychology as a philosophical base. It would be erroneous to represent humanistic psychotherapy as a single approach. Likewise, it would be incorrect for such diversity to be incorporated within a unifying integrative identity. The integrity of this diversity, whether mind, body or spirit in orientation, should not be compromised by the self-serving political interests of a minority.

In challenging the specific political aspirations of the IHP lobby, the authors of this chapter do not wish to alienate integrative practitioners, and want to explicitly acknowledge that integrative approaches (as defined by Norcross and Goldfried, 2005) should have equal standing.

The IHP lobby has repeatedly attempted to organize consent by postulating beliefs as if they were facts, and has continued to make a category error involving the fundamental philosophical basis of both approaches – subsuming them into each other for political convenience and without integrity. The time has come for those who hold elected office within our professional bodies to protect both humanistic *and* integrative approaches from such political manipulation. Whilst the emergence of a new modality called 'Integrative Humanistic Psychotherapy' has some plausibility, it must surely draw on its own merits, and not be allowed to devour the humanistic host from within. Likewise, the term 'integrative' deserves and warrants protection, whether as a component of Humanistic Psychology or as a stand-alone modality.

At the time of writing, the Association for Humanistic Psychology in Britain (AHPB) has announced that it will be celebrating 50 years of Humanistic Psychology with a conference in September 2013, co-hosted by the UKCP: Humanistic and Integrative College. It seems profoundly ironic that several of the announced speakers are figures who actively opposed Humanistic Psychology during the Skills for Health and statutory regulation debates, as described above. If Humanistic and Integrative Psychotherapy is not a sufficient UKCP college title, or if certain UKCP members (individual or organizational) cannot identify with Humanistic Psychology, then perhaps the solution is for those members to seek affiliation and accreditation with an alternative UKCP college. If the philosophical foundations of other colleges are not compatible, then perhaps it is time for those members who are at odds with Humanistic Psychology to break away and establish a new college: if there is a cuckoo within the humanistic nest, perhaps it is time for it to take flight and allow Humanistic Psychology to determine its future from an authentically humanistic perspective.

Note

If you are a client/person-centred counsellor or psychotherapist, you can participate in a survey looking at practitioner understanding and identity issues regarding 'person-centred' – log on to: www.survey.bris.ac.uk/hud/person-centred

References

Brodley, B.T. (1986) 'Client-centred therapy – what it is? What is it not?' Paper presented at the First Annual Meeting of the Association for the Development of the Person-Centered Approach, Chicago: University of Chicago, 3–7 September.

Cooper, M. (2008) *Essential Research Findings in Counselling and Psychotherapy*, London: Sage.

DH (2007) *Trust Assurance and Safety – The Regulation of Health Professionals in the 21st Century*, London: The Stationery Office.

DH (2011) *Enabling Excellence: Autonomy and Accountability for Healthcare Workers, and Social Care Workers*, retrieved 16 June 2013 from https://www.gov.uk/government/publications/enabling-excellence-autonomy-and-accountability-for-health-and-social-care-staff

Fonagy, P. (ed.) (2010) *Skills for Health: National Occupational Standards for Psychological Therapies*, London: Department of Health.

Health Act (1999) *Section 60, Regulation of health care and associated professions*, London: The Stationery Office.

Health Professions Council (2008) 'Aims and Vision', retrieved 16 June 2013 from http://www.hpc-uk.org/aboutus/aimsandvision/

Messer, S.B. (1992) 'A critical examination of belief structures in integrative and eclectic psychotherapy', in J.C. Norcross and M.R. Goldfried (eds), *Handbook of Psychotherapy Integration*, (pp. 130–165), New York: Oxford University Press.

Monk-Steel, J. (2010) 'UKCP members constitutional change: what it means for you – the individual member', *Psychotherapist*, 46 (Autumn): 37.

Norcross, J.C. (2005) 'A primer on psychotherapy integration', in J.C. Norcross and M.R. Goldfried (eds), *Handbook of Psychotherapy Integration*, 2nd edn, Oxford: Oxford University Press.

Norcross, J.C. and Goldfried, M.R. (eds) (2005) *Handbook of Psychotherapy Integration*, 2nd edn, Oxford: Oxford University Press.

Prime Minister's Office (2008a) *Prime Minister's Website*, accessed 16 June 2008 at www.pm.gov.uk/output/Page14969.asp. This page is no longer available.

Prime Minister's Office (2008b) *Prime Minister's Website*, accessed 16 June 2008 at www.pm.gov.uk/output/Page15454.asp. This page is no longer available.

Rogers, C.R. (1951) *Client-Centred Therapy*, London: Constable.

Rogers, C.R. (1959) 'A theory of therapy, personality, and interpersonal relationships, as developed in the client-centered framework', in S. Koch (ed.), *Psychology: A Study of a Science. Vol. 3: Formulations of the Person and the Social Context* (pp. 184–256), New York: McGraw-Hill.

Rogers, C.R. (1965) 'Some questions and challenges facing a Humanistic Psychology', *Journal of Humanistic Psychology*, Spring 1965, reprinted in Welch, I.D., Tate, G.A. and Richards, F. (eds) (1978) *Humanistic Psychology: A Sourcebook* (pp. 41–5). Buffalo, NY: Prometheus.

Rogers, C.R. (1973) 'Some new challenges to the helping professions', *American Psychologist*, 28 (5): 379–87; also in Rogers, C.R. (1980) *A Way of Being* (pp. 235–62), Boston: Houghton Mifflin.

Rogers, C.R. (1980) *A Way of Being*, Boston: Houghton Mifflin.

Rogers, C.R. (1987) 'Comments on Shlien's article "A countertheory of transference"', *Person-Centred Review*, 2 (2): 182–8. Reprinted (2002) in D.J. Cain (ed.) *Classics in the Person-Centered Approach* (pp. 453–7), Ross-on-Wye: PCCS Books.

Rowan, J. (2013) 'Early days in humanistic and transpersonal psychology', *Self & Society: International Journal for Humanistic Psychology*, 40 (2): 47–57.

Ryle, G. (1949) *The Concept of the Mind*, Chicago: University of Chicago Press.

Shlien, J.M. (1984) 'A countertheory of transference', in R.F. Levant and J.M. Shlien (eds), *Client-Centred Therapy and the Person-Centred Approach: New Directions in Theory, Research and Practice* (pp. 153–81), New York: Praeger. Reprinted (2002) in D.J. Cain (ed.) *Classics in the Person-Centered Approach* (pp. 415–35), Ross-on-Wye: PCCS Books.

The Times (2008) Letters to the Editor: 'Depression: might talk therapy be better than drugs?' London: Thursday 28 February: 18.

UKCP (2007) Humanistic and Integrative Psychotherapies Section, accessed 13 November 2007 from: www.psychotherapy.org.uk/humanistic_integrative
UKCP (2009a) *Constitution Documents: Memorandum of Association; Articles of Association; Byelaws; Standing Orders*, London: United Kingdom Council for Psychotherapy.
UKCP (2009b) *UKCP in Transition 2009–2015*, London: United Kingdom Council for Psychotherapy.
UKCP (2010) *Professional Occupational Standards: For Psychotherapists and Psychotherapeutic Counsellors*, London: United Kingdom Council for Psychotherapy.
UKCP: HIPS (2008a) *Minutes of the HIPS Delegates Meeting*, at UKCP AGM, Buxton, 14–15 March.
UKCP: HIPS (2008b) *Statement Prepared for Skills for Health National Occupational Modality Statement: Integrative Humanistic Psychotherapy*, 26 March.
UKCP: HIPS (2008c) *Brief Statement for Peter Fonagy, Chair of the Strategy Reference Group from UKCP: HIPS Executive Group*, August.
UKCP: HIPS (2009a) *The Future in Your Hands*, UKCP Political Action Group on behalf of the HIP Section, 27 September.
UKCP: HIPS (2009b) *Minutes of HIP Section Delegates Meeting*, No. 23, 20 October.
UKCP: HIPS (2009c) *Statement*, HIPS Political Group.
UKCP: HIPC (2010a) *Minutes of HIP College, Delegates Meeting*, No. 24, 27 January.
UKCP: HIPC (2010b) *Minutes of HIP College, Delegates Meeting*, No. 25, 27 March.
UKCP: HIPC (2011) *Minutes of HIP College, Delegates Meeting*, No. 30, 24 March .
UKCP: HIPC (2012) *Are We All Humanistic Psychotherapists Now?* UKCP: Humanistic and Integrative Psychotherapy College.
Weisz, J. (2010) 'UKCP Members, constitutional change: what it means for you – so, what is a UKCP College?' *The Psychotherapist*, 46 (Autumn): 36.

7 | Absence and Presence – Carl Rogers in 2013

Andy Rogers

> Like all good listeners, he has a way of attending that is at once intense and assuasive: the supplicant feels both nakedly revealed and sheltered, somehow, from all possible judgement. It's like he's working as hard as you. You both of you, briefly, feel unalone.
> (David Foster Wallace, *Infinite Jest*, 1996: 388)

Carl Rogers is everywhere and nowhere. As I write, it is 40 years since his controversial address to the American Psychological Association (APA), which he described without apology as 'an outpouring of pent-up criticism' (Rogers, 1980: 235). The speech has some of Rogers' best lines, not least the much-quoted yet routinely ignored observation that 'there are as many certified charlatans and exploiters of people as there are uncertified' (ibid.: 244). Given the scandalous scrabble for state regulation which we in the UK have just survived, it is tempting to revisit this potent critique of professionalism; but there is another neglected aspect of Rogers' relevance in and for our times, for which we need to go back beyond the APA address to a pivotal moment in the emergence of this Humanistic Psychology pioneer's thinking.

In the late 1930s, Rogers worked as a psychologist with the Society for the Prevention of Cruelty to Children in Rochester, New York. In one case, he found himself trying to convince a mother that her son's difficulties lay in her early rejection of the child but, as he wrote later, 'we got nowhere. Finally I gave up. I told her that it seemed we had both tried, but we had failed, and that we might as well give up our contacts' (Rogers, 1961: 11). Then, just as she was about to leave, the mother asked Rogers if he would see her for counselling. He agreed, so she returned to her seat and 'began to pour out her despair … all very different from the sterile "case history" she had given before' (ibid.).

'Real therapy began then' (ibid.), Rogers observed, and he would come to attribute considerable significance to the event, particularly in forming one of his core beliefs:

> [It] helped me to experience the fact – only fully realized later – that it is the client who knows what hurts, what directions to go, what problems are crucial, what experiences have been deeply buried. It began to occur to me that unless I had a need to demonstrate my own cleverness and learning, I would do better to rely upon the client for the direction of movement in the process.
>
> (1961: 11–12)

The incident is also a classic example of Rogers' trademark approach to developing ideas – listening to, trusting and learning from his own experience, rather than grappling with existing theories. As Rogers' biographer writes,

> He was always grateful that his thinking did not come from the teachings of one special mentor, nor out of the writings of one special person, nor out of endless philosophical debates on the merits of the various schools of therapy, or the nuances and changes in some 'master's' thinking over the years.
>
> (Kirschenbaum, 2007: 80)

So what happened next? Leap forward three decades to the APA address, then another 40 years to 2013, and we find a rather striking – if politically out-of-favour – structure in the professional landscape: a principled, well-researched and extensively articulated cluster of therapies, of which Rogers is the 'special mentor', the 'master' whose writing is 'endlessly debated', and whose 'nuances and changes' in thinking remain the reference point for contemporary divisions within the approach. Despite Rogers' caution about theory becoming a 'dogma of truth' (Rogers, 1959: 191), the person-centred approach is arguably as dogmatic as any other tradition. Debates rage about whether one thing or other is authentically 'person-centred', whether certain ideas and actions fit precisely with Rogers' practice, theories and beliefs at this or that point in his life, and there seems little to distinguish it from other therapies in this regard. When Rogers wrote of Freudian theory that, 'at the hands of insecure disciples … the gossamer threads became iron chains of dogma' (ibid: 191), he might easily have been predicting the future of his own creation.

Ironic, then, that one of Rogers' key insights came from operating without allegiance to a specific model of psychological theory, as happened with the mother in Rochester. This was an idiosyncratic encounter located within a particular personal, professional, cultural and historical moment. The subsequent success of the approach theoretically and professionally says less about the potential meaning of that experience than it does about the relationship between Rogers' character and career, and the facilitative social conditions necessary for the flourishing of his ideas, not least the impact of President Roosevelt's 'New Deal' response to the Great Depression in the 1930s (Barrett-Lennard, 1998) and the cultural revolutions of the 1950s and 1960s.

Clearly this context does not discredit anything Rogers said, wrote or did – it is the history of all 'big ideas' and the thinkers who have them; but it is important to distinguish between the growth of a movement and the potential meaning of its originator's eureka moments. The former does not own the latter, and it might be that the movement, with all its books, organizations, trainings and so on, is not the only, or even the best, expression of the insights from which it was born. In the case of the person-centred approach, the theory and other structures that evolved from the complex interaction of persons, places and moments in Rogers' lifetime potentially obscure something vital about his meeting with the mother, which is that 'real therapy' began – and was 'ultimately … very successful' (Rogers, 1961: 11) – when Rogers gave up knowing all sorts of things that someone in his position would normally be expected to know.

It is hard to picture Carl Rogers in this encounter, before client-centred therapy or the person-centred approach existed as 'things'. Rather than being grounded in the presence of well-established principles, propositions and practices, here his approach is defined by absence: an absence of psychological theory and treatment protocols; an absence of specific goals and intentions; an absence, importantly, of professional therapeutic expertise, which makes way for something yet to be identified. Presumably Rogers does not suddenly realise that this new 'way of being' will function in a particular way with regard to the mother's personality dynamics. More likely there is nowhere else to go – he is, in a sense, floundering. Professional psychological knowledge and skills have proven not up to the task, he does not know what to do, so he 'does' nothing. Or rather, he does nothing that would have been expected of someone in the role of psychological therapist. He does not attempt to 'treat' the mother, to alter the dynamics of her personality or guide her towards therapist-defined insight. Instead, Rogers meets her compassionately in her distress, as a fellow human being, from a position of not knowing what is wrong or how to make it right.

The story is no doubt important to some scholars and practitioners because it heralds the arrival of an idea that would be central in the development of an influential school of therapy, as if its value derived from it being a catalyst for construction. But if theory for Rogers was 'an attempt to give order and clarification' (Thorne, 1992: 42) to the subjective experiences of client and therapist, then what is fascinating about this event is precisely the fact that none of this imminent order and clarity existed at the time, nor proved necessary for therapy to occur. It is true that Rogers gets to the experiential moment itself by being trained and employed in psychology: he arrives there by being a more conventional therapist in the first place – but it is his letting go of all this which makes it uniquely interesting. Crucially, the thing Rogers suddenly found himself lacking at that pivotal point in his life and work was deference to external authority on the nature of distress and the meaning and purpose of therapy, a subordination previously internalized as individual professional expertise but which had now become redundant, opening the way for a shift in the source of authority to the client.

All of which begs an important question. What would it mean to meet a client in this way today? Perhaps there is no need, we might reply, because for us person-centred (or some other) therapy exists already, and provides an ideal philosophical and theoretical framework to enable us to meet each client as a person, with the utmost respect for their subjectivity, individuality, freedom and right to self-determination. But this rationale did not exist for Rogers in the moment we have been discussing and in any case it seems a rather lazy response that highlights the conundrum under consideration here.

In the session, Rogers experiences first-hand the limits, flaws and conceits of both psychological theory and 'theory-mindedness' (House, 2008), so from exasperation more than intellectual rigour he subverts the conventional therapy dynamic by letting go of his expertise and putting the client's reality first. We might describe this as an act of spontaneous experimental enquiry into human distress, personal relationships and indeed therapy itself, one arrived at not through commitment to an existing system of psychotherapeutic thought but through visceral experience and non-professionalized compassion. Following the event, however, Rogers tries to clarify and order his experiences back within the domain of psychological theory.

As we have seen, this clarification and ordering was a manifestation of the personal, professional and political influences that were in play in Rogers' life, and had little to do with the beginnings of 'real therapy' for the mother in Rochester. Rogers himself acknowledged the personal and political drivers of theoretical work when he identified his own 'need for order' (Rogers, 1959: 188) and the influence of 'insistent pressure from my colleagues [in the APA]' (ibid.: 185) as twin motivations for writing his most comprehensive theory statement. But the theoretical system that he needed personally and professionally developed a life of its own. Supported by helpful social changes, it gained traction in the field and growing popularity in the culture at large, the upside-down result being that for therapists following Rogers, his imposed order ended up functioning as an essential ('necessary and sufficient') touchstone for meeting others in their distress.

To put it another way, an unintended negative consequence of the success of the person-centred approach has been the creation of a new external authority – or in Rogers' own terms, 'external locus of evaluation' – which the events of therapy must satisfy. This might feel a more palatably human(e) authority and have been necessary at the time – as part of psychology's 'third way' challenge to the psychoanalytic and behaviourist strangleholds on the client's subjectivity – but in the contemporary environment it does not go far enough, as we shall see. Instead, it subtly contradicts and undermines Rogers' claimed shift to therapy being 'politically centred in the client' (Rogers, 1977: 14). Therapist deference to psychological theory is once again internalized as professional expertise, this time in the facilitation of specific changes in the dynamics of the client's 'self' by offering certain relational qualities that are hypothesized in the theory to have precisely this effect. So in trying to articulate and order his own experience, Rogers – the socially situated psychologist and scientist – unwittingly sets up a return to theory-centredness and instrumentalism, a freedom from which enabled him to meet the mother as a person, rather than as a 'case' or 'patient'.

I should say here that it is not my intention to denigrate the approach or its many committed practitioners. Contemporary person-centred therapy is no doubt valued by clients, and undertaken with degrees of artfulness and compassion by its adherents. It has never tired of critical reflection upon the intricacies of therapeutic work and the subtle ways in which power can become centred in the practitioner, and I know too that in their encounters with clients, person-centred therapists tend to be relatively unburdened by the weight of theory and the 'need to appear "clever"' (Mearns, 1994: 27), possibly because this aspect of the approach attracted them to person-centred work in the first place (ibid.). So it seems harsh to be critiquing the least obviously theory-centred of all therapies on the grounds that it is too bound by theory.

But we face a dilemma in the psychological therapies, and one that is particularly poignant for the person-centred approach. Our once-radical alternatives have been engulfed by our profession's success. The great achievements of Humanistic Psychology did not shift the mainstream anywhere near enough; instead, it co-opted us, granted us acceptance as long as we played the game, and now we confront the consequences. Do we chase what 'works', as if this were an unambiguously benign goal? Do we pursue certainty and knowing, via 'systematic outcome monitoring' and ever-more diagnostic theory systems? Do we accept the shift away from therapy as dialogue and toward therapy as a drug-like treatment for 'disorders' (Guy et al., 2011)? Do we do whatever it takes to sell our services to powerful social institutions? Is the pay-off of state endorsement via National Institute for Health and Care Excellence (NICE) guidelines – and subsequent employment in health service provision and back-to-work programmes – that desirable? Or do we risk taking a new stand against the medicalization of experience, against the self-defined authority of the 'evidence-based regime' (Rizq, 2013: 20), against the narrowing of what is deemed an appropriate therapeutic response to distress? Do we dare articulate therapy as uncertain, unpredictable and idiosyncratic – as the 'art of not knowing' (Schmid, 2001)? Can we generate new opportunities for reflection, respite and rejuvenation?

Given cognitive behaviour therapy's current dominance in the UK National Health Service (NHS), the pressure on other therapies is to pursue the same goals and with the same methods. Our 'interventions' must be 'evidence-based' and 'cost-effective'; we must 'treat disorders', return people to 'health' and 'productivity', and do it more quickly than everyone else. But the incongruence of adopting such a strategy is, for many practitioners, unsustainable, leaving us not only to critique current developments but also to create spaces for dialogue about an alternative future for our field. Efforts to do this from within conventional therapeutic debate are often hampered by its entanglement with forces that close down such spaces, most obviously when the interests of powerful individuals and groupings in the professions converge with dominant discourses of mental health, treatment and research. So in addressing the challenges ahead, a restatement of the radicalism of person-centred theory rings rather hollow, or at least seems nostalgic rather than present- or future-orientated, particularly when the approach is competing as a 'brand' by trying to find its way into NICE recommendations.

Just because we keep saying something is 'revolutionary' does not make it so. The battleground has shifted. The wars between Humanistic Psychology, behaviourism and psychoanalysis have been superseded, if not transcended. The immediate pressures facing the therapy field have opened up fault lines through the traditional schools (even the non-school of 'pluralism') to such an extent that there is increasingly as much difference within as between them. We see these divisions in the politics of our professions, most obviously in the uniting for common purpose that, in Britain, brought together psychoanalysts and humanistic counsellors – among others – to fight state regulation of the psychological therapies by the Health Professions Council. In the midst of that fierce debate, with Rogers' incendiary lament about 'certified charlatans' hovering nearby throughout, it was hard for some to see the implications for the wider scene, that the disagreements were not just about the proposed policy, but about the very meaning of therapy and, beyond that, human experience itself. It was startling and liberating to discover that the issue did not re-ignite feuds between the schools but revealed fundamental differences within, and commonalities between, them. When the environment becomes noxious enough, more meaningful differences emerge to transcend the competitive skirmishes of more comfortable times.

As well as in the politics, we see our fractured predicament in the philosophy of therapy, in the 'paradigm war' between modernity and postmodernism, and the welcome efforts to articulate 'post-professional', 'trans-modern' and 'post-existential' perspectives (e.g. House, 2010; Loewenthal, 2011). But we see it too in Carl Rogers' meeting with the mother in Rochester, and in how professional and cultural forces have overwhelmed some of the quiet meaning of that encounter. The story helpfully illuminates the experience of being a therapist, yet meeting clients with a curious and deeply respectful 'not-knowing', with an 'ordinary' – non-technical, non-instrumental – compassion (Lomas, 1999; Smail, 2005). This might sometimes look like person-centred therapy, but it could easily be psychoanalysis or something else entirely – it depends on the people in the room. Just as in the pivotal Rogers encounter, therapy becomes an act of research in itself (Mearns, 1994: 33), a 'co-operative enquiry' into the human condition (Postle, 2012), with direction, inspiration, meaning and rationale emerging not from a brand or the 'outcomes' it claims, but idiosyncratically within each moment, session and relationship.

Tellingly, this is not an approach that would curry much favour with the narrowly 'evidence-based' culture of the NHS, nor, thankfully, would it have a great deal to offer the British Government's back-to-work agenda. But it is also against the direction of travel in our own field, which is precisely the dilemma facing the person-centred approach. Can it express its radical potential in new ways and challenge this emerging trajectory, or will it seek state endorsement as an 'effective intervention' for 'mental disorders' by showing that it too 'works' (Cooper et al., 2010)? The danger being, of course, that in appeasing the demands of an increasingly medicalized and evidence-obsessed market in psychological treatment, it risks disconnecting irretrievably from the spirit of its inception, as embodied by Rogers' meeting with the mother in Rochester.

I guess we will never know how that session really went, or the sessions that followed, but the story is nonetheless a defiant allegory of all that is so beautiful and liberating yet simple and humble about the therapeutic encounter – 'the practice of freedom by free beings for free beings' (Grant, 2004: 163). In the embellishments I have given here, it is equally a tale of therapy's hubris. The further away from that moment in the late 1930s that person-centred and other therapies get, the further away they are, despite the countless pages of effort, from articulating what is so meaningful about our work.

As I said at the start, Carl Rogers is everywhere and nowhere. And it seems we have to find him and forget him all over again.

References

Barrett-Lennard, G. (1998) *Carl Rogers' Helping System: Journey and Substance*, London: Sage.

Cooper, M., Watson, J.C. and Hölldampf, D. (eds) (2010) *Person-Centered and Experiential Therapies Work*, Ross-on-Wye: PCCS Books.

Grant, B. (2004) 'The imperative of ethical justification in psychotherapy: the special case of client-centered therapy', *Person-Centered and Experiential Psychotherapies*, 3 (3): 152–65.

Guy, A., Thomas, R., Stephenson, S. and Loewenthal, D. (2011) *NICE under Scrutiny: The Impact of the National Institute for Health and Clinical Excellence Guidelines on the Provision of Psychotherapy in the UK*, University of Roehampton, Research Centre for Therapeutic Education: United Kingdom Council for Psychotherapy (UKCP) Research Unit.

House, R. (2008) 'Therapy's modernist "regime of truth": from scientific "theory-mindedness" towards the subtle and the mysterious', *Philosophical Practice*, 3 (3): 343–52.

House, R. (2010) *In, Against and Beyond Therapy: Critical Essays towards a Post-professional Era*, Ross-on-Wye: PCCS Books.

Kirschenbaum, H. (2007) *The Life and Work of Carl Rogers*, Ross-on-Wye: PCCS Books.

Loewenthal, D. (2011) *Post-existentialism and the Psychological Therapies: Towards a Therapy Without Foundations*, London: Karnac Books.

Lomas, P. (1999) *Doing Good? Psychotherapy Out of Its Depth*, Oxford: Oxford University Press.

Mearns, D. (1994) *Developing Person-Centred Counselling*, London: Sage.

Postle D. (2012) *Therapy Futures: Obstacles and Opportunities*, London: Wentworth Resources; available from Lulu.com.

Rizq, R. (2013) 'The language of healthcare', *Therapy Today*, 24 (2): 20–4.

Rogers, C.R. (1959) 'A theory of therapy, personality, and interpersonal relationships as developed in the client-centred framework', in S. Koch (ed.), *Psychology: A Study of Science, Vol. 3: Formulations of the Person and the Social Context* (pp. 184–256), New York: McGraw-Hill.

Rogers, C.R. (1961) *On Becoming a Person*, London: Constable.

Rogers, C.R. (1977) *Carl Rogers on Personal Power*, London: Constable.

Rogers, C.R. (1980) *A Way of Being*, Boston: Houghton Mifflin.

Schmid, P.F. (2001) 'Comprehension: The art of not knowing. Dialogical and ethical perspectives on empathy as dialogue in personal and person-centered relationships', in S. Haugh and T. Merry (eds), *Rogers' Therapeutic Conditions: Evolution, Theory and Practice, Volume 2: Empathy* (pp. 53–71), Ross-on-Wye: PCCS

Books; retrieved 16 January 2013 at: http://web.utanet.at/schmidpp/paper-compr.pdf

Smail, D. (2005) *Power, Interest and Psychology: Elements of a Social Materialist Understanding of Distress*, Ross-on-Wye: PCCS Books.

Thorne, B. (1992) *Carl Rogers*, London: Sage.

Wallace, D.F. (1996) *Infinite Jest*, London: Little, Brown & Co.

PART II

EXISTENTIAL, TRANSPERSONAL AND POSTMODERN PERSPECTIVES

8 | Humanistic Psychology's Chief Task: To reset psychology on its rightful existential-humanistic base

Kirk J. Schneider

While some in the field continue to believe that psychology proceeds purely on the basis of positivistic science (e.g. Baker et al., 2008), I contend that this is patently naïve. Psychology was, and probably always will be, a philosophically based discipline. In this light, the field of psychology has actually been 'reset' many times over its relatively brief 100-year history, and this resetting has had as much to do with philosophical fashion as it has had to do with empirical evidence (see Kuhn, 1962). The first time the field was reset was at the point where its standing as an explicit philosophy was replaced by its 'formalization' as an explicit laboratory science. This was the time when Wilhelm Wundt and his colleagues began basing psychology on the experimental method (or the philosophical approach of natural science) to evaluate laboratory findings. The second major time when psychology was reset was when psychoanalysis replaced laboratory science as the leading philosophical paradigm. This was a period, roughly the 1920s, when Freud and his colleagues emphasized the primacy of the so-called 'drive model' of human functioning over the conscious activities of laboratory investigation. The third major period of philosophical resetting was the usurpation of the psychoanalytic model by the behavioural model, where only overt and measurable human actions were considered the domain of legitimacy. The fourth major period of resetting was spearheaded by cognitive science, and the shift in emphasis from outward behavioural actions to inward informational processing. Now we are in a period where the predominant paradigm is quickly moving from cognitive science to neuroscience, from intellective processes to behaviour–brain correlates.

So where does that bring us to at present? How should psychology be reset in the emerging era, and what role does that leave for Humanistic Psychology?

I believe that psychology should now be reset on its rightful base in existence. It is high time that psychology recognized what the great poets and thinkers the world over have recognized for centuries – that the main problem of the human being is the paradoxical problem: that we are both angels and food for worms; that we are suspended between constrictive and expansive worlds; and that we are both exhilarated and stupefied by this tension. The role this leaves for Humanistic Psychology is the role that William James so deftly set for it back in 1902. That was the year James wrote his book *The Varieties of Religious Experience*, calling for a radically empirical, experientially informed inquiry into the human being's engagement with the world (Taylor, 2010). I also believe that Humanistic Psychology's role today is commensurate with the existential-phenomenological-spiritual tradition of successors to William James (see Mendelowitz and Kim, 2010), exemplified by Paul Tillich (1952), Martin Buber (1970), Rollo May (1981), R.D. Laing (1969), Ernest Becker (1973), and many others who called for a new 'whole-bodied' experience of inquiry and life. This whole-bodied psychology does not preclude other strands along its bandwidth, but it incorporates them as part of its awesome tableau.

In a nutshell then: The chief task for Humanistic Psychology going forward is to reset psychology on its rightful existential-humanistic base. By 'rightful', I mean that if mainstream psychology is to become the field that Nietzsche once dubbed the 'queen of the sciences', if it is to maximally apprehend lives and the transformation of lives, then it will need to show how mainstream psychology's present bases – cognitive, behavioural, and neuro-physiological – are wanting. It will need to show how one's relation to information processing, overt and measurable actions, and physio-chemical structures are but part-processes of an infinitely unfolding venture, a venture that comprises those part-processes, to be sure, but that also far exceeds them both in scope and consequence.

Consider, for example, how we have corrupted the term 'substrate' today. Substrate simply means underlying process or 'base on which an organism lives' (Webster's, 2003: 1246); and yet we have usurped the literal meaning of this term by reducing it to neurology. We have confused the physical base of organisms, e.g. 'neural substrates', with the phenomenological base of organisms – which is mystery. That is, the substrates of human behaviour are not merely traceable to a cell or a molecule or even an atom, but to an enigma that underlies all these overtly measurable processes – the groundlessness of existence. The groundlessness of existence is the *experiential* substrate of human behaviour/consciousness (see Schneider, 2013). The groundlessness of existence is the experiential base on which all things revolve, and we (that is, our mainstream culture, our profession) hardly ever speak of this problem, let alone acknowledge that it exists. Yet the substrates underlying neural substrates, the substrates that cause us the most problems and open us to the greatest possibilities – the 800-pound gorilla in our 'room' – is the groundlessness of existence.

I propose the following hypotheses. First: *most of our troubles as human beings can be traced to one overarching problem – our suspension in the groundlessness of existence*. Second, and a corollary to the first: *most of our joys, breakthroughs, and liberations can also be traced to our suspension in the groundlessness of existence*.

What is the rationale for these postulates? Just consider what we normally call 'psychopathology'. Consider what we experience following a great loss, or an illness, or a disruption. Consider the kinds of words we use to describe these upheavals – we feel the 'bottom has dropped out', that we have slipped into a 'black hole', that we are in 'free fall'. We feel 'crushed', 'sunk', or – in a word – 'groundless'. Further, consider how virtually all of these feelings drive us into 'disorders' characterized by our psychiatric manuals – e.g. depression, anxiety, mania and narcissism.

At the same time, consider what we experience when we can *confront* abysses of living, when we can sit with them, allow them to evolve, and potentially, incrementally, even become intrigued by them. How differently we can then experience the world; how fully we can then experience choice, possibility and poignancy, at every moment afforded to us.

That which I call 'awe-based' psychology is one possible inroad into the venture about which I speak (Schneider, 2004, 2009, 2013). By awe-based psychology, I mean a psychology that is grounded in humility and wonder – the adventure of living; and I mean a psychology that can radically enrich both *what* we discover, and *how we live* what we discover. Through awe-based psychology, we can impact every major sector of our lives, from child-rearing to education to the work setting to the governmental setting, and we can roundly enhance our science. Does this sound like a long-sought-after crossroad? Consider the following:

Mystery is a place where religion and science meet.

Dogma is a place where they part.

Awe-based psychology is a place where they can evolve and reunite.

Coda

We can talk until we're blue in the face about pat formulae and programmatic treatments. We can cite chemical imbalances in the brain, for example, or the lack of ability to regulate emotions, or the irrationality of conditioned thoughts as the bases for our disorders. However, until psychologists get down to the fundamental problem which fuels all these secondary conditions – our precariousness as creatures – they will be operating at a very restrictive level (and the results I'm afraid, are all too evident in our society). The question needs to be continually raised: Is helping a person to change behaviour patterns and recondition thoughts enough? Or do we owe it to that person to make available to him or her a deeper dimension of self-exploration? Do we owe it to that person to enable him or her to discover what really matters about his or her life, wherever that may lead? Do we owe it to his or her *society*? I believe so, and that the time for psychology to 'reset' is now.

Note

This chapter is adapted from the Special Section: The 50th anniversary of *Journal of Humanistic Psychology*, 'Reflections on the state of the field'. See *Journal of Humanistic Psychology*, 51 (4): 436–8. Copyright 2011, Sage Publishing Co.

References

Baker, T.B., McFall, R.M. and Shoham, V. (2008) 'Current status and future prospects of clinical psychology: toward a scientifically principled approach to mental and behavioral healthcare', *Psychological Science in the Public Interest*, 9 (2): 67–103.

Becker, E. (1973) *Denial of Death*, New York: Free Press.

Buber, M. (1970) *I and Thou* (transl. W. Kaufmann), New York: Scribner's.

Kuhn, T. (1962) *The Structure of Scientific Revolutions*, Chicago: University of Chicago Press.

Laing, R.D. (1969) *The Divided Self: An Existential Study in Sanity and Madness*, Harmondsworth: Penguin.

May, R. (1981) *Freedom and Destiny*, New York: Norton.

Mendelowitz, E. and Kim, C.Y. (2010) 'William James and the spirit of complexity', *Journal of Humanistic Psychology*, 50 (4): 459–70.

Schneider, K.J. (2004) *Rediscovery of Awe: Splendor, Mystery, and the Fluid Center of Life*, St Paul, MN: Paragon House.

Schneider, K.J. (2009) *Awakening to Awe: Personal Stories of Profound Transformation*, Lanham, MD: Jason Aronson.

Schneider, K.J. (2013) *The Polarized Mind: Why It's Killing Us and What We Can Do About It*, Colorado Springs, CO: University Professors Press.

Taylor, E. (2010) 'William James and the humanistic implications of the neuroscience revolution: an outrageous hypothesis', *Journal of Humanistic Psychology*, 50 (4): 410–29.

Tillich, P. (1952) *The Courage to Be*, New Haven, CT: Yale University Press.

9 | Humanism, Tragedy, and Humanistic Psychotherapy's Potential as the Destiny of Psychotherapy

Heward Wilkinson

Why does humanistic psychotherapy not embrace its natural destiny?

Why was not humanistic psychotherapy (I include counselling in this generic term) recognized as the natural alternative to the programmatic and outcome-based psychotherapies? Why did it not supersede psychoanalysis as the natural alternative to programmatic approaches? Should not, and does not, Humanistic Psychology contain within itself the full solution – at least at the other end of the spectrum from outcomes-based programmatic approaches – to the question, what psychotherapy is and does? Why did Humanistic Psychology end up with the reputation of being flaky or excessively 'New Age' – that is, irrational? What is Humanistic Psychology, anyway? Can this situation, in any measure, be repaired? Does humanistic psychotherapy perhaps still potentially hold within itself the solution to the dilemma of the non-programmatic psychotherapies? (My terminology will oscillate fairly freely between various formulations determined by context, as I progress. My opinions will of necessity, in this brief account of the problems, be quite emphatic and probably over-simplified.)

Some preliminary questions

Clearly there is a major historical, and indeed political, dimension to these questions. But it will be mainly the dilemmas or knots, within the *knowledge basis* of the approaches, with which I shall be concerned. Some of these are organized around the following issues: does humanistic psychotherapy suffer from an avowedly *optimistic* or utopian analysis of human existence; and/or is that really essential for it?

Does it suffer from an overly radical focus on the *present moment* (cf. Stern, 2004; Wilkinson, 2003), the here and now in process, in experience, at the expense of its recognition of the presence of the past? Is that part of the reason for a certain dogmatism, often anti-psychoanalytic dogmatism, which crept into humanistic psychotherapy? Is that the reason why integrative-humanistic approaches increasingly moved away from humanistic roots and returned to assimilate psychoanalytic insights, albeit mainly from relational psychoanalytic traditions, and also freely drawing in depth on insights from developmental psychology and developmental neuroscience? But why could not these developments within the integrative movement have been apprehended as humanistic? And how does Humanistic Psychology propose to solve its profound dilemma concerning the relationship between its secularist elements, and its transpersonal leanings?

Has it, latterly, essentially opted out of the philosophical struggle by embracing a sort of postmodernist relativism, instead of articulating its own philosophical base, its own epistemology and concept of truth? (Is, indeed, relational psychoanalysis tempted to follow it in this, too?!) Did it, in the hands of brilliant and philosophically aware men, like Carl Rogers and Fritz Perls, and Abraham Maslow, nevertheless, in its focus on feelings, senses and embodiment at the expense of mind and intellect, take up an anti-philosophy position, just as did the great literary critic F.R. Leavis, at much the same time as Humanistic Psychology was coming into its own, when he had dubbed himself an anti-philosopher (Wilkinson, 2013)? Is there not, oddly against its own aspirations, something overly empiricist and Anglo-American about this?

So, then, why did it not full-bloodedly embrace and develop a phenomenological analysis of its own praxis, the philosophical tradition intrinsically and most uniquely most germane to it, and to the psychotherapy field as such – something admitted, even, by Peter Fonagy?!

And with that I return to my original question; what really *did* prevent humanistic psychotherapy from successfully taking up the office of being the flag-bearer of the articulation of narrative and process-based approaches, the non-programmatic approaches? Why was that left to psychoanalysis, with its contradictory hankerings for scientific paradigms, to the extent that anyone took it on at all?

Might there not, even now, be *another* potential understanding of humanistic psychotherapy, profoundly phenomenological, one free of ideology, which embraces the 'what just is' or 'what simply is, purely descriptively simply is', of existence, without trying to push towards a particular solution, ideology, belief framework or primary methodology, and in which consists the latent *truth* of humanistic psychotherapy's embrace of optimism, secularist elements and the present moment?

Might the secret of Humanistic Psychology's problem be, precisely, that inadvertently, and without quite intending it, in the full flush of its peak moment and experience in the 1960s, it ended up as a *quasi-belief system*, and consequently lost its intrinsic power of infinite openness, negative capability, which it needed to occupy and retain a sufficiently comprehensive position?

I must of course declare an interest here, which is my own sense that the poetic shaping of experience (Wilkinson, 2009a, 2009b) offers a genuinely non-partisan non-programmatic perspective upon these issues, and that this leads me to a potentially different understanding of the basis of Humanistic Psychology. But I shall return to this.

But this also suggests a beginning way in to the problem: is there something about Humanistic Vision which prevents it recognizing the human and literary dimension of *tragedy*? Does the dimension of tragedy have something in it, must it have something in it, which transcends the humanism of the humanistic belief framework, at any rate? Can we, in the light of it, ask whether there may even be something nihilistic in the vision of orthodox Humanistic Vision, which we need to transcend?

Joseph Conrad's *Nostromo*

To start to address this, I begin with a passage from Joseph Conrad's great political novel, *Nostromo* (Conrad, 1904/1951), one of the serious contestants for the greatest 20th century English language novel, describing a revolution set in the imaginary city of Sulaco in the fictional South American Republic of Costaguana (think about that name). As indicated, I shall use whatever terminology is contextually appropriate. The invention of the generic term 'human potential' indicates that the earlier founders also struggled to define what it is we are talking about here, as distinct from 'straight' 'humanism' or 'Humanistic Psychology'. We have difficulties with names here, which perhaps correspond to the fault lines with all the issues involved.

In general the tragic atmosphere of the novel is represented well in the following powerful passage, where Hernandez – the bandit by virtue only of necessity in the face of injustice – who controls the Campo, the uplands above Sulaco, has offered the townspeople refuge from the insurrectionary forces of the Montero brothers. Charles Gould is the mining entrepreneur whose San Tome silver mine holds the key to the wealth of this 'Occidental' province (about to become independent by a bold stroke). He is with Antonia, the daughter of the elder statesman Don Jose Avellanos, inspiration of the constitutional grouping and forces:

> 'I must leave you now,' repeated Charles Gould to Antonia. She turned her head slowly and uncovered her face. The emissary and compadre of Hernandez spurred his horse close up. 'Has not the master of the mine any message to send to Hernandez, the master of the Campo?'
>
> The truth of the comparison struck Charles Gould heavily. In his determined purpose he held the mine, and the indomitable bandit held the Campo by the same precarious tenure. They were equals before the lawlessness of the land. It was impossible to disentangle one's activity from its debasing contacts. A close-meshed net of crime and corruption lay upon the whole country. An immense and weary discouragement sealed his lips for a time.
>
> 'You are a just man,' urged the emissary of Hernandez. 'Look at those people who made my compadre a general and have turned us all into soldiers. Look at those oligarchs fleeing for life, with only the clothes on their backs. My compadre does not think of that, but our followers may be wondering greatly, and I would speak for them to you. Listen, senor! For

> many months now the Campo has been our own. We need ask no man for anything; but soldiers must have their pay to live honestly when the wars are over. It is believed that your soul is so just that a prayer from you would cure the sickness of every beast, like the orison of the upright judge. Let me have some words from your lips that would act like a charm upon the doubts of our partida, where all are men.'
> 'Do you hear what he says?' Charles Gould said in English to Antonia. 'Forgive us our misery!' she exclaimed, hurriedly.
> 'It is your character that is the inexhaustible treasure which may save us all yet; your character, Carlos, not your wealth. I entreat you to give this man your word that you will accept any arrangement my uncle may make with their chief. One word. He will want no more.'
> On the site of the roadside hut there remained nothing but an enormous heap of embers, throwing afar a darkening red glow, in which Antonia's face appeared deeply flushed with excitement. Charles Gould, with only a short hesitation, pronounced the required pledge. He was like a man who had ventured on a precipitous path with no room to turn, where the only chance of safety is to press forward. At that moment he understood it thoroughly as he looked down at Don Jose stretched out, hardly breathing, by the side of the erect Antonia, vanquished in a lifelong struggle with the powers of moral darkness, whose stagnant depths breed monstrous crimes and monstrous illusions. In a few words the emissary from Hernandez expressed his complete satisfaction.

That climactic phrase, 'vanquished in a lifelong struggle with the powers of moral darkness, whose stagnant depths breed monstrous crimes and monstrous illusions', could be echoed in intent from Shakespeare's *King Lear*, from Dostoyevsky's *Crime and Punishment*, from *The Oresteia* of Aeschylus, or from Orwell's *Nineteen Eighty-Four*. None of those works is nihilistic, in the sense of repudiating or denying a moral purpose to existence (whether or not they implicate any divinity), but all of them in some sense envisage the reality of evil, and of goodness or moral resolve, defining itself over against evil.

Why do I quote these examples? Is it naïve and foolish of me to think that Humanistic Vision may have a problem with accepting that there is evil and moral darkness, tragedy, and demonic elements in existence? Is there an element of absolutism in Humanistic Vision, which brings it near to denying the primary human reality of morality? Surely wise Humanistic Vision does not *deny* these realities, it just makes sense of them in a different way? Surely, in particular, existential versions of humanism, which lie, for instance, behind the visions of Carl Rogers (1961) and Fritz Perls (1969), absolutely do not deny these realities? But does that work – what are the questions we need to ask here? With these examples, to work my way into a critique of Humanistic Vision and consideration of the way it might respond to these challenges is my intention here; and I am not going to put all my eggs into the basket of one example, but keep asking questions and allow it all to accumulate incrementally, exploring Humanistic Vision.

Arguably, three dimensions initially play out through our reflections on humanism; the first of them we are, in a manner, looking at through the above example:

Essential goodness versus *inherency of evil*

Immanence versus *transcendence*

Creative feeling versus *objective truth*

These could all be formulated in various ways, but I shall start from here. Is humanism a value system, an expression of optimism and Promethean hope? Or is it an epistemology, a worldview? 'We are all humanists now.' Well! – are we? Is humanism, or the Human Potential Movement, the victim of its own success, so that it can no longer, and no longer needs to, articulate itself as a movement? *Indeed, is its aspiration to be a movement actually counter to its essential power and influence?*

I shall allow the different tendencies to emerge in how I label what we are talking about at different points, tracking that as far as necessary. I used 'Human Potential Movement' just here, because 'humanistic psychotherapy' or 'Humanistic Psychology' seemed too narrow, and on the other hand simply to use 'humanism' too strongly implies merely humanism in the philosophical sense, which is commonly equated with atheist secularism.

If we take humanistic approaches in the psychotherapy context, they raise fundamental questions, going back long before the modern age, which enable us to understand some of the struggles and dilemmas played out in the Human Potential Movement. If, then, we review our options in individual narrative psychotherapy (I initially assume that mainly encompasses both analytic and humanistic-integrative approaches, and deal with greater complexities later) in the light of the history of Christian theology, with its Greek and Greek Tragic background (at work in the Crucifixion narratives of the Gospels, also in the background of the dramatic-dialectic framings of Paul's Epistles), then at first sight we are dealing with a modern version of the 4th century argument between Pelagius and Augustine of Hippo. Rogers or Maslow are Pelagius, Freud or Klein are Augustine (Jung is an interesting transitional case). Pelagius, it is commonly claimed at any rate, says that man's original capacity of will for good or innocence remains, intrinsically, still available behind the consequences of the Fall; Augustine (Schaff, 1956) says the Fall has, like a virus, invaded all human volition, action and motivation, and we can only be restored by God's grace in Christ. Luther reiterated this latter position emphatically at the Reformation, and the argument played itself out again in his argument (Luther, 1525/1957) about the Freedom of the Will with one of the founders of humanism, Erasmus.

But the whole issue is not at all simple, and its lack of simplicity has manifested itself in the evolution of Humanistic Psychology. We are, therefore, probably, once we start digging deeper here, engaging with a historically very ancient *ongoing dialectical process*, of which there are various versions, Christian and post-Christian. Nietzsche (1887/2007) describes it as Israel versus Rome; Karl Barth evokes it as pagan or implicitly pagan absolutism versus grace in the Christian sense (Barth, 1952/2002); René Girard evokes it as scapegoating-based human stances versus non-scapegoating stances, which he sees in the Jewish-Christian evolution towards the Gospel (Girard, 1978) – in all these and other variants, it is not primarily about transcendence, but about a fundamental ethical difference. Is René Girard a Pelagian? Or an Augustinian? What about Nietzsche? Is Nietzsche a humanist? No easy answers, but there is a complex dialectic here about morality and tragedy which humanism, apart from existentialism, has hardly engaged in. Freud undoubtedly did fringe into it, in particular, in *Civilisation and its Discontents*, another of the founding texts of the modern world (cf. Lionel Trilling, 'The teaching of modern literature', in his *Beyond Culture*, 1965), and such texts as *The Theme of the Three Caskets* (Freud, in Gay, 1989).

Has humanism engaged adequately in this? And if not adequately, might that be something which would deepen and authenticate its relationships and existence in the modern world? What would it have lost by engaging in it? If contact functions, attachment, empathy and other humanistic or nearly humanistic values and impulses are intrinsic to human beings, how is it possible for humanity to become, again and again, up to and including Auschwitz, so utterly alienated from those primary dimensions of human existence? If that alienation were accepted as a mystery, as it is in much Christian tradition, and in existential philosophy, would that annul the humanistic understanding? And as for psychoanalysis with its supposed pessimism about human nature (which Humanistic Psychology has a tendency to mock) in such texts as Freud's above, and in such texts as Melanie Klein's commentary upon Aeschylus' *The Oresteia* (Klein, 1975): surely here, psychoanalysis is simply manifesting what Freud always affirmed, its profoundly human roots in literature and poetry, and in the tragic-mythic tradition? Is it a black mark against psychoanalysis that it can do this? But the example of existential understanding suggests that, if existentialism is humanistic, as surely it is (e.g. Sartre, 1946/2007), Humanistic Vision in principle is not debarred from addressing the tragic, in these senses. Is it, then, merely a popular and caricature humanism that hinted at Humanistic Vision's transcendence of the tragic?

If tragic vision can be included, given then that tragic vision – *Macbeth* or *Hamlet*, for instance – no more than the Crucifixion narratives in the Gospels (because of its sheerly *enactive* or life dimension) does not deal in any simple antithesis of this world against a higher world, immanence against transcendence, we could also, at a stroke, put aside the humanistic dilemma about the transpersonal, and the strong tendency in the humanistic tradition to accept the transpersonal dimension as humanistic would fall into place. We would also gain a perspective upon the emphasis on feeling in Humanistic Vision; it would have to do, intrinsically as opposed to popular caricature, with *the recognition of the accessibility of the sense of the whole, and the ontological intuition of existence*, primarily to feeling-apprehension, and this would accord with the primacy of feeling and mood in cognition in writings as various as those of D.H. Lawrence, Heidegger, Buber, Bowlby, John Heron, Suzanne Langer, and, going back a bit, Hume and Spinoza. And many others. This, then, does not constitute an irrationalism.

All right! I move briefly, and to end, to another key, then!

Humanism and humour, comedy and irony

Does Humanistic Vision have a problem with humour and irony, including black humour? Is it overly earnest, a bit four square, in its vision of the world? Can it accommodate *Waiting for Godot*? What does humanism do with it, when Nietzsche (1883/2006: Aphorism §1) writes about the teachers of belief and purpose in existence:

> There is no denying that *in the long run* every one of these great teachers of a purpose was vanquished by laughter, reason, and nature: the short tragedy always gave way again and returned into the eternal comedy of existence; and 'the waves of uncountable laughter' – to cite Aeschylus – must in the end overwhelm even the greatest of these tragedians. In spite of all this laughter which makes the required corrections, human nature has nevertheless been changed by the ever new appearance of these teachers of the purpose of existence: It now has one additional need – the need for the ever new appearance of such teachers and teachings of a 'purpose'.

Or even, to come down to the quite banal in a sense, what does humanism do with something as basically ironic – and yet utterly open-ended and enactive, read the final lines! – as T.S. Eliot's (1917/1967) *The Love Song of J. Alfred Prufrock*?

> No! I am not Prince Hamlet, nor was meant to be;
> Am an attendant lord, one that will do
> To swell a progress, start a scene or two,
> Advise the prince; no doubt, an easy tool,
> Deferential, glad to be of use,   115
> Politic, cautious, and meticulous;
> Full of high sentence, but a bit obtuse;
> At times, indeed, almost ridiculous –
> Almost, at times, the Fool.
>
> I grow old … I grow old …   120
> I shall wear the bottoms of my trousers rolled.
>
> Shall I part my hair behind? Do I dare to eat a peach?
> I shall wear white flannel trousers, and walk upon the beach.
> I have heard the mermaids singing, each to each.
> I do not think that they will sing to me.   125
> I have seen them riding seaward on the waves
> Combing the white hair of the waves blown back
> When the wind blows the water white and black.
>
> We have lingered in the chambers of the sea
> By sea-girls wreathed with seaweed red and brown   130
> Till human voices wake us, and we drown.

A humanism of the human

If humanism can embrace the total communication of humour and the comic in all their significance, then a *'Humanism of the Human'* is genuinely possible. Therefore, if there were to be found, and if we were to consider:

1. a humanism which is primarily based in *being with and in process*, though it may also use programmatic and teaching elements, not dogmatically excluding them in the name of modality;

2. a humanism, therefore, which freely assimilates, and is in that sense integrative, without any sense of conflict;

3. a humanism which, whilst it may have, in the light of its heritage, a most acute sense of the present moment, whether Rogerian, Perlsian or any other form, does not dogmatically exclude either the widest possible recognition of context, the full recognition of the past and future as living presences in the now, and the full recognition of the value of texts, including extra-psychotherapeutic texts, as germane to its reality;

4. a humanism based in fundamental tolerance of what is, and acceptance of the cross-grained nature, partly consciousness based, partly beyond consciousness in various ways, of human existence, in all its absurdity, horror and wondrousness, including (not condoning but knowing the existence of) evil as well as good, without reaching for dogmatic solutions or beliefs;

5. a humanism which is fully enactive, in the literary sense, not the reductive sense acting out or in, which is derived from classical psychoanalysis;

6. a humanism which therefore can fully embrace human comedy and tragedy without trying to turn them into something else;

7. a humanism truly committed to open-endedness, spontaneity and creativity, without denying method, any method, but without deifying it either;

8. a humanism of which it could truly be said, 'All human life is there'; and

9. a humanism which thinks as well as feels, and which therefore takes seriously the responsibility to think out what it is in philosophical and therefore primarily phenomenological terms, including thinking responsibly, neither dogmatically exclusively nor over-deferentially, about its relationship to science and research; …

… then, such a humanism would be free, mature, non-ideological, and 'come of age'; and to the extent that it already exists, I welcome it. Such a humanism, of course, would be coterminous in essence with psychotherapy itself. I myself would be, and am, happy to call myself a humanistic psychotherapist, in the sense of such a humanism. For such a humanism, there would not be a dogmatic differentiation from psychoanalysis or integrative approaches; there would be rapprochement with many approaches, but free also of their dogmatic elements.

Such a humanism would, indeed, simply be a manifestation of Being Human!

References

Barth, K. (2002) *Protestant Theology in the Nineteenth Century*, Grand Rapids, MI: Eerdmans Publishing. (Original work published 1952)
Conrad, J. (1951) *Nostromo*, New York: Modern Library. (Original work published 1904)
Eliot, T.S. (1967) *Prufrock and Other Observations*, New York: Harcourt, Brace & World. (Original work published 1917)
Gay, P. (ed.) (1989) *The Freud Reader*, New York: W.W. Norton.
Girard, R. (1978) *Things Hidden since the Foundation of the World*, Palo Alto, CA: Stanford University Press.
Klein, M. (1975) *Envy and Gratitude and Other Works*, New York: Simon and Schuster.
Luther, M. (1957) *The Bondage of the Will* (A New Translation of *De Servo Arbitrio* (1525), Martin Luther's Reply to Erasmus of Rotterdam, trans. J.I. Packer and O.R. Johnston), Old Tappan, NJ: Fleming H. Revell Co.
Nietzsche. F.W. (2006) *The Gay Science*, Mineola, NY: Dover Publications. (Original work published 1883)
Nietzsche, F.W. (2007) *The Genealogy of Morals*, Cambridge: Cambridge University Press. (Original work published 1887)
Perls, F. (1969) *In and Out the Garbage Pail*, Cleveland, OH: Gestalt Journal Press.
Rogers, C.R. (1961) *On Becoming a Person: A Therapist's View of Psychotherapy*, London: Constable.
Sartre J.-P. (2007) *Existentialism Is a Humanism* (trans. Carol Macomber), New Haven, CT: Yale University Press. (Original work published 1946)
Schaff, P. (ed.) (1956) *A Select Library of the Nicene and Post-Nicene Fathers of the Christian Church*, Grand Rapids, MI: W.R. Eerdmans Pub. Co.
Stern, D.N. (2004) *The Present Moment in Psychotherapy and Everyday Life*, New York: W.W. Norton.
Trilling, L. (1965) *Beyond Culture: Essays on Literature and Learning*, New York: Viking Press.
Wilkinson, H. (2003) 'Review Article: The Shadow of Freud: Is Daniel Stern still a psychoanalyst? The creative tension between the present and the past in psychoanalytic and existential psychotherapies, in Daniel Stern's *The Present Moment*, and his humanistic-existential partners in dialogue', *International Journal of Psychotherapy*, 8 (3): 235–54.
Wilkinson, H. (2009a) *The Muse as Therapist: A New Poetic Paradigm for Psychotherapy*, Karnac: London.
Wilkinson, H. (2009b) *Primary Process of Deconstruction: Towards a Derridean Psychotherapy*, in R. Frie and D.M. Orange (eds), *Beyond Postmodernism: New Dimensions in Clinical Theory and Practice*, London: Routledge.
Wilkinson, H. (2013) 'A Cyclops in the Philosopher's Cave: Leavis and the Coleridgean Function in our Time', 26 January; retrieved from http://hewardwilkinson.co.uk/cyclops-philosopher%E2%80%99s-cave-leavis-and-coleridgean-function-our-time

10 | The Future of Humanism: Cultivating the humanities impulse in mental health culture

James T. Hansen

In this chapter I argue that the future of humanism is dependent upon the cultivation of the humanities impulse in mental health culture. Certain orientations to helping can be categorized as humanities approaches because their focus is on human meaning systems. The dominant medical model, in contrast, purposefully eschews human meaning systems. Unfortunately, humanities approaches are generally disconnected from each other, which weakens their ability to impact mental health culture. Humanism will have a bright future if it is conjoined with other humanities-based orientations. This would create a powerful, unified humanities response to the technical approaches that currently dominate the helping professions.

I am pleased and honored to have been invited to share my thoughts on the future of Humanistic Psychology. I have given this topic a great deal of thought over the past couple of decades, so I appreciate the opportunity to consolidate my ideas into a succinct essay. In short, I believe that the future of humanism is dependent upon the ability of helping professionals to cultivate the humanities impulse in mental health culture. To understand what I mean by this, I provide a brief history of humanism below.

Brief history of humanism

The humanistic revolution in psychology echoed many of the themes present in Renaissance humanism, which emerged centuries before (Davidson, 2000). Rather than understanding human beings as pawns of God or as scientific specimens, Renaissance humanists endeavored to appreciate people on their own terms (Tarnas, 1991). Analogously, the mid-20th century psychological humanists revolted against the reductionist image of human beings proffered by psychoanalysis and behaviorism, which were the dominant treatment orientations at the time (deCarvalho, 1990). According to the psychological humanists, human experiences (e.g. love, anxiety, aesthetic awe) should not be reduced to psychic parts or stimulus–response contingencies, but could only be adequately understood holistically, as unique elements of the human condition (Matson, 1971).

There are potentially many ways to conceptualize the changes in mental health culture that the pioneering psychological humanists hoped to achieve. For various reasons (which I elaborate below), I prefer to think of Rogers (1957), Maslow (1968) and their colleagues as advocating for a mental health culture based on the humanities (Hansen, 2012). Indeed, the psychological humanists argued that the humanities (e.g. history, literature, philosophy), not science, should serve as the intellectual foundation for the helping professions (Fishman, 1999). This is a sensible proposition because the fundamental data of both the humanities and the helping professions are human meaning systems.

Naturally, as an outgrowth of their conceptual emphasis on unreduced human experience, the psychological humanists viewed the therapeutic relationship as the central area of concern in the helping encounter (Rogers, 1957). Rogers (1957), for instance, theorized that the establishment and maintenance of certain relational conditions is all that is needed for successful client outcomes. Indeed, decades of outcome research has consistently verified the humanistic premise that the therapeutic relationship, not specific techniques, is the most important variable in treatment outcomes (Wampold, 2001).

Why, then, given the tremendous amount of research that supports humanistic conceptualizations of the helping situation, has humanism been suppressed in contemporary mental health culture? To ask this question another way, why has the humanities emphasis in the helping professions, which is known to be the conceptual path to positive outcomes, been replaced by a supposedly scientific emphasis on techniques, which has been consistently shown to contribute little to treatment outcomes?

The answers to these questions are complex, and a full exploration of them is beyond the scope of this chapter. However, Elkins (2009), in his outstanding book, offered insightful opinions about the fall of humanism that are worth reviewing. Humanistic Psychology, Elkins argued, empowered clients, a move that threatened the established power base of mental health professionals. Humanism made helping client-centered instead of expert-centered. Mental health professionals, hoping to re-establish their power, reacted against this egalitarian view of the therapeutic relationship. As a result, the helping professions became increasingly scientific and medicalized, thereby fortifying the supposed expertise of practitioners and diminishing the power of clients. Contemporarily, the humanities vision of the founding humanists has been buried under a scientific, technical and medicalized view of the therapeutic encounter (Hansen, 2009).

Humanities impulse in contemporary mental health culture

The humanities impulse (which emphasizes human meaning systems over techniques) has been an omnipresent force throughout the history of mental health (Hansen, 2009, 2012). However, the manifestation of this impulse has varied, depending on the era in which it arose. During the mid-20th century, the humanities impulse gave rise to psychological humanism. Although humanism has been suppressed in modern times, the humanities impulse continues to be an important force in contemporary mental health culture. Arguably, this contemporary humanities impulse has taken the form of the postmodernist movement. In order to understand postmodernism, the basic assumptions of modernism must be reviewed.

Briefly, modernism presumes that: (a) there are singular truths that human beings can objectively apprehend; and (b) each person has a self, which is the center of their human agency (Hansen, 2004). Both of these modernist assumptions are present in traditional psychological humanism (Hansen, 2005b). That is, psychological humanism presumes that: (a) psychological truths about clients can be apprehended by an empathic therapist; and (b) clients have a true self, with mental health being equated with fidelity to one's congruent, actualized self (Hansen, 2005b). Postmodernists reject these modernist assumptions about truth and self (Gergen, 1999). For postmodernists, truth and self are human creations that shift and change as a function of the community in which one is currently participating (McNamee, 1996).

A number of innovative approaches to practice and research were formulated as a result of the introduction of postmodernist ideas to mental health culture. For example, solution-focused (de Shazer, 1985) and narrative therapies (e.g. White and Epston, 1990) have direct conceptual ties to postmodernism because these therapeutic systems emphasize the creation of new, adaptive meaning systems, rather than the discovery of fixed truths. Qualitative research, as another example of a movement informed by postmodernism, is a method of inquiry that does not presume universal laws, but attempts to understand people in their local environments (Berg, 2004).

The general emphasis of postmodernism, then, at least as it has been applied to the helping encounter, has been on the *creation* of human meaning systems (Hansen, 2006). New meanings are judged by their adaptive utility within the therapeutic relationship, not by their epistemological proximity to a supposed objective truth about clients (Hansen, 2007a). In contrast, psychological humanism, because it remains steeped in modernist assumptions, is epistemically aimed at the accurate, empathic *discovery* of truths about clients (Hansen, 2005b). Psychological humanism, therefore, is a mid-century manifestation of the humanities impulse that has generally not been philosophically updated to embrace contemporary ideas about truth and self. As I note below, these conceptual divisions among humanities orientations play a role in preventing the humanities impulse from rising as a strong, unified force in contemporary mental health culture.

Cultivating the humanities impulse

To review, I have argued that an emphasis on human meaning systems (which I have called the *humanities impulse*) regularly arises in mental health culture. This humanities impulse is also regularly suppressed by a technical, medicalized view of human nature. Indeed, mental health history can be read as a continual battle for dominance between humanities and technical views of the helping encounter (Hansen, 2009). Contemporarily, humanism is suppressed, and technical approaches are dominant (Elkins, 2009).

In this regard, there are strong conceptual advantages to defining psychological humanism as a particular instance of the humanities impulse in mental health culture, rather than as an isolated theoretical orientation. Specifically, by making this conceptual move, humanism can be conjoined with, and thereby fortified by, other humanities-based orientations, such as postmodernist approaches. Also, the humanities represent an established disciplinary category that has larger implications for the professional life of helping professionals than a single theoretical orientation, such as humanism. There are, therefore, wider professional implications of adopting a thoroughgoing humanities mindset than there are for simply endorsing humanism as a treatment orientation (Hansen, 2012).

From this conceptual vantage point, the future of humanism is dependent upon the ability of helping professionals to cultivate the humanities impulse in contemporary mental health culture. In order for humanism to re-emerge as a vital helping orientation, this cultivation must occur in several professional realms: (a) theoretical, (b) empirical, (c) practice and (d) professional culture.

Theoretically, as mentioned above, humanism continues to be steeped in modernist assumptions (Hansen, 2005b), a situation which keeps humanism theoretically sequestered from other humanities orientations. Arguably, humanism should be brought up to speed with postmodernism, so that movements that emphasize human meaning systems can become a unified humanities force in mental health culture (Hansen, 2005b). For instance, the consolidated self of humanism makes little sense in a postmodern world, wherein selves are continually bombarded by multifarious identity opportunities (Gergen, 1991). Diverse masks of self that adapt to various communal demands should arguably be the new standard for mental health, not the stubborn, unyielding consolidated self of traditional humanism (Gergen, 1995).

The humanistic ideal of therapists finding the truth about their clients also smacks of an outdated modernist view of the helping encounter. In this regard, I have suggested that the traditional humanistic ideal of 'accurate empathic understanding' (Rogers, 1957: 99) be replaced by the concept of 'emotional resonance' (Hansen, 2005b: 10), a phrase that conceptually subtracts the truth ideal inherent in the concept of *accurate* empathic understanding, yet retains the idea that therapists should intervene in ways that are experientially meaningful to clients. In turn, therapeutic systems based on postmodernist assumptions can be significantly enriched by the traditional humanistic focus on the therapeutic relationship (Hansen, 2005b). After all, meanings are not constructed in a vacuum; they require certain relational conditions (which were best articulated by the traditional humanists) to emerge and take hold.

Humanism, then, needs to be theoretically updated so that it can join forces with other manifestations of the humanities impulse in mental health culture. There is strength in numbers. Humanism stands a much better chance of survival if it is theoretically brought into the fold with other humanities-based orientations. Although there has been work done in this area (e.g. Hansen, 2005b), there is still much to do.

Of course, there are other, more practical actions that can be taken to strengthen the humanities impulse in contemporary mental health culture. Psychotherapy researchers, for instance, should abandon the failed empirically supported treatment movement, which was designed to discover optimal treatments for particular conditions (Elkins, 2009). The problems with this anti-humanistic movement are too numerous to detail in this chapter. Wampold (2001), however, provides some excellent suggestions for alternative research agendas, which, in my estimation, are congruent with a humanities-based conceptualization of the helping encounter.

Practitioners can cultivate the humanities impulse in mental health culture by carefully considering whether to participate in anti-humanities-based realms of practice. For instance, the medical model, with its emphasis on biological reductionism, disorders and techniques, is the antithesis of humanities ideals (Hansen, 2005a, 2007b). Of course, I am fully aware that the medical model is a reality of contemporary practice, and that practitioners may have difficulty making a living if they do not participate in it. Therefore, I am not advising practitioners to boycott the medical model, only to think critically about the ideological impact of participating in it.

Professionally, the structure of the helping professions has been founded upon a hierarchical model that is reminiscent of technical/scientific professional culture (Hansen, 2012). Research knowledge from on high is disseminated to the lowly practitioners below; licensure, approved continuing education credits, and mandated supervision are culturally entrenched components of professional life for helping professionals (at least in the United States). My humanities colleagues (e.g. English and history professors) operate in professional cultures that are far less hierarchical and rule bound. No one tells them how to think and practice, or the proper way to educate themselves after graduation. Cultivating the humanities impulse would mean bringing elements of the humanities' professional culture to the helping professions. Some ideas about reconfiguring professional life for helping professionals have been offered (e.g. Hansen, 2012; House, 2003), but there is still a good deal of work to be done in this area.

Conclusions

I have argued that the future of humanism depends upon the ability of helping professionals to cultivate the humanities impulse (i.e. emphasis on human meaning systems) in mental health culture. Conceptualizing humanism as a manifestation of a larger humanities impulse has at least two conceptual advantages over regarding humanism as an isolated theory: (a) humanism can be theoretically conjoined with other humanities-based orientations, thereby creating a powerful and united humanities response (rather than a weak, conceptually disjointed one) to the technical, medical ideologies that currently dominate mental health culture; and (b) the humanities, as an organizing construct, is richer and more theoretically inclusive than humanism. Therefore, ideas from the humanities can provide mental health professionals with greater guidance and direction than humanism alone, particularly with regard to professional culture (i.e. mental health professionals can consider adopting elements of long-established humanities' professional cultures). In my opinion, then, humanism has a bright future if theoreticians, researchers and practitioners focus their professional energies on human meaning systems instead of the technical aspects of the helping encounter.

Perhaps, though, there is a better, simpler reason to believe that humanism has a bright future than the ones I have offered. In this regard, I regularly invite my students and supervisees to engage in an introspective task. Specifically, I ask them to recall a time when they felt emotionally burdened, spoke to someone (e.g. a friend, family member, minister, counselor, etc.) about their troubles, and left the conversation feeling renewed. After providing a few minutes of silence, I ask them to tell me what the person to whom they spoke did to help them feel better (as part of the initial instruction, I deliberately tell them not to reveal the nature of their problem to me, just the type of responses that the helper provided). At this point, I would like to invite you, the reader, to take a break from reading, and engage in this introspective task for a few moments.

I suspect that your responses are very similar to the responses of my students and supervisees. Indeed, over the many years that I have conducted this experiment, there has been almost universal agreement that the helper listened intently with a non-judgmental attitude, tried to see the problem from the individual's point of view, validated the concerns of the individual, and, perhaps, through empathy, gently helped the person to see a side of the issue that she or he had not seen before. No one has ever said that the helper corrected irrational thoughts, told the person that she or he had a particular disorder, or made a list of goals for the person to accomplish with accompanying strategies and timelines. This, then, is the fundamental reason that humanism has a bright future: everyone knows that it works.

References

Berg, B. (2004) *Qualitative Research Methods for the Social Sciences*, 5th edn, Boston: Allyn & Bacon.

Davidson, L. (2000) 'Philosophical foundations of humanistic psychology', *The Humanistic Psychologist*, 28: 7–31; reprinted in *Self & Society: International Journal for Humanistic Psychology*, 40 (2), 2013, pp. 7–17.

DeCarvalho, R. (1990) 'A history of the "third force" in psychology', *Journal of Humanistic Psychology*, 30 (4): 22–44.

De Shazer, S. (1985) *Keys to Solution in Brief Therapy*, New York: W.W. Norton.

Elkins, D. (2009) *Humanistic Psychology: A Clinical Manifesto. A Critique of Clinical*

Psychology and the Need for Progressive Alternatives, Colorado Springs, CO: University of the Rockies Press.

Fishman, D. (1999) *The Case for a Pragmatic Psychology,* New York: New York University Press.

Gergen, K. (1991) *The Saturated Self: Dilemmas of Identity in Contemporary Life,* New York: Basic Books.

Gergen, K. (1995) 'The healthy, happy human being wears many masks', in W. Anderson (ed.), *The Truth about the Truth: De-confusing and Re-constructing the Postmodern World* (pp. 136–50), New York: G.P. Putnam's Sons.

Gergen, K. (1999) *An Invitation to Social Construction,* Thousand Oaks, CA: Sage.

Hansen, J.T. (2004) 'Thoughts on knowing: epistemic implications of counseling practice', *Journal of Counseling and Development,* 82: 131–8.

Hansen, J.T. (2005a) 'The devaluation of inner subjective experiences by the counseling profession: a plea to reclaim the essence of the profession', *Journal of Counseling and Development,* 83: 406–15.

Hansen, J.T. (2005b) 'Postmodernism and humanism: a proposed integration of perspectives that value human meaning systems', *Journal of Humanistic Counseling, Education and Development,* 44: 3–15.

Hansen, J.T. (2006) 'Discovery and creation within the counseling process: reflections on the timeless nature of the helping encounter', *Journal of Mental Health Counseling,* 28: 289–308.

Hansen, J.T. (2007a) 'Counseling without truth: toward a neopragmatic foundation for counseling practice', *Journal of Counseling and Development,* 85: 423–30.

Hansen, J.T. (2007b) 'Should counseling be considered a health care profession? Critical thoughts on the transition to a health care ideology', *Journal of Counseling and Development,* 85: 286–93 (reprinted in the October 2007 edition of *Therapy Today,* British Association for Counselling and Psychotherapy).

Hansen, J.T. (2009) 'On displaced humanists: counselor education and the meaning-reduction pendulum', *Journal of Humanistic Counseling, Education and Development,* 48: 65–76.

Hansen, J.T. (2012) 'Extending the humanistic vision: toward a humanities foundation for the counseling profession', *Journal of Humanistic Counseling,* 51 (2): 131–44.

House, R. (2003) *Therapy beyond Modernity: Deconstructing and Transcending Profession-centred Therapy,* New York and London: Karnac Books.

Maslow, A. (1968) *Toward a Psychology of Being,* 2nd edn, New York: Van Nostrand Reinhold.

Matson, F. (1971) 'Humanistic theory: the third revolution in psychology', *The Humanist,* 12: 7–11.

McNamee, S. (1996) 'Psychotherapy as a social construction', in H. Rosen and K. Kuchlwein (eds), *Constructing Realities: Meaning-making Perspectives for Psychotherapists* (pp. 115–37), San Francisco: Jossey-Bass.

Rogers, C.R. (1957) 'The necessary and sufficient conditions of therapeutic personality change', *Journal of Consulting Psychology,* 21: 95–103.

Tarnas, R. (1991) *The Passion of the Western Mind: Understanding the Ideas that Have Shaped Our World View,* New York: Harmony.

Wampold, B. (2001) *The Great Psychotherapy Debate: Models, Methods, and Findings,* Mahwah, NJ: Erlbaum.

White, M. and Epston, D. (1990) *Narrative Means to Therapeutic Ends,* New York: W.W. Norton.

11 | Creating Space:
The future of Humanistic Psychology

Caroline Brazier

The development of counselling and psychotherapy practice in the last 50 years has had substantial effect not only within the field of mental health provision, but also far more broadly in fields such as education, social provision, business and politics. With such wide-ranging impact, it is the duty of those engaged in the psychological professions to reflect on this influence, and on the implicit and explicit value systems which are being communicated. This chapter addresses the questions raised by this expansion of interest, and in particular reflects on the impact of Buddhist models and the Other-Centred Approach in this context.

Psychology has, arguably, been one of the major influences upon society in the 20th century and beyond (Furedi, 2004). Its reach has gone far beyond the consulting room and the treatment of mental and psychosomatic illness with which it started, and has impacted upon the fabric of modern life in all manner of ways, far divorced from its origins. Whether in the growing subtlety of advertising and propaganda, which we are exposed to through the plethora of media available today, or in the concern for the emotional and physical wellbeing of children growing up in our education and welfare systems, psychology has influenced us for better or worse. In the extreme it has, on the one hand, enabled the calculation of methods of torture and population management engaged in by various regimes to be maximally efficacious, supporting such regimes in the maintenance of their values and power bases. On the other, it has been employed in the development of a sporting elite, not only coached in body but also sharply honed in their mind states.

The use of psychology in social understanding takes different forms. These can aid social cohesion or create division. Psychological theory may, for example, be used to solve crimes and understand causes of such events in the psyche of the perpetrators, but it may also result in creating labels which separate the bad from the rest of the population, insulating us from knowledge of our own capacity to harm. It can be used to protect the vulnerable and avoid some of the crass treatment of children in earlier ages, but it can also create a culture so anxious about repressing the young or exposing them to possible dangers that it fails to set boundaries, overlooks common-sense responses, and effectively imprisons young people in their own homes in front of computers or televisions, rather than allowing them the freedom previously associated with childhood.

The impact of psychology, though, has infiltrated our lives in both public and private spheres to an extent that we have ceased to even question. From birth, to marriage and parenting, through to bereavement, people's experience is interpreted through the medium of a therapeutic ethos. Numerous studies of this subject have noted that conventional moral meanings attached to concepts such as guilt and responsibility lose their salience in circumstances where the therapeutic ethos gains influence (Furedi, 2004: 12).

The trend towards the psychologization of society has been amplified by the tendency over the second half of the 20th century towards increasing dependence on the expert. In the past, in contrast, people trusted their own judgement, based on behaviour learned from parents, grandparents and peers, as well as from direct personal observation. Just as 21st century young people trust sell-by dates on food products more than their own ability to distinguish what is safe to eat and what is not, so too, they resort to the self-help manual and to the therapist for advice on how to live their lives, and manage the lives of those for whom they have responsibility. This phenomenon is not new, for self-help manuals have been in circulation for centuries, but as Furedi points out (2004: 12), it has escalated substantially.

In a climate where the role of the expert as advisor and guru has grown, as it has in recent years, the potential for social manipulation through the provision of advice and information increases. Just as, in the past, compliant groups have succumbed to the propaganda of governments and religious leaders (one only has to think of the way in which women's working habits changed before, during and after the Second World War),[1] so too the potential influences of therapy culture are a factor for concern, both to the profession and to society at large. We need to ask ourselves, if therapy is influential, how is it influential? What effect is its influence having? What sort of therapy is being promoted by mainstream services, and how are its philosophy and values representative of the corporate or governmental values of its providers?

It seems to me that there are two levels of influence actually taking place. First, there is a level of influence which comes simply from the fact that therapy itself has become an important factor in the creation of social process. This seems to be observable in trends such as, for example, a tendency to fragmentation in society. The growth of individualism is evidenced in an increase of single-person households, changes in patterns of family life and marriage, and more emphasis on personal fulfilment in the rhetoric of popular media. Whilst causality for such big-scale trends must remain a matter of speculation, it seems reasonable to imagine a link between these

---

1. The original film, *Rosie the Riveter* (Redd Evans and John Jacob Loeb, Paramount Music Corporation, 1942), led to many real-life stories of women who helped the war effort but later returned to domestic duties as the men came back from war.

changes and the rise of personal-growth movements through the 1960s and 1970s, and beyond.

A second level of influence may be seen in the preferred type of therapy on offer. In particular, in the UK over the last couple of decades in mainstream services, we have seen a move away from the predominance of humanistic counselling models, and towards a growth in the use of cognitive behaviour therapy (CBT). An interest in 'happiness' in recent times, and the use of mindfulness methods, both seem to suggest a re-framing of the understanding of psychological health, away from the exploration of problems and unconscious process, and towards a more functional view in which mental process is adjusted through active intervention.

Highlighting the fact that such trends occur, whether or not one accepts the specifics of my broad-brush interpretations of their nature, poses questions for those of us engaged in the practice of therapy and the training of therapists. What influences do and could our methods have on society? How can we evaluate and improve what we offer? And do different humanistic therapies create different conditions for change?

Of course, much is unpredictable. The same psychological theory can, in different cultures, be used or subverted in different ways to support positive or harmful positions. Often a meta-level of values and assumptions within which the therapy is operating is even more influential on such processes than the therapy itself. Methods can be divorced from their roots, as we see with mindfulness practices, which often go to some lengths to remove themselves from their Buddhist origins, for example.

I would like to take this opportunity, then, to reflect on the potential impact at a social level of the therapy which I am involved in teaching. It does itself come from Buddhist roots and, having its origins in the values and culture of that faith, presents a somewhat different worldview to that of many Western humanistic therapies, whilst at the same time upholding other values which I see as very compatible with that movement.

This approach is other-centred therapy (Brazier, 2009). This model is based in a Buddhist understanding of mind, and in particular to the notion of the conditioned self. The model sees identity as contingent upon perceived objects, which are viewed in such a way as to confirm the sense of self. Thus, each person surrounds themself with a protective world of relationships; of 'others', human and non-human, all of which support the identity. This is like a protective bubble made up of distortion and delusion, and it forms a defence structure, created to ward off anxiety about the uncertainty of life and our existential position as mortal beings.

The view of the self as a defence structure is not new to Western thought, but the other-centred model does create a challenge to those therapies which regard the strengthening of the sense of identity and self-esteem as paramount. It takes the focus of the client's attention away from the self towards investigating the objects of perception. The client is more likely to be asked 'How did your friend feel?' than 'How do you feel?'

Buddhist psychology views perception of, and attachment to, significant objects as the basis by which, on the one hand, people feel safe enough to function, but, on the other hand, are psychologically restricted. Objects are the anchors on which we pin our sense of our existence, mirrors of the self and supports to its continuity. They are more often perceived in self-confirming ways, not as existent in their own right. They form a world perceived as 'my world' rather than a world which is objectively present.

With its orientation towards perception and the relationship with an object world, other-centred methods tend to focus predominantly on an enquiry into how the client perceives. The view of others conditions the mentality, so altering that view will bring about psychological change. The methodology is concerned with exploring the distortions which perception inevitably introduces, which reflect personal patterns of worldview, and also with facilitating a clearer view of others and real connection with them. The self, or identity, is reflected in the worldview which maintains it. In Buddhist theory, self-structures are associated with rigidity, and their relinquishment with increasing fluidity and clarity. Rather as with Carl Rogers' description of the fully functioning person (Rogers, 1961), the person inhabits the flow of their experience.

Because the method is concerned with relationship, in particular it helps the client to explore and develop empathy for the important others in their life. It encourages a shift from a self-orientated viewpoint to multiple perspectives through techniques which invite the client to step into the shoes of those people who are significant in their lives. Whether through empathic reflection or role reversal, the client attempts to see the world and even themselves through the eyes of the people to whom they are closest. Other other-centred methods derive from Japanese therapies such as Naikan (Krech, 2001), which offers a life review process in which contemplating one's early relationships typically results in an increasing sense of gratitude and appreciation rather than, as is common in many Western therapies, feelings of personal entitlement and a sense of things having been done wrong by others.

Other-centred methodologies break up the client's sense of being a special case, and build the sense of relatedness. They question the self-story, and push the client to investigate the truth of their history, their impact on others and their current situation. They also tend to focus on relatedness and to value the person's connection with others, promoting values of social context and cohesion.

The other-centred approach also places the client in the context of an environment. The others which create supports for the identity may be environmental as well as human. In fact, this model lends itself particularly well to environmentally based work (Brazier, 2011) and eco-therapy (Tariki Trust, 2013). Whilst this sort of work can be done in a way that is human-centric and uses the environment as ground for personal projection, with an other-centred framework the methodology is once again more concerned with direct encounter and relationship. Where methods are projective, they involve exploring the limits of perception, its embeddedness in conditioned views, or use of collective myth and story as a basis for creative work. Such work takes seriously the client's relationship to the planet, not just as a screen for personal growth, but as the inhabitant of an eco-system for which they have a shared responsibility.

Therapies can shape the way that individuals and groups view the world. They can collude with prevailing trends both of popular culture and of government policy, or they can challenge them. They themselves create cultures which may or may not be conducive to the good of individuals or society. The detailed argument of what benefits and insights particular therapies bring is something beyond the scope of a short chapter, but I have reviewed in brief the ethos and values of an other-centred approach in the hope that by doing so, I have offered some indication of the sort of issues which may be at stake, and of how these may vary greatly according to the therapeutic model adopted.

So this is a starting point. By flagging up the possibilities and also the pitfalls, I invite discussion of ways forward for the profession, not only in continuing its powerful influence into the 21st century, but also in responsibly and critically reviewing it.

References

Brazier, C. (2009) *Other-Centred Therapy: Buddhist Psychology in Action*, Ropley: O-Books.
Brazier, C. (2011) *Acorns among the Grass: Adventures in Ecotherapy*, Ropley: Earth Books.
Furedi, F. (2004) *Therapy Culture*, London: Routledge.
Krech, G. (2001) *Naikan: Gratitude, Grace, and the Japanese Art of Self-reflection*, Berkeley, CA: Stone Bridge Press.
Rogers, C.R. (1961) 'A process conception of psychotherapy', in *On Becoming a Person* (pp. 125–62), London: Constable.
Tariki Trust (2013) Ten Directions course programme, http://buddhistpsychology.typepad.com/amida_france/ten-directions.html

12 | Directions for Humanistic Psychology

John Rowan

I have been involved in Humanistic Psychology since 1970, have been to conferences in the USA and elsewhere, have met some of the leading figures, and been to groups led by these people. I have also been writing about Humanistic Psychology since 1975.

There have been some changes along the way. The great reliance on expressing feelings, so prevalent in the 1970s, has diminished. The emphasis on the individual, such a key issue in those days, has shifted. We are all relational now.

One of the most interesting changes has been the increased interest in the transpersonal. Humanistic and Transpersonal Psychology have always been close – after all, Abraham Maslow founded both of them – but in recent years, in the USA there have been some organizational moves which have brought the two into closer proximity. In Europe, too, there has been a huge growth in EUROTAS (the European transpersonal umbrella), which now has about 30 national organizational members. The EUROTAS conferences look and feel very much like humanistic conferences. In England, the United Kingdom Council for Psychotherapy (UKCP) has recently formed a sub-section devoted to transpersonal psychotherapy.

At the same time there has been an increased interest in the relationship between the humanistic and the existential. The current editor of the *Journal of Humanistic Psychology* is the author of several books bringing together humanistic and existential ideas in the field of psychotherapy. James Bugental had the unique honour of being admitted to the editorial boards of both the *Journal of Humanistic Psychology* and the *Journal of Existential Analysis*. Rollo May is another important writer with a foot in both camps. In this country Mick Cooper is someone who has contributed to person-centred, experiential and existential writings, and to research too (e.g. Cooper, 2003, 2008).

One of my own contributions has been the chapter in *The Handbook of Humanistic Psychology* (Rowan, 2002), where I outline some of the similarities and differences between the humanistic and the existential, and in the next chapter Ernesto Spinelli (2002) presents some arguments with a different position in the same area. To me it seems obvious that the humanistic and the existential share an outlook which Ken Wilber calls the Centaur (e.g. 2001) – a belief in bodymind unity, an appreciation of authenticity, a way of thinking which is essentially dialectical. This is what Maslow (1994) called self-actualization.

It is interesting that in a recent book describing the newer tendencies in psychoanalysis, the writer says: 'Self-actualization, a term developed by humanistic psychologists, is one way to characterize the broadest aim of most psychoanalytic psychotherapists' (Curtis and Hirsch, 2011: 82). It is amazing to realize how many different schools of psychotherapy are now adopting a relational approach. Even the behavioural schools are starting to do this, as for example with ACT (acceptance and commitment therapy), which has aspirations to be the humanistic face of CBT and its relatives. I am giving a paucity of academic references here, because this is not a technical matter, but rather a human matter.

But we are under threat today. The problem is that most of us do not believe that randomized controlled trials (RCTs) are the right way to research psychotherapy. Such approaches are good for measuring the efficacy of techniques of treatment. But the techniques of treatment only account for a small percentage – about 15 per cent in most findings – of the efficacy of therapy. Why get involved in the very expensive trappings of the RCT, if that way of working in research is not going to measure anything that is worth measuring? Mick Cooper, who is a good friend and someone I respect, seems to have fallen for the blandishments of the RCT, but I don't really understand how.

There is now a serious attempt in motion to complain to the UK Health Service's National Institute for Health and Care Excellence (or NICE), who idolize the RCT, that this is not the way to go. It is to be hoped that this movement succeeds (and there are signs that it will) – otherwise, we are all going to be deprived of government funding and acknowledgement. There are serious signs that the humanistic therapies are being downgraded in many areas – for example, a recent compendium of therapies, the previous editions of which had chapters on Gestalt and on transactional analysis, has dropped these chapters from its current edition.

I got so worried about this that I wrote around to the chairs of all the humanistic organizations in the UKCP, asking them if they wanted to get together to fight this tendency. I even sent them a copy of my *A Guide to Humanistic Psychology* (2005) to remind them of what that speciality contained. I only got one reply. Whether this is apathy or adherence to a different approach, I do not know. What I do know is that I am a bit disappointed, and even disgusted, by such a low level of response. Who cares about this question?

So do we just concentrate on the transpersonal approach, and let the humanistic organizations stew in their own juice? One of the difficulties of the transpersonal approach is that in academia, it is even less known and even less welcomed than is Humanistic Psychology. Part of the reason for this is that it is about spirituality, and there is no consensus as to what spirituality is, nor how it is to be treated. We thought in the 1970s that everyone accepted the perennial philosophy: there was really only one spiritual journey, even if people used different names to describe it. But in recent times this has been challenged, particularly by Jorge Ferrer of the California Institute of Integral Psychology (e.g. 2001). He has brought up huge academic batteries of argument to prove that the perennial philosophy is wrong. I have in fact engaged in wordy battles with him in the British Psychological Society's *Transpersonal Psychology Review* on this very point. But this is a contested area, and the final shape of the understanding of spirituality is still to come.

In view of all this, how can we regain our optimism? I don't have the answer. But I do have the question, and perhaps questions are more important than answers. Certainly, they are more stimulating and more full of the divine dissatisfaction that may lead to new ideas and, as we say, new vistas.

References

Cooper, M. (2003) *Existential Therapies*, London: Sage.

Cooper, M. (2008) *Essential Research Findings in Counselling and Psychotherapy: The Facts are Friendly*, London: Sage.

Curtis, R.C. and Hirsch, I. (2011) 'Relational psychoanalytic psychotherapy', in S.B. Messer and A.S. Jurman (eds), *Essential Psychotherapies: Theory and Practice*, 3rd edn (pp. 72–104), New York: Guilford Press.

Ferrer, J.N. (2001) *Revisioning Transpersonal Theory: A Participatory Vision of Human Spirituality*, Albany, NY: State University of New York Press.

Maslow, A. (1994) 'Self-actualizing and beyond', in *The Farther Reaches of Human Nature* (pp. 40–54), New York: Arkana/Penguin.

Rowan, J. (2002) 'Existential analysis and humanistic psychotherapy', in K.J. Schneider, J.F.T. Bugental and J.F. Pierson (eds), *The Handbook of Humanistic Psychology: Leading Edges in Theory, Research, and Practice* (pp. 447–64), Thousand Oaks, CA: Sage.

Rowan, J. (2005) *A Guide to Humanistic Psychology*, 3rd edn, London: Association for Humanistic Psychology in Britain.

Spinelli, E. (2002) 'A reply to John Rowan', in K.J. Schneider, J.F.T. Bugental and J.F. Pierson (eds), *The Handbook of Humanistic Psychology: Leading Edges in Theory, Research, and Practice* (pp. 465–71), Thousand Oaks, CA: Sage.

Wilber, K. (2001) *No Boundary: Eastern and Western Approaches to Personal Growth*, Boston: Shambhala.

13 | An Accidental Affiliation

Alexandra Chalfont

In 1965 the brochure for the seminar programme at Esalen in California laid out what is perhaps the fundamental question posed by Humanistic Psychology: 'What are the limits of human ability, the boundaries of human experience? What does it mean to be a human being?' (Anderson, 2004).

In that year, as a teenager living in England, I was confronting that very question when trying to understand the East–West situation in Europe. A number of school students had won places in an essay-writing competition on aspects of international understanding, and the prize was a trip to Berlin to learn about the city and its situation, to be guests of the Mayor, and to visit East Berlin. This visit was one of the markers of my life, and the experience of going through Checkpoint Charlie at the height of the Cold War was one I would not forget. I only realized decades later how much it influenced what became key refrains in my life – an individual and personal study of, and search for, deeper intercultural understanding, and the potential for a more peaceful being together in the world.

Meanwhile in California, according to Walter Anderson, Esalen adopted the phrase 'human potential movement' around this time. People like Alexander Lowen and Joseph Campbell came in. Fritz Perls was energetically developing Gestalt, and Ida Rolf and Will Schutz were installed at Esalen. Schutz recognized that society was in need of 'openness and honesty, a willingness to take personal risks and accept responsibility for one's acts, a deeper capacity for feeling and expressing emotions and greater freedom from false morality' (Anderson, 2004: 157). By 1968 Esalen had become a centre for the resolution of racial conflict in America. It was also a year of 'giddiness' for the American Association for Humanistic Psychology's annual meeting in the USA, where one saw such people like Abraham Maslow, Herbert Marcuse and Thomas Szasz, and which included Rankians, Adlerians, Jungians and neo-Freudians (ibid.: 184).

In Europe at this time, I found myself in Paris in the throes of the student revolution. As I read about the growth and development of Esalen, I noticed small resonances with my own life and interests, and recognized names of people appearing at Esalen that I had only known from my reading at the time. Ronnie Laing was, according to Walter Anderson, enjoying a bawdy life there, and I had read *The Divided Self* as a 15-year old. I found great solace (as well as disquiet) in noticing that, while I was not schizophrenic in the pathological sense, there were others who were experiencing similar things to me. At the same time I was reading Huxley's *The Doors of Perception* and *Heaven and Hell*, and was surprised that other people needed drugs to experience what my brain seemed to do of its own accord from time to time!

In the mid-1970s, teaching English literature in Germany, I enjoyed Maxwell Maltz's book *Psycho-Cybernetics* (1969) and now I read that Werner Erhard, the founder of est and another Esalen visitor, was particularly moved by this book. At the same time I was teaching Shakespeare's *Macbeth*, and took Berne's *Games People Play* (1968) to study the human interactions in the play together with my students. Little did I know then that Eric Berne would be known as the father of transactional analysis, one of the three main streams to form and inform Humanistic Psychology, along with Gestalt and the person-centred approach. I could go on, tracking developments in Humanistic Psychology and finding parallels in my own life. I think, though, that I have listed enough to make the point: that I have found myself to be an 'accidental affiliate' of Humanistic Psychology throughout my life.

A while ago I was thinking of a particular artist I used to like in the 1980s, but his name refused to come to mind. A few days later I found myself leafing through a book I had not looked at for years – Piero Ferrucci's *What We May Be* (1982) – and my eyes were drawn to an exercise called 'Inner Beauty', which invites us firstly to think of a trait, a capacity or an attitude in ourselves which we consider beautiful, whether it be fully manifest or just the seed of an attitude. I thought of my love of art. The second step is to acknowledge and enjoy this element, and let an image appear in our mind's eye that symbolizes what we have chosen. The image that came up for me was the memory of a landscape painting, and with a flash of recognition the name that had escaped me now danced before my eyes: Kaspar David Friedrich.

Friedrich was known as a significant artist and exponent of Romanticism in the 'Age of Goethe', at the beginning of the 19th century. His moody landscapes have been at times assigned to kitsch art, have been appropriated for albums of Goth music, and, I learned more recently, have been the subject of attention in psychoanalysis.

For me, these paintings simultaneously express both the transpersonal dimension and the subjective experience of an inner landscape; perspective seems to shift unexpectedly, and a dark foreground shadows against a clear and luminous distance. This art seems thus to hold an inversion of the present and the past, and a sense of our vulnerability in the face of an immaterial nature that we believe to be both a given, and something commonly known to us in our everyday experience of living. Although his depiction of nature is based on empirical observation, Friedrich himself says that an artist shows not 'what he sees before him, but what he sees within him'. It is thus not only the case that nature imposes boundaries on us, but also that we impose limitations on ourselves – through our internal understandings of the world outside – just as much as we are limited by conditions beyond our skin.

The ultimate and inevitable existential boundary is imposed on us by death. George Berguno, Professor of Psychology at the American University in London, discusses in the journal *Existential Analysis* (Berguno, 2008), the two kinds of boundary situations that humans are confronted with, which he considers relevant for 'existentialist thought for our times and the possibility of a new existentialism' (p. 246). As noted above, these are those boundaries that are imposed upon us, as well as those that are brought about by our own actions. Berguno claims that self-imposed boundary situations such as conflict, guilt, historicity or fidelity are 'more expressive of the paradoxical nature of our human condition' (p.248). To survive such boundary situations, organisms need to develop an ability to adapt to life's challenges. We, as organisms, need to adapt to what the situation asks of us, and in the process we move towards becoming fully functioning.

Barrett-Lennard, in a wonderful book on person-centred therapy (Barrett-Lennard, 1998), cites attributes of the fully functioning person as follows: an 'openness to experience'; 'Living in an existential fashion … fluid motion, unpredictability and an ongoing quality of becoming and transcendence' (p. 129). A person who lives thus will experience their 'Self becoming emergent from experience … would find his organism a trustworthy means of arriving at the most satisfying behaviour in each existential situation' (Anderson, 2004: 184). Working out 'the most satisfying behaviour' presupposes that we are able to identify the challenge in the situation. We need to be able to recognize whether our senses are telling us 'the truth'.

Jordan B. Peterson, Professor of Psychology at Toronto University, asks us in *Maps of Meaning: The Architecture of Belief* (1999a) to presuppose that all experience, the objective as well as the emotional and subjective, is real. He goes on to wonder whether human beings are 'adapted to the significance of things, rather than to "things" themselves' (1999b: 3, para. 6). Peterson traces back the preoccupations of our human mythologies. He finds that even in going back to the most ancient mythologies that we know, these narratives have common denominators. The stories tell of challenges in living, and there seem to be two fundamental domains that human beings need to adapt to, if we are to survive and live successfully: the known and the unknown.

Our brains seem to have one mode of operation when faced with known and predictable 'familiar territory', and another mode when confronted with the unknown and the unexplored. Faced with a challenge, we try to ascertain what it is. However, it is not enough to work out what it is; we need also to work out what it means, what it signifies. Is it something which belongs to the order we have learned through our cultural conditioning to expect, or is it chaos, something unexpected, unmet and out of our experience? As soon as something unknown appears or happens, we attribute meaning by analogy. If it seems like a snake, a dragon, we know to fear it and to have a fear response which will trigger fight or flight. We use our creative imagination to mediate between the known and the unknown, between order and chaos, in order to be able to deal with the unexpected. This is exemplified in the language of metaphor, and has always been our human way of making sense of the world. Jordan Peterson points out that the 'objective world is something that has been conjured up for us recently' (1999b: 1, para. 1) through the process of science. This implies that the environment of humans can be regarded as spiritual as well as well as material.

One of my favourite authors is Franz Kafka. In his 'Aphorisms' he writes: 'There is nothing other than a spiritual world; what we call a sensory world is the Evil in the Spiritual, and what we call evil is simply the necessity of a single moment in our eternal development' (cited in Friedländer, 2012: 228, my translation). The connection I want to make between Friedrich, Berguno, Peterson and Kafka is that they could all be regarded, like me, as 'accidental affiliates' of Humanistic Psychology; I could think of many others.

My most recent accidental affiliation was more direct, and took place three years ago. After a couple of decades abroad, involved in adult personal development, philology, translation and cross-cultural understanding, I had returned to England and trained in various modalities of psychotherapy. One of the additional activities I took on was as managing editor of *Self & Society*, journal of our Association for Humanistic Psychology (AHP). After six years it was time to leave, and I needed to acknowledge a frustration and disappointment with what I felt was sometimes a shadow side of Humanistic Psychology associations. The notion that process is more important than product seemed to sit deep in some people's psyche. I felt that discussions tended to stretch into the ether, and decisions seemed sometimes impossible to make, let alone to carry out. Along with this, there seemed to come an occasional belief for some that commerce is inherently a very bad thing, and that words such as 'profit', 'outcome', 'efficiency' and 'technology' were unacceptable concepts, the application of which would imply an adoption of these concepts as values rather than useful tools.

A few years later, in 2009, I received a phone call from the editor of *Self & Society*. The Association was to be closed, there was no money – *Self & Society* was to disappear. A small group was gathering to try and save AHP. Would I be involved? Loving *Self & Society* as I did, I said 'yes', for its sake alone. People in the group came and went, and through hefty cost-cutting and support from good friends, the Association gained an even keel by the autumn of 2010. At the Annual General Meeting, the co-chairs stepped down to resume their earlier lives. We needed new co-chairs; John Rowan, our stalwart guardian and early adopter of Humanistic Psychology in Britain, offered to take on one role, and somehow I found myself in the other. From being a person of accidental affiliation, I was now in the thick of it.

For over two years I felt less a co-chair than a servant. With a dearth of volunteers, and coffers that emptied as soon as a penny was tossed in, trustees acted simultaneously as members of the Board as well as Management Committee and odd-job people. Some of us felt that what we needed was a clear vision of what might be, and a determination to do whatever we could to reach it. Our aim was to eventually reach beyond a core constituency, as various groupings had developed directions which they felt were autonomous and markedly different in some way. Thus, although we still consisted of a strong number of gestaltists, existentialists, transactional analysts, transpersonal practitioners and person-centred people, some had wandered away from the community to concentrate on their more specialized direction. One of the consequences was that many more recent colleagues in the counselling and psychotherapy world had never heard of AHP or *Self & Society*. Did the term 'Humanistic Psychology' still hold currency for the future? This question still needs to find its answer, I feel. It may go some way to doing this if it creates some new spaces where practitioners of broadly similar philosophy and practice – including those whose affinity with Humanistic Psychology may be more accidental than deliberate – can explore their common factors, as well as recognizing potential for common growth, collaboration and development.

Self & Society has now been re-designed and re-launched, and holds much potential for the future as a meeting place for our texts. The 2013 joint conference with the Humanistic and Integrative College of the United Kingdom Council for Psychotherapy (UKCP) could be an interesting step in this direction, and may already be showing some promise as this book is published.

The inherent beauty of the humanistic approach lies for me in its acceptance of the wholeness of living beings and life. If Humanistic Psychology can consign its stereotypical 'hippie' public image to its formative phase as a beginning movement; if it can loosen its attachment to individualism in favour of an individuality that pays equal attention to exploring and accepting the collective nature of being human; if it can relax its sometimes wholesale antipathy to scientific method and accept science as one essential way of learning among many; and if it can allow itself to continue becoming in a vital, bold and experimental undertaking, then why would it not grow and develop?

In the AHP, we can continue to engage fully with the personal, political, social and spiritual in an inclusive and differentiated way. As transpersonal beings, as individuals as well as collectives, some of us have been able to tap into a consciousness beyond the dual, in deepening awareness of non-duality and a vast nothingness beyond time and space, beyond matter and non-matter. But we can also choose to keep returning, as material organisms ourselves, to the level of all the various manifestations of matter in the world, in order to live towards and beyond whatever may be our present understanding of our human potential. As humans we are still only at the beginning of being, of doing and of learning. History keeps repeating this lesson. I suspect many of us would agree with Berguno when he says, 'the debt that history imposes on us in the form of the past can be transformed through our responsible actions into a creative commitment to the future' (2008: 249). Humanistic Psychology could make a contribution.

References

Anderson, W.T. (2004) *The Upstart Spring: Esalen and the Human Potential Movement: The First Twenty Years,* Bloomington, IN: iUniverse.
Barrett-Lennard, G.T. (1998) *Carl Rogers' Helping System: Journey and Substance,* London: Sage.

Berguno, G. (2008) 'Towards a new conception of the human condition', *Existential Analysis*, 19 (2): 246–53.
Berne, E. (1968) *Games People Play: The Psychology of Human Relationships*, Harmondsworth: Penguin.
Ferrucci, P. (1982) *What We May Be: The Vision and Techniques of Psychosynthesis*, Harmondsworth: Penguin.
Friedländer, S. (2012) *Franz Kafka*, Munich: C.H. Beck.
Maltz, M. (1969) *Psycho-Cybernetics*, New York: Simon and Schuster.
Peterson, J.B. (1999a) *Maps of Meaning: The Architecture of Belief*, London: Routledge.
Peterson, J.B. (1999b) *Maps of Meaning: The Architecture of Belief, Précis.* Retrieved 24 May 2002 from psycoloquy.99.10.033.maps_of_meaning.1.peterson. Now available at http://psych.utoronto.ca/users/peterson/pdf/Peterson%20JB%20Maps%20of%20Meaning%20Precis%20Psycoloquy%201999.pdf

14 | On the Future of Humanistic Psychology: Possible avenues for exploration

Robin Shohet

In this brief chapter I am describing my four current interests in psychology/spirituality. These are forgiveness, the effects of shock, the future of the planet, and non-duality, or questioning the existence of a separate 'I'. Obviously these are huge topics and I do no more than touch on them, but I think each can have a place in the future of Humanistic Psychology.

Having been associated with Humanistic Psychology for 35 years, I was delighted to be asked to write something on this theme. The topic of 'the Future of Humanistic Psychology' is quite a daunting one. I barely know my own future for the coming months, so I have decided to describe some of my interests and hypothesize why they might be relevant.

The first is forgiveness. I ran a forgiveness conference at Findhorn in 1999, and I will be doing another this year, in 2013. As part of my research I came across a short article in which the author described how the future of humanity depended on forgiveness. This was not just his or her opinion – computer programmes had been run which said that the biggest danger to humanity was, in fact, the cycles of revenge that seemed to have been going since 'the year dot', but now the weaponry was so powerful that the danger was not localized.

The second topic that I think bears study is shock. I am in the middle of a book called *We Are All in Shock* by Stephanie Mines (2003). The title speaks for itself. My belief is that an inability to forgive reflects an inability to let go. What makes it so difficult to let go is partly shock. The whole body/mind system has contracted, and before it can loosen itself, the need for safety is paramount. And the world in many ways is less safe (although we should not exaggerate this – if we think of illness, mortality rates, world wars even as little as 60 years ago. What I think has happened is that our expectations have increased, so that the world feels less safe.) Humanistic Psychology with a focus on bodywork would seem to play an important part in helping the release of shock. And this will open up the possibility of forgiveness.

The third area relates to the future of the planet. It would appear that we are fast running out of resources – well I don't need to go into detail. About 20 years ago I wrote an article called 'How green is your mind?' In it I asked the reader to imagine that they were a car and that their mind was the exhaust. Every time they had a negative thought, any negative thought, they would be polluting the planet. In other words, I put the responsibility for pollution not on to managing resources or global warming, but on the way our minds work, on the way we do not recognize our interdependence, how we create separation, and in doing so increase fear, which stresses our adrenals, making us more likely both to be shocked and to stay shocked. The *Upanishads* have a saying: 'Where there is another there is fear'. What I think they mean is that if I see you as separate, then you are potentially a threat. If I come from seeing you as connected, then even if it does not appear like it, we are on the same side, and just holding that possibility makes it more likely to happen. You cannot be green and have vengeful thoughts. And so connecting back to Humanistic Psychology, mindfulness, the work of such people as Eckhart Tolle, seems very relevant.

My final strand is the field of non-duality, there being no separate 'I'. This is commonly associated with Buddhism, but I came across it through the Hindu path of Advaita Vedanta. In truth the non-dual approach transcends all approaches and paths. Teachers in this field include the great Indian sage Ramana Maharshi, and more recently Jeff Foster, Byron Katie, Roger Linden, Jac O'Keeffe (these can all be found by googling Conscious TV). Ramana Maharshi used to describe this approach as using a thorn to get out another thorn – using mind to go beyond mind. And this idea is quite radical for the future of Humanistic Psychology – using it to go beyond it, to question the existence of the separate 'I' is to question the need for a psychology of it. This is a huge topic, one worthy of a book in its own right, I think.

As I finished writing this chapter I was teaching a module on a supervision course, and I revisited John Rowan's *The Reality Game*, written in 1983. John was very instrumental in helping to spread Humanistic Psychology in Britain, and the book has a timeless simplicity in explaining some of the core concepts. I strongly recommend it. It is good to see that even though Humanistic Psychology might have grown and changed and will continue to do so, the foundations seem as sound to me now as they did all those years ago.

References

Mines, S. (2003) *We Are All in Shock: How Overwhelming Experiences Shatter You ... And What You Can Do About It*, Pompton Plains, NJ: New Page Books.

Rowan, J. (1983) *The Reality Game: A Guide to Humanistic Counselling and Therapy*, London: Routledge & Kegan Paul (2nd edn, 1998).

PART III

FUTURE PROSPECTS

15 | The Future of Humanistic Therapy

Nick Totton

Introduction

Based on the book *The Problem with the Humanistic Therapies* (Totton, 2010), this chapter explores a number of questions relevant to the future of the humanistic therapies, and it reaches the conclusion that two futures need to be considered: the more likely but less attractive, where humanistic therapy increasingly conforms to the mainstream; and the more attractive but less likely, where humanistic therapy reasserts its core values. 'The Problem With …' is the overall title of the book series in which the book on which this chapter is based appears, and the series includes volumes on psychodynamic therapy, coaching and other modalities. Each book in the series considers the positive as well as negative aspects of its subject, and ends with suggestions as to how things might move forward.

In my book *The Problem with the Humanistic Therapies*, I offered six questions for discussion:

- Is the autonomous status of humanistic therapy still important?
- What, if any, bridges should be built between humanistic therapy and other modalities?
- Are the differences between humanistic schools themselves still significant and worth preserving?
- What could be improved in humanistic therapy on a clinical level?
- What could be improved in humanistic therapy on a theoretical level?
- What does the future seem likely to bring?

I will explore each of these in turn.

Is the autonomous status of humanistic therapy still important?

There is a powerful tendency – related to, but distinct from, the drive for regulation – towards increasing integration of the various approaches to psychotherapy and counselling: an ironing out of differences, an emphasis on what we share, a simplification of the field – perhaps ultimately creating a generic occupation in which differing modalities play only a minor role. In the UK at least, this movement towards integration is driven largely by the demands of state and private managerial systems, which would ideally like all practitioners to be doing the same thing, in the same way, demonstrating the same 'competencies'. The existing situation, with many dozens of schools and approaches all doing some of the same things, in some of the same ways, but also all diverging from each other in a variety of different ways, is a bureaucrat's nightmare.

Humanistic therapy is an obvious potential victim here, since it has paid less attention than other therapy modalities to clarifying and defining its unique positions in terms recognizable to administrators. This is in itself a reason to defend the independence of humanistic work, as a terrain where freedom is recognized as an inherent value – a powerful position worth defending, but also a vulnerable one in the current context of positivist hegemony. The state does not want to hear about the inherent truth value of each person's experience, it wants to hear about how they can be got back to work with their symptoms alleviated.

We can seldom make absolute distinctions in the therapy world, but here are some pretty strong ones. Unlike most cognitive behaviour therapy (CBT) and all medical-model therapies, humanistic practice is oriented towards growth, not cure. Unlike most psychodynamic therapies, humanistic practice is actively relational and egalitarian. These two distinctions are key to its unique identity; if it were to be subsumed into a generic version of therapeutic practice, this is what would be lost.

The existence of different modalities and approaches benefits not only the client, but also the practitioner (which is of course therefore also good for clients, who benefit from having happy practitioners). Different clients need different approaches which best suit their problems, life situation and personality. But it is equally important for practitioners to work in a style which suits their personality, and hence enables them to give their best. If all the psychoanalysts were asked to do CBT, all the CBTers to do humanistic therapy, and all the humanists to do psychoanalysis, then even after retraining it is unlikely that either the practitioners or their clients would be satisfied with the result!

What, if any, bridges should be built between humanistic therapy and other modalities?

Despite the above, there is an authentic need to strengthen the interconnections between modalities, and for each to learn from the others while still recognizing and preserving the real differences of approach. The humanistic therapies have plenty to learn and plenty to teach. What they have to learn is perhaps primarily about containment and restraint; while what they have to teach is perhaps primarily about spontaneity, mutuality and trust.

This doesn't describe best practice in each modality, where the finest practitioners have already incorporated all or much of what they need from the other modalities. But the average practitioner is often very ignorant of what is going on elsewhere, and not equipped to invent for themselves what is missing or under-emphasized in their own training. I will stick my neck out and say that many humanistic practitioners need to learn more restraint, while many psychodynamic and behavioural practitioners need to achieve more spontaneity and mutuality.

Humanistic therapy is rooted in an appreciation of people and their innate tendency to heal and grow; it displays a valuing of individual quirks and foibles, a principled willingness to follow where the client leads, and an optimism which is itself conducive to therapeutic success. The weaknesses which can follow from this attitude include impulsiveness, over-involvement with the client, a distrust of theory (especially if it involves 'putting people in boxes') and a reliance on charisma. Here humanistic practitioners can usefully learn from the other models, which have evolved effective ways of stepping back from the immediate relationship and from identifying with, rather than just identifying, the feelings and reactions it evokes in us. This is one of the things theory is good for: it encourages us to think, to fit the immediate experience into a wider context, to interrogate our first impulse for what it tells us rather than immediately transform it into action.

Of course the humanistic therapies already have the tools for this sort of thinking – script theory, for example (Steiner, 1990), or process work's concept of 'dreaming up' (Mindell, 1987), or Gestalt's analysis of contact disturbances (Latner, 1992), or the Reichian theory of character (Totton and Jacobs, 2001: Chapter 3). Psychodynamic conceptualizations of relational issues in terms of transference and countertransference also have a great deal to offer, as is indicated by their very wide influence on humanistic and integrative work. But such frameworks are not always applied to help the therapist 'cool off' and consider the implications of their immediate responses.

The least useful import from other modalities is unfortunately the most prevalent: various psychopathologies and diagnostic systems are increasingly a part of humanistic practitioners' mental furniture. This stems largely from intense external pressure: the British National Health Service on the one hand, and insurance companies and their case management offshoots on the other, demand a diagnosis if they are going to underwrite treatment – understandably, given that both institutions exist to address medical problems, and therefore need a medical definition of what is going on in therapy. Since they, alongside voluntary organizations whose funders have largely adopted the same approach, are the only sources of subsidy for therapy, this demand has largely been accepted, and therapy's heritage of medico-pathological labels has been dusted off – even though the humanistic therapies have stated over and over again that their central task is to work with growth rather than cure.

Are the differences between humanistic schools themselves still significant and worth preserving?

Like any beleaguered group, humanistic practitioners have increasingly tended towards mutual support, huddling together for comfort and protection. This encourages 'integrative' approaches – not only between humanistic and psychodynamic theory, but between different humanistic schools. Integration fits with the overall humanistic ethos; as Eric Whitton says, 'one of the most important aspects of humanistic therapy is that it is inclusive rather than exclusive' (Whitton, 2003: 38).

However, humanistic therapy can resemble the Church of England: if inclusiveness is a strength, woolliness is a corresponding weakness. A united front between modalities which share values does not mean that they are interchangeable. There are significant differences between the humanistic therapies, philosophically, theoretically and clinically; and these will be experienced by clients primarily as differences of atmosphere. A 'typical' Rogerian therapist, for example, will be accepting, letting the client set the pace and content of the work; while a 'typical' transactional analysis (TA) therapist will lay out their stall to a greater or lesser extent at the start of the work, explaining to the client how TA works and how it understands people. A 'typical' Gestalt therapist (and in each modality many practitioners are not typical) will focus on style more than content, challenging the client to track their immediate experience and how they process it. All roads lead to Rome, but these are three very different maps for the journey! There are also humanistic therapists who work primarily with embodiment, or different forms of creative expression, or in some self-developed individual style.

What could be improved in humanistic therapy on a clinical level?

My suggestions here cluster around issues of relationality and unconscious process. Humanistic practitioners tend to overplay the role of consciousness and intention in therapy: the only aspects of relationship to be explored may be those available to immediate awareness. To go further into 'relational depth' (Mearns and Cooper, 2005), alongside the positions of client and therapist there needs to be present the third position of witness, fostered by external and internal supervision.

A strength of humanistic therapy is its culture of ongoing clinical supervision. It is regarded as a norm, and enforced by many organizations, that practitioners at every level of experience have supervision on their client work. 'The basic humanistic position is that all therapists need supervision all the time' (Rowan, 1998: 192). In my view this is very valuable, contrasting with the much more ambiguous role of supervision in psychoanalytic work, where 'needing supervision' can be regarded as a sign of clinical immaturity, to be replaced with ad hoc 'consultation'; and also with many employment contexts where line management competes with or replaces clinical supervision.

However, there are far too many humanistic practitioners with questionable supervision arrangements. I still encounter therapists whose supervision is part of their personal therapy! Short of this extreme of potential collusiveness, some humanistic supervision styles seem designed to protect the therapist's ego more than their clients. There are some very useful books on humanistic supervision (Proctor, 2000; Page and Woskett, 2001; Hawkins and Shohet, 2007), which need to be widely read and applied.

But what of the internal supervisor? This concept was developed by Patrick Casement (1985, 1990), who sees it as 'more than self-analysis and more than self-supervision', based in an essentially playful capacity to identify with the client and with other people whom the client mentions, and to synthesize these points of view along with one's own (1985: 34ff). For example, if the client talks of being angry with a friend, the internal supervisor muses that 'someone is angry with someone' (1985: 38), rather than being drawn into the soap opera plot. Although I have serious criticisms of how Casement carries out this project in practice (Totton, 2000: 144–5), his theoretical account is exemplary, and feeds into the recent 'relational turn' in psychoanalysis (Greenberg and Mitchell, 1983; Mitchell and Aron, 1999). This has been paralleled in several other psychotherapy modalities (e.g. Hargarden and Sills, 2002; DeYoung, 2003; Dworkin, 2005; Mearns and Cooper, 2005; Spinelli, 2007). One of the exciting aspects is that it brings together psychodynamic and humanistic practitioners, including body psychotherapists, who all agree that relationship is at the heart both of people's problems and of the solutions to those problems. The humanistic tradition has much to contribute to relational psychotherapy, having always emphasized what radical analysts are calling the 'now moment' in therapy, when the practitioner has to abandon theory and respond from their own authenticity (Boston Change Process Study Group, 1998, 2003).

Humanistic practitioners, one might say, have always specialized in leaning forward – offering warm human contact to the client, being interested in and committed to their process and willing to offer themselves to the relationship. The analytic tradition is now recognizing the value of this aspect of the work. But in order to make the best use of these strengths, humanistic therapists perhaps need to learn more about leaning back, creating an internal space for thinking and fantasizing about what is going on with and for the client, in parallel with being part of that process. This does not necessarily involve the sort of interpretation of which many humanists are suspicious. At the most basic, it is a resource for our own authentic relating.

What could be improved in humanistic therapy on a theoretical level?

This internal space of leaning back is, of course, the space of theory itself, where we think about the world rather than simply being part of it. I believe theory is underdeveloped in humanistic therapy: in integrating body, mind, spirit and emotion, mind is too often the poor relation. There is plenty of what passes for theory; but much of it strikes me as verbiage, a windy rehearsal of the obvious and the dubious, with little bearing on the practice of therapy. Humanistic therapy has Big Ideas in plenty; it also has a lively and powerful clinical practice. What seems in relatively short supply is a method of connecting the two. Those who teach the modalities of humanistic therapy may be surprised and offended by this statement; but if they lean back rather than forward, they may see some truth in it.

TA, in particular, has no philosophical overview: all of the many, often elaborate concepts are essentially operational, ways of describing rather than explaining what happens. Stewart and Joines say quite explicitly that 'an ego-state is not a thing. Instead it is a name, which we use to describe a set of phenomena' (Stewart and Joines, 1987: 18). But the same applies to any noun – 'tree' or 'mountain', say; and this does not remove the responsibility to make coherent sense of the names we use and their relationship with other names. Without theories of internalization and projection, for example, ego-states (Parent, Adult and Child) are mysterious and inexplicable. They also contain imported and unexamined theories of human nature and development. TA places too high a priority on being easy to understand (Stewart and Joines, 1987: 8): some realities (quantum mechanics, for instance, or human consciousness) are inherently not easy to understand!

Gestalt therapy does indeed rest on a set of philosophical positions. In fact, there are perhaps rather too many of them. Perls identified phenomenology and (a little surprisingly) behaviourism as the key philosophies behind his work; existentialism, field theory, and of course Gestalt psychology are also often mentioned, while the trace of psychoanalytic ideas is everywhere present but scarcely ever referred to. Gestalt has perhaps still to achieve a maturity where its emphasis on here-and-now awareness can articulate fully with its intellectual position. Instead, it trails a bag of theories behind it – a bag which may even be the unintegrated shadow of its insistence on immediate experience.

The essence of Rogerian theory can be – and has been – written on one side of a sheet of paper: the 'six conditions for therapeutic change', or even more so the three 'core conditions', are very brief, but their unpacking takes a lifetime. As Pete Sanders puts it, the conditions for therapeutic change are 'attitudes, not skills' (Sanders, 2006: 9) – what Amy Mindell (2003) calls 'metaskills', in some ways close to what we used to call 'virtues'. So there is a certain incongruity in the elaborate theoretical structures which have been built on this foundation; at its best, Rogerian work is the Quakerism of psychotherapy, concerned with presence, not theology.

I suspect that if the humanistic therapies are to transcend their theoretical limitations, they will need to take the courageous step of letting go of their inherited language and terms of reference, and reinventing themselves from the ground up: a difficult and frightening move for any institution, and especially hard at a moment when humanistic therapies are so much on the defensive back foot.

What does the future seem likely to bring?

We are experiencing a powerful trend, in therapy and in Western society generally, towards regulation, monitoring and control of all activities. This is often justified by appealing to two goals: security and effectiveness. People must be protected, it is argued, from the incompetent and the ill-intentioned; therefore all activities must be conducted in ways which 'expert' opinion deems to be effective and safe, and everyone who carries them out must be trained and tested for competence in following these safe and effective methods.

Although the attempt to regulate therapy as a form of medical practice has, for now, been defeated, the state's involvement in the future of psychotherapy is wider than this. It has committed itself to a major investment in training and deploying practitioners in the public sector. However – in line with the ideology of expertise and 'evidence-based practice' – it has been persuaded to privilege CBT over both psychodynamic and humanistic approaches.

The humanistic therapies may be handicapped in their principled opposition by twin Achilles' heels: their hunger for recognition, and their desire to be of use. Currently, energy which might have gone into opposing oversimplified notions of evidence-based practice is being used to campaign for continuing recognition of humanistic therapy within the National Health Service; while a whole range of humanistic training organizations have hurriedly organized bolt-on courses in CBT. This can only dilute and disguise the real point of humanistic therapy, which is 'therapeutic personality change' (Rogers, 1957) – transformative movement in the whole structure of the human being, rather than the alleviation of specific symptoms.

So we can talk of two futures: the more likely but less attractive, and the less likely but desirable. The less attractive future involves an increasing conformity to the social mainstream, and the loss of much of what makes humanistic work valuable, so that these modalities eventually continue only as shells. The desirable future, I suggest, is one in which humanistic practitioners and organizations reassert the principles on which their tradition is based: recognition of the client's inherent tendency to grow, respect for the client's inherent intelligence and autonomy, and integration of the different aspects of being human. At least for now, these are minority values; but the minority can often exercise a crucial influence on the mainstream.

References
Boston Change Process Study Group (1998) 'Non-interpretive mechanisms in psychoanalytic therapy: the "something more" than interpretation', *International Journal of Psychoanalysis*, 79: 903–21.
Boston Change Process Study Group (2003) 'Explicating the implicit: the interactive microprocess in the analytic situation', *International Journal of Psychoanalysis*, 83: 1051–62.
Casement, P. (1985) *On Learning from the Patient*, London: Routledge.
Casement, P. (1990) *Further Learning from the Patient: The Analytic Space and Process*, London: Routledge.

DeYoung, P. (2003) *Relational Psychotherapy: A Primer*, London: Brunner-Routledge.
Dworkin, M. (2005) *EMDR and the Relational Imperative*, London: Brunner-Routledge.
Greenberg, J. and Mitchell, S. (1983) *Object Relations in Psychoanalytic Theory*, Cambridge, MA: Harvard University Press.
Hargarden, H. and Sills, C. (2002) *Transactional Analysis: A Relational Perspective*, London: Brunner-Routledge.
Hawkins, P. and Shohet, R. (2007) *Supervision in the Helping Professions*, 3rd edn, Maidenhead: Open University Press.
Latner, J. (1992) 'The theory of Gestalt therapy', in E.C. Nevis (ed.), *Gestalt Therapy Perspectives and Applications*, Cleveland, OH: Gestalt Institute of Cleveland Press.
Mearns, D. and Cooper, M. (2005) *Working at Relational Depth in Counselling and Psychotherapy*, London: Sage.
Mindell, A. (1987) *The Dreambody in Relationships*, London: Routledge & Kegan Paul.
Mindell, A. (2003) *Metaskills: The Spiritual Art of Therapy*, Portland, OR: Lao Tse Press.
Mitchell, S.A. and Aron, L. (1999) *Relational Psychoanalysis: The Emergence of a Tradition*, Hillsdale, NJ: The Analytic Press.
Page, S. and Wosket, V. (2001) *Supervising the Counsellor: A Cyclical Model*, 2nd edn, London: Brunner-Routledge.
Proctor, B. (2000) *Group Supervision: A Guide to Creative Practice*, London: Sage.
Rogers, C.R. (1957) 'The necessary and sufficient conditions of therapeutic personality change', *Journal of Counseling Psychology*, 21: 95–103.
Rowan, J. (1998) *The Reality Game*, 2nd edn, London: Routledge.
Sanders, P. (2006) *The Person-Centred Counselling Primer*, Ross-on-Wye: PCCS Books.
Spinelli, E. (2007) *Practising Existential Psychotherapy: The Relational World*, London: Sage.
Steiner, C. (1990) *Scripts People Live*, New York: Grove Weidenfeld.
Stewart, I. and Joines, V. (1987) *TA Today: A New Introduction to Transactional Analysis*, Nottingham: Lifespace Press.
Totton, N. (2000) *Psychotherapy and Politics*, London: Sage.
Totton, N. (2010) *The Problem with the Humanistic Psychotherapies*, London: Karnac.
Totton, N. and Jacobs, M. (2001) *Character and Personality Types*, Buckingham: Open University Press.
Whitton, E. (2003). *Humanistic Approach to Psychotherapy*, London: Whurr.

16 | Humanistic Psychology: Possible ways forward

Windy Dryden

Introduction

In this chapter, I outline and discuss four tasks with which I would like to see this therapeutic tradition engage, the purpose of which would be the strengthening of Humanistic Psychology: (a) carry out an inventory of strengths and weaknesses; (b) publish up-to-date texts on Humanistic Psychology; (c) consider whether or not to align with pluralistic developments in the field; and (d) engage with reality.

I am perhaps known as a practitioner within the cognitive behaviour therapy (CBT) tradition and thus it may seem strange, at first glance, to find me writing about the future of Humanistic Psychology. Actually, it's not that strange. I have quite an affinity with humanistic therapy dating back to 1975 when I did the one-year, full-time Diploma in Counselling in Educational Settings course at Aston University, the core theoretical model of which was client-centred therapy.[1] In retrospect, I was far more drawn to client-centred theory than I was to client-centred practice, which I found quite restricting and with which I did not resonate as a person. So I embarked upon an exploration of other approaches, and settled on what is now known as Rational Emotive Behaviour Therapy (REBT), which enabled me to be more active as a practitioner, but which was also rooted in a humanistic approach which encourages unconditional acceptance of self, others and the world (Ellis, 1973).

Having established my credentials, let me modify the task I have been given before I engage with it. I was originally invited to speculate on the future of Humanistic Psychology. My reaction to doing this was the same as my reaction to doing something similar for my recently published book on different CBT approaches (Dryden, 2012).[2] In the preface of that book I said the following:

---

1. Now known as person-centred therapy.
2. This book entitled *Cognitive Behaviour Therapies* (Dryden, 2012) is a British-based update of a book that I edited with Bill Golden called *Cognitive-Behavioural Approaches to Psychotherapy*, that had British and North American contributors (Dryden and Golden, 1986).

> I was tempted to write a concluding chapter in the current volume speculating on the likely future direction of CBT. I have resisted this temptation for one major reason. There was no way Bill Golden and I could have foreseen the developments that have taken place in CBT in Britain and in the world over the 25 years since the original book was published. Should I be around to edit this book again in 25 years' time (I will be 86 then!), then my guess is that CBT, as it exists then, will be as unrecognisable to me now as CBT now would have been to Bill and I back then.
>
> (Dryden, 2012: xiii)

So rather than speculating on the future of Humanistic Psychology, let me outline a number of tasks with which I would like to see this therapeutic tradition engage – with the purpose of such engagement being the strengthening of Humanistic Psychology. Actually, a lot of what I have to say has been said by Nick Totton in his excellent book entitled *The Problem with the Humanistic Therapies* (Totton, 2010; see Totton's Chapter 15, this volume).

Carry out an inventory of strengths and weaknesses

In order to move forward, it would be useful if there were broad consistency about the strengths and weaknesses of Humanistic Psychology. Although not himself a humanistic practitioner, Totton (2010) outlined his view of the strengths and weakness of this therapeutic tradition. These are outlined in Table 16.1. This list might be a good place to begin the dialogue amongst practitioners of Humanistic Psychology, although as can be seen, each strength can be seen as a weakness and vice versa, depending on one's point of view.

Table 16.1 Totton's (2010) view of the strengths and weaknesses of Humanistic Psychology

Strengths	Weaknesses
Takes a positive view of human nature	Demonstrates a Pollyanna complex
Focuses on growth, not cure	Tends to deny pathology
Empowers clients	Gives undue responsibility to clients
Adopts a style which is closer to ordinary communicating	Misses transferential issues
Adopts a contactful way of relating	Has boundary problems
Is spontaneous and improvising	Glorifies impulsiveness
Demonstrates a positive attitude to embodiment, to emotions	Has a negative attitude to rationality and theory
Demonstrates a positive attitude to spirituality	Is prone to mysticism and 'uplift'
Offers an inherent social critique	Is out of the mainstream
Favours an experiential paradigm of practice and research	Is weak on research

It may be that humanistic therapists will come up with a different set of strengths and weaknesses and may well regard what Totton sees as weaknesses as misconceptions about the humanistic tradition. That is not the point. Developing an agreed list of strengths and weaknesses will lead the humanistic field to capitalize on the former, and mobilize its resources to deal in an orchestrated way with the latter.

Publish up-to-date texts on Humanistic Psychology

While preparing this chapter I asked for reading suggestions from the book's co-editor Richard House, and looked for up-to-date texts on Humanistic Psychology written by British authors.[3] Apart from the book by Totton (2010), which is a critique of the humanistic therapies rather than a text outlining its principles and practice, the most recent example of the latter I could find was written a decade ago by Eric Whitton (2003) for a publisher which is now defunct. The two most recent editions of major texts written by the indefatigable John Rowan are well over ten years old: *The Reality Game: A Guide to Humanistic Counselling and Therapy*, 2nd edition (Rowan, 1998) and *Ordinary Ecstasy: The Dialectics of Humanistic Psychology*, 3rd edition (Rowan, 2001). While there is a comprehensive edited text entitled *The Handbook of Humanistic Psychology: Leading Edges in Theory, Research, and Practice* (Schneider, Bugental and Pierson, 2002), this is written largely for those already committed to the field, and is quite expensive.

If Humanistic Psychology is going to get its message across to professionals from other therapeutic traditions, and particularly if it is going to appeal to prospective practitioners, then it is very important, in my view, for up-to-date accessible texts to be available and consistently updated so that Humanistic Psychology has a current 'feel' to it. If you compare this state of affairs with the plethora of up-to-date books on CBT available, then the size of the problem becomes stark.

I mentioned Totton's (2010) book earlier. This book is an excellent example of someone who is enthusiastic and knowledgeable about the field of Humanistic Psychology, but who does not align himself with it. He writes sensibly, critically and above all empathically about the field. Totton's book is now sadly out of print, which means that it may not get the wide readership that it deserves [but see Chapter 15, this volume – Eds].

As Totton (2010) argued, Humanistic Psychology is a broad and diverse church, and yet it is difficult to get a current sense of the field's breadth and depth. I edit a series entitled 'CBT: Distinctive Features'.[4] This series is designed to show the distinctive theoretical and practical features of a number of approaches within the CBT tradition. It is written for people who may be interested in CBT as well as for CBT therapists from a specific approach who

---

3. I am referring here to the broad field of Humanistic Psychology. I am well aware that more recent texts on specific humanistic approaches have been published.
4. There are currently ten books in the series, with more in the pipeline.

want to learn about the distinctive features of other CBT approaches. Each book has the same structure to facilitate comparison.

I had planned to co-edit a similar series on Humanistic Psychology with John Rowan, but our plans did not materialize. I still think, however, that such a series would help to revitalize Humanistic Psychology, both from within and without, and I would encourage interested parties to pick up the publishing mantle here. Failing that, I would like to see one edited text which outlines the main humanistic approaches in Britain. I have edited such a book on CBT (Dryden, 2012), and again authors of each CBT approach have written to a set chapter structure to facilitate comparison. In summary, perhaps the field of Humanistic Psychology needs a Windy Dryden to co-ordinate these latter efforts!

Pluralism: To align with or not?

In my view, one of the most exciting trends to emerge recently in the field of counselling and psychotherapy has been that of pluralism (Cooper and McLeod, 2011; House and Totton, 2011; Samuels, 1993). There are three core principles of pluralistic counselling and therapy. These are:

1. There are different pathways to therapeutic change; it follows from this that there is no one best therapeutic orientation/method; and different clients are likely to have different therapeutic needs at different points in time.

2. If therapists want to know what is likely to be most helpful for individual clients, they should start by exploring it with them.

3. Pluralistic therapists demonstrate understanding of the views of practitioners from other therapeutic orientations, and respect for and acceptance of these practitioners even when they disagree with some of their views.

The question for the field of Humanistic Psychology is whether, and to what extent, it should align itself with pluralism. This development has recently been spearheaded by Cooper and McLeod (2011), who are most closely connected with the humanistic-existential therapeutic tradition. This means that Humanistic Psychology would have less difficulty 'hitching its wheels' to the pluralistic 'wagon' than the psychodynamic and CBT traditions, particularly with respect to the second core principle listed above. In addition, humanistic therapists should be best placed to adhere to the third core principle, at least in theory. Whether they do so in practice is another matter (cf. Loewenthal and House, 2010). Perhaps it is with the first principle that humanistic practitioners would have the most difficulty. For example, Totton (2010) noted that such practitioners tend to downplay unconscious and rational factors in the change process.

Assuming that obstacles to pluralism can be successfully addressed, the question remains as to whether or not Humanistic Psychology should align itself with the pluralistic movement. Whatever happens, I believe that it should seriously debate this issue. My view is that it should align itself with the pluralistic movement as long as it promotes simultaneously its distinctive features in a jargon-free way to the rest of the therapeutic world.

Engaging with reality

One of the challenges for those therapy approaches not represented in the Increasing Access to Psychological Therapies (IAPT) initiative is how to respond to this programme. Do they criticize CBT that largely comprises the initiative, do they petition the government, play politics, or carry out the kind of research that is acceptable to the National Institute of Health and Care Excellence (NICE) so that it can become a part of the therapeutic establishment as conceived by the government? My point here is that whatever stance or combination of stances the Humanistic Psychology movement decides to take, it would be best if it demonstrates the core conditions of empathy, acceptance and congruence in doing so. Thus, it is possible to mount a cogent critical response to CBT that is based on an understanding of CBT from its internal frame of reference and accept and show respect to CBT therapists while criticizing aspects of CBT theory and practice to which one objects. In my view, these attitudes were not demonstrated by the majority of contributors to Loewenthal and House's (2010) edited book entitled *Critically Engaging CBT*, which should serve as a model of how not to engage CBT practitioners in a meaningful dialogue.

In summary, the future of Humanistic Psychology is largely within the hands of its adherents – no doubt including many readers of this book! If you practise what you preach while engaging with other approaches with which you disagree, if you capitalize on the strengths of Humanistic Psychology and are honest about its weaknesses and address these in a concerted manner, then the future of Humanistic Psychology will be rosy. If not ... well let's not go there!

References
Cooper, M. and McLeod, J. (2011) *Pluralistic Counselling and Psychotherapy*, London: Sage.
Dryden, W. (ed.) (2012) *Cognitive Behaviour Therapies*, London: Sage.
Dryden, W. and Golden, W.L. (eds) (1986) *Cognitive-Behavioural Approaches to Psychotherapy*, London: Harper & Row.
Ellis, A. (1973) *Humanistic Psychotherapy: The Rational-Emotive Approach*, New York: McGraw-Hill.
House, R. and Totton, N. (eds) (2011) *Implausible Professions: Arguments for Pluralism and Autonomy in Psychotherapy and Counselling*, 2nd edn, Ross-on-Wye: PCCS Books.
Loewenthal, D. and House, R. (eds) (2010) *Critically Engaging CBT*, Maidenhead: Open University Press.
Rowan, J. (1998) *The Reality Game: A Guide to Humanistic Counselling and Therapy*, 2nd edn, London: Routledge.

Rowan, J. (2001) *Ordinary Ecstasy: The Dialectics of Humanistic Psychology*, 3rd edn, Hove: Routledge.
Samuels, A. (1993) *The Plural Psyche: Personality, Morality and the Father*, London: Routledge.
Schneider, K.J., Bugental, J.F.T. and Pierson, J.F. (eds) (2002) *The Handbook of Humanistic Psychology: Leading Edges in Theory, Research, and Practice*, Thousand Oaks, CA: Sage.
Totton, N. (2010) *The Problem with the Humanistic Therapies*, London: Karnac Books.
Whitton, E. (2003) *Humanistic Approach to Psychotherapy*, London: Whurr.

17 | Humanistic Psychology: How it was and how it may be

Dina Glouberman

Humanistic Psychology was a wonderful thing when I was coming up in the psychotherapy/personal development world in the late 1960s and early 1970s. I was attending Brandeis University where Abraham Maslow was teaching, and partly as a consequence I was profoundly influenced by the writings of Erich Fromm, Carl Rogers, Fritz Perls, Rollo May, Jacob Moreno, and all the Humanistic Psychology pioneers.

Humanistic Psychology at that time meant everything that was young, progressive, open to change and politically on the side of the angels. It encouraged us to begin a lifetime of development and expansion, without ever having to label ourselves as ill or lacking.

Some of the things I am talking about here may not be associated in everyone's mind with Humanistic Psychology, so perhaps this is a broad picture of a movement and a way of thinking that characterized that time and which I associate with Humanistic Psychology. I want to give a feel of what it was like for us at that time, and then to explore a few possibilities of what the way forward might be. I also want to express my immense gratitude for the ways in which Humanistic Psychology inspired me to become what I am, both personally and professionally.

My work on imagery, or Imagework (Glouberman, 2010), as I call it, the focus that has significantly defined my approach, my writing, and my life, had its roots in Humanistic Psychology. I can still picture the first time I was in a workshop and someone introduced Fritz Perls' method of becoming the image in a dream and speaking as that image. It was an astounding moment, one in which a new window on life opened for me. And I remember too the moment my friend Robin, who was in a personal development group with me, told me she was working on her 'stuff' at home. What? It's not just in a group? The idea of self-help Imagework, indeed of giving away the secrets of psychotherapy to be used by anyone anywhere, probably had its seed thought there.

My commitment to group work also came from that background. My father, who was a genuine seeker way ahead of his time, introduced me to humanistic group work at a group work conference in New York in the late 1960s. In fact, he was partly responsible for my being at Brandeis University, because he loved Maslow.

At the time of the conference, I'd been trying to work on my feelings about my mother's death a year or so before in my psychoanalytic therapy, with not much success. I found myself attending a workshop called 'The Psychodrama of Death', with the wonderful psychodramatist, Hannah Weiner. I talked about the way my mother's presence was haunting me, and Hannah stood on a table, becoming my mother. She asked me what I wanted. I told her I just wanted her to be alive somewhere, even if I could never see her. Hannah, as my mother, replied, 'I can't do that for you'. I heard myself saying, 'Well if you can't be alive, then I want you to be dead!'

At her suggestion, I pushed Hannah/mother out of the room. I must have done it with incredible force because it seemed easy, and yet Hannah was a very big woman, and she told me later that she was doing her best to resist. Then I slammed the door, three times, to the cheers of the group. Could you really push your dead mother out the door and be cheered for it? At that moment, I let go of her ghost, and could honour my love for her. My analyst, Joe Sandler, got it when he saw me in London afterwards and I told him what had happened. He said, 'You must be very disappointed in our work together.'

Fritz Perls actually invited me to participate in his first training course in California. I didn't go. Instead, I chose to come to the Henderson Hospital in Sutton and work as a lowly social therapist, the equivalent of an assistant nurse, in the therapeutic community set up by founder Maxwell Jones, who was, however, no longer there. At the same time I turned down an opportunity to be a clinical psychologist working with Maxwell Jones himself in Dingleton Hospital in Scotland.

Why did I make such an odd choice? My reasoning was that I wanted to learn the most I possibly could, and totally innocent of normal social considerations, I thought that the best idea was to go to a new country (more difference), and be lower status and therefore closer to the patients (more connection). I was in search of truth, and I felt I couldn't know the truth if I was blinded by my culture and my assumptions.

In some ways it was a rather mad choice, knowing what I know now, and there were certainly moments when I regretted it. But perhaps unconsciously I was not only ignorant about the uses of status but was also avoiding the charismatic leaders in order to forge my own path. This path led to Skyros,[1] Imagework, and, for that matter, to burnout, and then *The Joy of Burnout* (Glouberman, 2007). This probably would not have happened if I had followed the leaders. Perhaps that was part of the legacy of Humanistic Psychology – to attract those of us who were seekers and initiators and not simply followers.

So what about the future? To be sure, the future of Humanistic Psychology cannot mimic the past, because by its nature it was a new phenomenon responding to what was around. It expanded our limits, broke open our

---

1. Skyros Holistic Holidays, founded in 1979 by Dr Dina Glouberman and Dr Yannis Andricopoulos, www.skyros.com; www.dinaglouberman.com/approach/skyros/

normal ways of thinking. If we try to hold on to what we have, which is an attitude you find in so many institutions and schools, we end up with an ossified way of thinking.

I am reminded of my stay at the Henderson Hospital. It had been created by Maxwell Jones in 1958 as a revolutionary community environment in the setting of an NHS hospital, where each person, no matter their rank, had one vote. As such, it had had a big international impact (Rapoport et al., 1979). But by the time I worked there for six months in 1968, not only was he absent, but the new and revolutionary were no longer welcome.

I discovered through bitter experience that to get anything changed, you had to either get a psychiatrist to agree with you, since they were highest in the supposedly non-existent pecking order, or you had to say it five times until they thought it was familiar and not new. One of the nurses literally said, 'If it was good enough for Maxwell Jones, it's good enough for me.'

I wouldn't want that for Humanistic Psychology. And yet though we cannot mimic the past, the underlying approach of expanding limits and challenging limiting categories must guide us, and the basic foundations of Humanistic Psychology do need to be honoured. My utopic vision would be of a whole-person psychology based on seeing how we can be at our best, with a central core of meaning and value in the driving seat, with a many-faceted interior world that represents many different ways of seeing and being, and a connected, empowered and creative relationship to the world around. As Merleau-Ponty (2002) said, our consciousness is not in our head but in our relationship to the world. That world includes the social, emotional, mental and spiritual worlds, as well as the physical world.

When we were starting Skyros in Greece, I became excited about the ancient Greek idea of health, which was a Western form of holism. It spoke not only of health as based on mind, body and spirit being in harmony with each other, but also, and this was more surprising, with the natural environment, and with the social environment. To be healthy, you needed good politics and good ecology. Indeed, according to Hippocrates (e.g. Hippocrates, 1983), the way the wind is blowing needed to be factored into a diagnosis. This kind of holistic notion of health is what Humanistic Psychology has always espoused; we are keeping good company with Hippocrates.

Much of what we are known for in Humanistic Psychology has now seemingly been accepted in the mainstream. This is our success as visionaries, and also our challenge. But if we look closely at some of the areas where we have been pioneers, we will see that the ideas may have been adopted, but the application has narrowed so that they no longer represent the original vision.

Here are a few of the many areas in which we could be said to be pioneers, and where we could take up the baton again and run with it. I have chosen the following because these are the areas with which I am most familiar through my own work. There are so many others, for example in the fields of political psychology and of ecopsychology, which are crucial. Some of this is already being worked with and written about in the AHP journal *Self & Society* and in other Humanistic Psychology forums, but perhaps we need to toot our own horn more.

Coaching

The success of coaching is based, at least in part, on the fact that it implies that you are a go-getting person with nothing wrong with you, except that you could use some visioning and hand-holding to 'do' your job and life better. This idea, that we can be normal healthy people who want to expand, is what Humanistic Psychology pioneered, except that this has become rather aligned with the business and personal success world. My own response to this has been to offer 'Mind, Heart and Soul Coaching'. Humanistic Psychology can more generally pioneer the kind of coaching that develops the whole person, in the context of spirit, society and nature. This means that we include psycho-spiritual, creative, ecological and social transformation development among the aspects in which we want to get coaching, not just traditional success.

Mindfulness

Like coaching, mindfulness has exploded as a panacea, and has been taken up most obviously by the CBT people for healing depression and other problems, often with excellent results. Yet my own first memory of an experience of mindfulness was in the early 1960s, reading the seminal book *Gestalt Therapy: Excitement and Growth in the Human Personality* by Fritz Perls, R.F. Hefferline and Paul Goodman (1951). The first exercise in the book was simply to say sentences that began, 'Right now I am aware of …' again and again. I can still remember the altered state I moved into as I really saw my kitchen for the very first time. The purpose was to bring us into the present moment and expand our consciousness, rather than to fix us. I have also followed the Vietnamese Buddhist Thich Nhat Hanh, who was one of the major figures who introduced mindfulness in the West as part of a spiritual discipline (e.g. Thich Nhat Hanh, 1991). I have been surprised to find that he is hardly mentioned in traditional psychology mindfulness circles. A new Humanistic Psychology take on mindfulness that preserves a wider and deeper vision could be remarkable.

Imagery

My own introduction to imagery was, as I said earlier, via Fritz Perls and Gestalt therapy. I was also inspired by Jung's active imagination (1997) by David Spangler's *Laws of Manifestation* (2008), by the imagery precision of Grinder and Bandler's neuro-linguistic programming (NLP) (1989), and by many similar broad and deep approaches. Imagery has a wonderful function as a way of understanding and guiding the whole person within a multi-level environment. One image can have a meaning on a physical, mental, emotional, social, spiritual and ecological level. Amazingly, you can often find images travelling from one person to another in a group because on a deep level there is no real boundary between us; in one of my groups, nine people sitting near each other had images of trees, and no on else in the room did. We also use each image as a perspective, to see ourselves and the world from as many perspectives as there are images, i.e. infinite. I could go on and on. But as in coaching and mindfulness, the original breadth of approach has been narrowed down either to a kind of spiritual materialism, as in some of the creative visualization, law of attraction and NLP approaches, or to heal psychological problems, as in CBT and, again, NLP. Could Humanistic Psychology now pioneer a broader approach to the humanistic uses of imagery?

Community

Humanistic Psychology always included within it the importance of the environment and the community, and the idea that we need to create worlds that heal, not just good therapy. This was certainly my intention in creating Skyros Holidays, which represented all my own yearnings to be part of a larger whole. The first principle of Skyros was community; not a traditional community where we get care, belonging, connectedness and approval in exchange for social control, but rather a step forward into a new kind of community where we can celebrate individuality as well as connectedness. Caring and belonging and connectedness need to be predicated on honouring each other for what we are and are becoming, not how we fit in. And we need to give each member a voice in determining how the community will be. Again, revisioning community is a ripe field for Humanistic Psychology.

Holistic approaches applied to particular fields

Burnout has been one such area for me. Out of my own experience of burnout I discovered that it isn't about working too hard, but about our heart going out of what we are doing, and driving ourselves to do it anyway because our identity is tied up in the old path. It is our ability to find the meaning in what we are doing that carries us through. When that stops, we are truly unable to continue. The therapy here is basically stepping back and considering how to become whole-hearted again (Glouberman, 2007). In my work on fear of the future, I discovered that our very worst fear is not what we think it is, poverty or illness or loss, but of losing ourselves. Unless we can find in us that which will be there when all else fails, we will be frightened (Glouberman, n.d.). Again, we are talking of the whole person, not the problem. In how many such fields can we create a unique and specifically humanistic approach?

More generally, for me, the future of Humanistic Psychology is to peep through everything we do and create an inspiration for a different approach to life. It includes so many wonderful windows to see the world as one in which we are each in our own process of personal development throughout our lifetime, and that rather than be ashamed that we need it, we can wear this as our badge of courage. It reminds us that the personal, the spiritual and the political are all part of the same human yearning to move beyond the status quo to new understandings and new realities.

It tells us that we will never, never, succeed if we simply box ourselves up in old categories and old diagnoses, nor will we be able to help others if we don't give them a chance to define themselves, rather than telling them who they are and what they need.

And above all, it reminds us always to challenge our own limits, to go beyond what we think is true to that which we don't yet know. The pioneers of Humanistic Psychology did that for us. We must do this for the generation that follows.

References

Glouberman, D. (2007) *The Joy of Burnout: How the End of the World Can Be a New Beginning*, London: Skyros Books.

Glouberman, D. (2010) *Life Choices, Life Changes: Develop your Personal Vision with Imagework* , London: Skyros Books; (see also http://www.dinaglouberman.com/approach/imagework/; Glouberman, D. (in preparation) *We Are What We Imagine: From Difficult Times to New Beginnings*).

Glouberman, D. (n.d.) Future fear. Available at www.dinaglouberman.com/approach/future-fear/

Grinder, J. and Bandler, R. (1989) *The Structure of Magic, I and II*, Palo Alto, CA: Science and Behavior Books.

Hippocrates (1983) *Hippocratic Writing* (trans. J. Chadwick and others), London: Penguin Classics.

Jung, C.G. (1997) *Jung on Active Imagination* (ed. Joan Chodorow) (Series: 'Encountering Jung'), Princeton, NJ: Princeton University Press.

Merleau-Ponty, M. (2002) *Phenomenology of Perception: An Introduction*, New York: Routledge Classics.

Perls, F.S., Hefferline, R. and Goodman, P. (1951) *Gestalt Therapy: Excitement and Growth in the Human Personality*, New York: Gestalt Journal Press.

Rapoport, R, Rapoport, R, and Rosow, I. (1979) *Community as Doctor*, London: Ayer Co. Pub.

Spangler, D. (2008) *Laws of Manifestation: A Consciousness Classic*, Newburyport, MA: Weiser Books.

Thich Nhat Hanh (1991) *The Miracle of Mindfulness*, London: Rider Books.

18 | The Future of Humanistic Psychology

Gaie Houston

This chapter moves from memories of the early days of the journal *Self & Society*, to making a case for radically different attitudes in theories of people, and in educational focus. The importance of integrating neuroscience, anthropology, political science and every other related discipline is acknowledged, into a co-operative endeavour towards creating the psychological conditions most conducive to community, creativity and sense of fulfilment. Uneasy with much that is attributed to the idea of spirituality, I prefer that education should be co-operative, learning as much as teaching, and making people aware of the importance of groups of every size, along with an understanding of their own likely responses in differing contexts.

Being invited to write this piece was to me affirming of my sense of connectedness with like-minded people. Very warming. This sense had sometimes waned since the early days of *Self & Society* journal. At that time the Editorial Board, of which I was one, would meet monthly to eat a malodorous Chinese takeout meal in the editor's office, and talk excitedly. Vivian Milroy, *Self & Society*'s first editor, always spoke of recording our talk and publishing it, but I cannot remember whether this ever happened. I suspect that our conversation was a little like singing at a party: wonderfully touching in its emotion and quality to the singers as they sang, but cacophonous if replayed at a more sober and isolated moment.

So what would I like to happen next? The worst might be for there to be a humanistic party which sang and talked to itself in its own room, until it thought it was the bee's knees and the cat's pyjamas. Put more positively, I fervently hope for an integration and/or a coalition of the major branches of psychology and psychotherapy. Rather than seeing Humanistic Psychology as a third force, I would like there to be one force which made use of the insights and skills of behaviourist and psychoanalytic thinking, of sociology and anthropology, of every damn thing conducive to our better understanding and skills with getting on with each other and the rest of the planet. Some of this is happening openly already. Some is happening covertly, with accompanying cries of plagiarism or thievery of ideas and methods.

The sober and isolated moment, out of the swim of *Self & Society*, has lasted a good many years for me, as the editorship changed and I showed as a name on a list but had no other presence. In the interval I have sometimes groaned at articles which have struck me, in my own well-preserved prejudice, as wafty, or separatist, or generally Spiritual with a big 'S'. So one of my hopes is for integration of disciplines as earthy as neuroscience into Humanistic Psychology. I do not really understand what people mean when they use the word 'spiritual'. When people describe it to me, it sounds like a fusion of what I experience as hope and of love, in some of its various senses. I cannot see that it needs a separate word.

To me there is something called 'mind', which I understand to be the functioning of the brain in the same way that body movement is the functioning of the muscles. This word 'brain' is in some ways a shorthand, standing for the myriad and amazing processes of every part of the body, resulting in the aware and unaware process of that organ itself. It seems to me that in our evolution, we have needed will, determination, optimism, hope, in massive measure, to be represented in our mental processes. Otherwise we might have jacked it all in and settled for peaceful oblivion when opposing sub-species turned up at the cave entrance, or when another horrendous Ice Age set in. So I incline to think that hope, the perhaps steady, perhaps heady belief, that There Is Something Better, that there will be summer, there will be a healthy mate, a child born, there will be peace, recovery from illness, harvest, a fat pig to eat – all these hopes have held up enough times to help form this construct, Spirituality. From being a yearning or hope, it has sometimes coalesced into a belief, a Knowing, that there is a god or heaven or higher plane or Something Beyond Us or whatever, outside ordinary reality.

Now I think ordinary reality is so mind-bogglingly amazing that it is quite enough to be getting on with, without any mystery add-ons. My unease with the word is partly when it seems to denote something outside of the body. And a bit superior – something for the elect, perhaps to be honed by periods of retreat from the world. Well, as far as I can see, the world is all we have got. And the world is all the extraordinary riches of the planet, and it is other people. Neuroscience is showing us some of the amazingness. I could fill this piece with examples, but will offer just one.

Sympathy, empathy, whatever we call intuitive response to each other, turns out often to be a function of perfectly observable mirror neurons, dancing away as we interact with other people or the world, and creating internal glimpses and hints of what it is to be the other. How remarkable and how vital to our social existence is this physical system, so recently discovered. This leads to my hope that Humanistic Psychology will embrace the new understandings made possible by this science and, if necessary, discard what is more esoteric. Spirituality has the word 'higher' often associated with it. 'Higher' sounds like 'off the ground'. It is then the opposite of humility, which in its root means 'on the ground'. Neuroscience has the capacity to keep us on the ground, gradually accounting for all we have built into our species over countless generations, rather than putting that responsibility outside of ourselves.

There is some of my hope for Humanistic Psychology as a theory of people. Then comes the hope of how we make use of our theory, our understandings. The saying that it makes more sense to build a fence at the top of a cliff than just to have an ambulance at the bottom of it appeals to me as a slogan for all trained therapeutic practitioners now. I think that, sadly, it will be a long time before we can retire the ambulance. The appalling divide still widening between rich and poor will partly account for that. So what do I want us to do prophylactically, at the top of the cliff?

What seems to me the best place to intervene is at the beginning. I would like to see humanistic practitioners working with parents and families and to support teachers in the social part of schooling. I have seen excellent things happening in this way in primary and junior schools. Later, the national curriculum and public exams seem very often to drive humanity out of the window. Sometimes this is to do with the individualistic stance of all concerned.

Long ago I saw a Chinese film which showed in detail the working of a self-criticism group in a school. It gave flesh to what I had witnessed in China myself, when I was there in 1977. The teacher came into the playground and blew the whistle to end the break. A boy threw a ball which hit her as she turned away. She threatened some punishment, as I remember. Then the whole class and teacher met as a self-criticism group, and gradually the background to the incident was revealed. The teacher spoke of the humiliation of the hit, and the pain, and asked for an apology. After hesitation, the culprit told how the teacher had lost his exercise book the week before, and not believed that he had handed it in. When she found it, the teacher had not apologized. This she now did, sincerely, and the boy followed suit. This seemed to me a very proper resolution, which left people closer to each other than before, with no rancour left in them. That same film showed how, when a boy got very low marks for arithmetic, the whole class stayed behind to help him master what he had not understood. His bad marks were seen as a product of the group, and a slur on the group.

An instance I quote often to students is of the pupils at Winchester, one of the most academically successful schools in England. When doing their prep, they are encouraged to leave their study doors open, and confer and discuss together. As in China, social learning is recognized. Collaborating is seen to be of at least as great if not a great deal more value as competing.

I would like to see us running groups with collaborative values and openness, both for pupils and for teachers. The teachers of a London Comprehensive school used their own money to have me in for a weekly session, which was in part a support group, and in part a learning group for finding more ways of fulfilling what can be called the pastoral care part of their work. Those teachers approached me. I would like more of us to invent and advertise ways of helping directly like this, to strengthen teachers and show them and students how to recognize, and how to be more appropriately open with, each other. Whenever I have seen school classes encouraged to sit and talk in the ways familiar to humanistic practitioners, but still foreign to very many others, the outcomes have been excellent. Helping this to happen is a future I would love to see.

In this same vein, but at a wider level, my largest hobby-horse is to educate everyone about group membership. Perhaps as you read what I wrote about China, you made a quick judgement, about Mao and Communism and Tiananmen Square, and thus my naïveté in being taken in by anything to do with that regime. I hope not. We are group animals. The group exists before the individual, who is indivisible from the whole. However, we have invented computers and the Internet and mobile phones. Virtual relating, virtual contact, virtual danger and reward and all manner of stimuli make it possible to be busy and interested without one single jot of eye or skin contact. With music stuffed into both ears, we are encouraged to disappear into a closed inner world, beguiled with these room-fresheners of the psyche.

It looks as if it will get harder for people to engage, or even want to engage directly, with anyone else. But we are interdependent atoms, cells, whatever, in a system. That sense of interdependence needs urgently to be brought into everyone's awareness, if we are to make any kind of a fist at saving the planet, let alone making loving lives.

As ever, children are more likely than grown-ups to be open to this truth. Learning more about government and political systems seems to me a crucial part of education. Taking a class to a local Council meeting, and then having time with counsellors and officers, and being set to solve whatever problems face the Council at that moment is one economical way to introduce the idea of interdependence at more than person-to-person level. Humanistic Psychology is holistic. If no one else notices what is essential in education, it is up to us to act.

There is more that I would like to view as necessary, rather than elective, education about groups. Wilfred Bion said that the pair was a denial of the group. Much of the social structure, and indeed the architecture of the present, bears out this statement. Harry Stack Sullivan said that the pair is the building block of society. And it is that too. But the pair and the singleton lack the buffeting and emoting and range of opinions and responses that is there at any moment in a group. I am speaking here of a small group, one where the people know each other well enough to be fairly free. Such small groups challenge prejudice and provide stimulus, excitement, novelty, and so enlarge the lives of the members. Humanistic practitioners are in my experience good at introducing the values and skills needed to make such small groups enormously enhancing. But they more often are seen as ambulance groups than top-of-the-cliff groups that will help prevent a fall. I would like to see them stalking out into the community and surprising more and more people into such warmth and rewarding experience.

Sociologists have often shown that if two groups are doing roughly the same task, but out of sight of each other, they will feel scared and hostile towards each other. So it is not enough to establish countless, cosy loving groups who want to lurk indoors and hate their neighbours. We shall need to help them find ways of communicating, or at least of recognizing, that their feelings towards another group may stem from their own fear, rather than some strange quality of the others.

As if that is not enough, I want us to find ways, a bit as Jacob Moreno did so brilliantly, of working with communities, large groups, to familiarize everyone with the good and bad possibilities of reaction and behaviour in such a configuration. Because we have been raised with an inflated and false sense of autonomy, it is difficult to take on board how quickly we can become part of a mob. That is an important learning. Another is about how to hold on to autonomy in a crowd, and find a voice. 'Democracy' is a word thrown about grandly by politicians. But it will work better when more people think and trust themselves, and dare to speak out. And that is more likely when their feelings and thoughts have been tested and supported in intimate groups, reference groups, whatever you like to call them.

I have been offered carte blanche, and have chosen to speculate and daydream a future for us. It would have been as easy to interpret the title another way, and talk about power struggles within the therapeutic world, and the tendency of the loudest voice to win. Instead, I have described what is certainly radical, but also perfectly practical. It will involve a lot of work, and a preference for humility rather than pride, and enormous creativity. It could be fun.

19 | From Humanism to Humanistic Psychology and Back Again

Keith Tudor

Introduction

This chapter reviews the origins of 'Humanistic Psychology' and critiques the view that it represents a 'third force' in psychology as, in philosophical terms, a 'category error'. The chapter argues that it is clearer and more congruent for practitioners who identify as 'humanistic' to return to principles and theories of humanism which underpin diverse psychological and therapeutic practice that may encompass working with unconscious as well as conscious material, the dynamics of the psyche, and working both cognitively and behaviourally.

Personal background

Some time in the early 1980s, I remember discussing with a fellow political activist our different experiences of therapy and our mutual interest to train in psychotherapy. As someone who had enjoyed a liberal upbringing and education, and was then actively involved in libertarian socialist politics, I was drawn to Gestalt and transactional analysis (TA) which, I understood, were forms of therapy in the humanistic 'school' or tradition. Interestingly, my friend, who was involved in a Trotskyist socialist group which was more focused on the political party than class or movement, went on to train as a psychoanalyst – and, gradually and unfortunately, we parted company.

Although much of my training was framed as 'humanistic', it clearly drew on a number of ideas, concepts and practices from psychoanalysis which, historically, is the 'first force' of psychology (Freud's first paper on psychoanalysis was published in 1896), and behaviourism, the 'second force' (Watson's article 'Psychology as the behaviorist views it', which has been referred to as the behaviourist manifesto, was published in 1913), although Sutich (1968) has 'positivistic or behavioristic theory' as the first forces, and 'classical psychoanalytical theory' as the second force. This sense that humanistic therapies drew on, came from and, indeed, represented aspects of other traditions or forces was epitomized for me when, some years later (in 1999), when I was applying for full membership of the UK Association of Humanistic Psychology Practitioners (AHPP) as a Group Psychotherapist (an accreditation I maintained for some ten years), I met at my interview John Rowan, whose first question to me was, 'How come you think TA is a *humanistic* psychotherapy?'! I responded robustly, and my successful interview and application was the beginning of a happy association and identification with the AHPP.

Organization, argument and terms

For many years, the three forces of psychology have been a major organizing principle, and whilst, these days, the term 'force' is rarely used in this context, these traditions or approaches have formed both the literature in the field of psychology, psychotherapy, counselling and counselling psychology and the organization of the profession, e.g. the United Kingdom Council for Psychotherapy (UKCP) and its Sections, now Colleges. They have, however, also led to 'turf wars' based on theoretical orientation or modality whereby, for instance, practitioners from one particular theoretical orientation have been excluded from placements and employment by practitioners from another. As I have trained, worked, reflected, read and written, I have become increasingly sceptical that the three 'forces' are so clearly differentiated as such (see Hinshelwood, in Rowan and Hinshelwood, 1987) or, more fundamentally, that they are, or represent, the same category of things.

Following some brief comments on the history of Humanistic Psychology, and on differences and similarities, I put forward the argument that viewing Humanistic Psychology as a third force is, in philosophical terms, a category error, and that therapists – and their clients – would benefit from those 'humanistic' practitioners who identify as such being clearer about the philosophy or philosophies, including humanism, that underpin and inform their practice – which may be psychodynamic (if not psychoanalytic) and/or behavioural.

As a field and a discipline, 'psychology' is, of course, wider than its clinical or therapeutic applications. In this chapter, as I am predominantly concerned with humanistic counselling, psychotherapy, and counselling psychology, I use the term 'humanistic therapies' to encompass these therapeutic fields and activities; and reserve the term 'Humanistic Psychology' to when I refer to the history and background to my present concerns or to other authors' use of the term. The same logic, of course, also applies to therapies rooted in the other forces; thus it is more accurate to refer to 'psychoanalytic therapies' (from psychoanalysis) and 'behavioural therapies' (from behaviourism).

A brief history

Humanistic Psychology has commonly been referred to as 'third force' psychology. This phrase goes back to the early 1960s when the (then) American Association for Humanistic Psychology (AAHP) reported what it sought to represent:

> Humanistic Psychology may be defined as the third branch of the general field of psychology (the two already in existence being the psychoanalytic and the behaviorist) and as such, is primarily concerned with those human capacities and potentialities that have little or no systematic place, either in positivist or behaviorist theory or in classical psychoanalytic theory.
>
> (Sutich, 1962)

The background to the foundation of the AHPP was the fact that in the 1950s, a number of psychologists, most notably Abraham Maslow, were finding it difficult to get published, due to the dominance in psychology of behaviourism. In response to this, Maslow began to contact other like-minded psychologists and, in 1954, compiled a mailing list of about 125 people with a view to exchanging papers. In the early 1960s the individuals on this list became the first subscribers to the *Journal of Humanistic Psychology* (see DeCarvalho, 1990; and, for the history of Humanistic Psychology in Britain, see Rowan, 2013). Maslow called the list 'the Eupsychian Network' because, as he later reflected (Maslow, 1968):

> all these groups, organizations and journals are interested in helping the individual grow toward fuller humanness, the society grow toward synergy and health, and all societies and all peoples move toward becoming one world and one species. This list can be called a network because the memberships overlap and because these organizations and individuals more or less share the humanistic and transhumanistic outlook on life.
>
> (p. 237)

DeCarvalho (1990) has dated the emergence of Humanistic Psychology as a 'third force' in American psychology to November 1964, when a conference was held in a small country inn in Old Saybrook, Connecticut, attended by George Allport, Jacques Barzun, James Bugental, Charlotte Bühler, George Kelly, Robert Knapp (chair), Abraham Maslow, Rollo May, Carl Moustakas, Gardner Murphy, Henry Murray, Carl Rogers, and others.

Third-force psychology has a rich and complex history (see DeCarvalho, 1990, 1991; Moss, 1999; Schneider, Bugental and Pierson, 2001; Cain, 2001), not least as Humanistic Psychology in America and in Britain draws on different views of philosophical traditions and, specifically, existentialism, and thus has different flavours. One aspect of the history of Humanistic Psychology which is particularly significant for this present discussion is that it began as a 'discontent', especially with behaviourism, and as an alternative, both to psychoanalysis and to behaviourism. As DeCarvalho (1990) has noted, 'At first ... the AHPP was little more than a protest group. Its early organizational meetings were colored by a deep dissatisfaction with and rebellion against behaviourism' (p. 28). The fact that, in the early days of this association, there was a distinct group that wanted and tended to define Humanistic Psychology in terms of what it did *not* stand for has left us, well, 'third'! One example of this was published in the first number of the (American) Association of Humanistic Psychology (AHP)'s *Newsletter*:

> If you are dissatisfied with a psychology that views man as a composite of part functions, a psychology whose model of science is taken over from physics, and whose model of a practitioner is taken from medicine – and you want to do something to change this state of affairs, fill out this application.
>
> (AHP, 1963: 3)

Despite the fact that, over the years, humanistic therapies have presented themselves more positively, I think this early sense of identity in opposition has left a certain legacy and, if you like, an organizational psychology of opposition and, to a certain extent, marginality.

Claims and territory, roots and branches

As Humanistic Psychology became more confident, it began to claim its distinctiveness. Thus, Sutich (1962) suggested that Humanistic Psychology was humanistic because it derived from values and ideas such as:

> love, creativity, self, growth, organism, basic need-gratification, self-actualization, higher values, being, becoming, spontaneity, play, humor, affection, naturalness, warmth, ego-transcendence, objectivity, autonomy, responsibility, meaning, fair play, transcendental experience, psychological health, and related concepts.

Some 30 years later, the AHPP suggested that humanist practitioners share certain fundamental core beliefs about:

- The theory of human nature and of self – that the individual is unique, truth-seeking, an integrated and self-regulating whole, with a right to autonomy with responsibility.
- The aims of therapy and of growth – which is self-awareness and actualisation, which, in turn, includes: wholeness and completion, authenticity, emotional competence, the furtherance of creativity, respect for difference, and integrity and autonomy whilst acknowledging interdependence.
- The nature of the therapeutic relationship – as the primary agent of change, and founded on the therapist's genuineness, empathy, openness, honesty, and non-judgemental acceptance of the client (see AHPP, 1998/2009).

In a more detailed contribution, Cain (2001) identified a number of characteristics which, he asserted, define humanistic psychotherapies. With regard to views of the person, these are:

- That she or he is self-aware, free to choose, and responsible.
- That she or he is holistic – 'The person is viewed *holistically*, as an indivisible, interrelated organism who cannot be reduced to the sum of his or her parts' (ibid.: 5) – and as embodied, and contextual beings.
- That she or he needs to make sense and find meaning, and to construe her or his realities.
- That she or he has a capacity for creativity.
- That, as primarily social beings, we have a powerful need to belong.

Cain also discussed the importance in humanistic psychotherapies of: the actualizing tendency, a relational emphasis, phenomenology, empathy, the concept of 'the self' (which, in my view, is often unthinkingly and uncritically reified as 'the Self'), and anxiety.

Such claims and lists, however, imply that neither psychoanalysis nor behaviourism (nor psychoanalysts or behaviourists) hold these beliefs and views – which, simply, is not true. In his correspondence with John Rowan, Hinshelwood (Rowan and Hinshelwood, 1987: 143) wrote that 'I am not sure that you are altogether correct in implying such a radical division between psychoanalysis and humanistic psychotherapy', adding that: 'The act of appropriating the term "humanistic" for one sector of psychotherapy is itself a little provocative'. I have some sympathy with Hinshelwood's objection as, similarly, I object to the kind of territorialism that is implied by 'cognitive behaviour therapy', as if no other therapies are cognitive or behavioural! – for a critique of which and a response to which, see Tudor (2008a).

Such claims and divisions also ignore history. John Rowan's question to me about TA was, in part, probably based on his understanding of the centrality in TA of ego state theory, which derives from Federn's ego psychology, which, in turn, has its roots in psychoanalysis. Not many people would see any link between contemporary person-centred approaches and classical psychoanalysis, and yet Carl Rogers, who was influenced by Otto Rank (see Kramer, 1995), is only two degrees of separation from Sigmund Freud; and, whilst Rogers' (1942) 'newer psychotherapy' is a long way from Freud's psychoanalysis, there are elements of psychodynamic thinking in Rogers' theory, especially his concepts of defences, i.e. denial and distortion. Whilst I agree with Rowan (in Rowan and Hinshelwood, 1987; Rowan, 2001) that there are roots of Humanistic and certainly transpersonal psychotherapy which are independent of psychoanalysis, when humanistic psychotherapists are tracing their therapeutic lineage, both theoretically and personally (in terms of the influence of their therapists and supervisors and *their* therapists and supervisors, and so on), thereby acknowledging what Traue (1990/2001) has referred to as 'ancestors of the mind', most of us would be only a few handshakes away from the Viennese Doctor. (I myself am personally only three handshakes away from Sigmund Freud, via my Godmother, Margaret Proctor, who met Anna Freud; and, professionally, four degrees away, via Natalie Rogers, from Carl Rogers and Otto Rank.)

It is worth noting that Maslow (1962), who coined the phrase 'third force' psychology, described Humanistic Psychology as 'epi-behavioural' and 'epi-Freudian' (*epi* meaning 'building upon'). Bugental (1964) also did not see Humanistic Psychology as a competitor to the other two 'forces': 'Humanistic psychology generally does not see itself as competitive with the other two orientations; rather, it attempts to supplement their observations and to introduce further perspectives and insights' (p. 22). Similarly, Bühler (1965), an early feminist and one of the largely unacknowledged founders of Humanistic Psychology, wrote: 'Humanistic psychology ... does not necessarily deny that many accomplishments and creations may be the by-product of procedures meant ultimately to satisfy an ambitious ego and indirectly a pleasure-seeking id' (p. 54).

As Hinshelwood (in Rowan and Hinshelwood, 1987) has observed, the criticism of psychoanalysis in the United States of America by American humanists is somewhat misplaced when translated to Britain – and, for that matter, to other countries in the world. As he put it:

> The character of the British schools of psychoanalysis (like many of the Continental ones) is deeply humanistic and is concerned with the struggling human being, and has left behind all the mechanistic trappings that Freud's nineteenth-century background encumbered him with .... The opposition between psychoanalysis and humanistic psychology has so much less relevance over here.
>
> (p. 144)

Whilst there are some obvious differences between aspects of psychoanalytic, behavioural and humanistic theories, there are, I would argue, more and significant similarities, especially between 'humanistic' and 'psychoanalytic' traditions (see Tudor, 2009) – and there are certainly differences between and within different humanistic theories, therapies and therapists (on which see, for instance, Mearns and Thorne, 2000). Rowan (in Rowan and Hinshelwood, 1987) identified that the overlap between psychoanalysis and humanistic psychotherapy would include: projection, the importance of countertransference, the emphasis on the therapeutic alliance, and the use of therapy for the therapist. In her excellent article on this theme, Gomez (2004), who describes herself as a humanistic *and* psychoanalytic psychotherapist, reviews the respective flag statements of the Analytic Psychology, Psychoanalytic & Psychodynamic (APPP), and the Humanistic & Integrative (HIP) Sections of the UKCP, and finds little to which practitioners from either Section would object. Finally (on this point), there are theoreticians and practitioners who have been very much identified with psychoanalysis, who are writing, as it were, across the divide (see, notably, McWilliams, 2005; Orange, 2010).

The old first, second and third force categorization is simply too general, and too generalized, to be relevant or useful in contemporary debates about psychotherapy and its practice.

Categories

Traditionally, there are five branches of philosophy: metaphysics, which deals with fundamental questions of reality; epistemology, which deals with concepts of knowledge (how we know things); logic, which studies the rules of valid reasoning and argument; ethics or moral philosophy, which is concerned with human values; and aesthetics, which deals with the notion of beauty and the philosophy of art. In logic, there are various rules by which reasoning is said to be valid, or not, and argument judged to be sound, or not. The term 'category mistake' or 'category error' is a mistake or error about ontology (the essence of things) or about semantics (meaning). For example, to claim that most readers of this book are humanists may or may not be true; it is not a category error since it could be contingently the case. On the other hand, to claim that most apples are humanists would be to make a category error since apples belong to a category of things that cannot be said to have beliefs or values. Although there are debates within philosophy about the enterprise of categorization and the approach to establishing a category error, here I use the concept of category to raise the question: is 'Humanistic Psychology' of the same nature of things as 'psychoanalysis' and/or 'behaviourism' – and, by implication, whether the first two 'forces' are the same category?

The first category error is, then, that the three 'categories', psychoanalysis, behaviourism and Humanistic Psychology (which is generally how the three forces have been named), are not the same order of things. Psychoanalysis, literally, the analysis of the psyche, is, fundamentally a *method* of psychological investigation (through free association and interpretation). The term, however, also refers to a therapeutic technique, which has gone through a series of modifications by Freud himself and others since; and to a body of facts and theories. Behaviourism is an approach to psychology which combines elements of philosophy, methodology and theory. Humanistic Psychology is also an approach to psychology which defines its description of and relation to psychology with reference to humanism, which encompasses a group of philosophies and ethical perspectives which emphasize certain values and the agency of human beings. Earlier, I acknowledged that psychology as a field and a discipline is wider than its clinical or therapeutic applications; this also applies to psychoanalysis and humanism, and these probably more so than behaviourism. If we are referring to three (four, or more) forces of *psychology*, then this category error is resolved by renaming the forces: psychoanalytic psychology, behavioural psychology, and Humanistic Psychology – with their respective therapies.

In the previous section I quoted Bühler (1965); she continued: 'But humanistic psychology conceives of the human being differently. It conceives of man as living with intentionality, which means as living with purpose' (pp. 54–5) – and, indeed, Bühler herself had advanced a theory of four basic tendencies (Bühler, 1959). My point here is that if 'Humanist Psychology' is different from other forms of psychology by virtue of its conception of human beings, then that is a difference about human nature (see DeCarvalho, 1990) and, more fundamentally, about ontology or the essence of things –

differences which are more accurately and better described as *philosophical*, and not *psychological*.

In their work on paradigm analysis, Burrell and Morgan (1979) provided a way of understanding such differences. They identified four assumptions in social science and placed them on a subjective–objective continuum (see Table 19.1). I have added 'method' and changed the order of the terms so that it reads from the bottom (the more fundamental, underlying assumptions) to the top.

Table 19.1 The Nature of Social Science *(based on Burrell and Morgan, 1979)*

The subjectivist approach to social science	Assumptions	The objectivist approach to social science
Qualitative	Method	Quantitative
Ideographic	Methodology	Nomothetic
Anti-positivism	Epistemology	Positivism
Voluntarism	Human nature	Determinism
Nominalism	Ontology	Realism

Drawing on this work, it seems to me more useful to name differences between practitioners and practice, theories and models as differences of ontology, human nature, etc., than of 'force'.

One reviewer of this chapter suggested that the commonly held view of the distinctions between the three forces were that:

> psychoanalytic psychology is based on a view of the essence of the person as 'basically destructive'; behavioural psychology is based on the view of the essence of the person as 'basically tabula rasa'; and humanistic [psychology] is based on the view of the essence of the person as 'basically intrinsically directional to maintain/enhance itself'.
>
> (Anon.)

I think that this is a good summary of what are broad and commonly held differences and, as such, are ontological differences. The problem is that they are too broad and 'common': there are psychoanalytic and behavioural psychologists and therapists who are humanistic in their outlook; there are behavioural psychologists who are very analytic; and there are certainly 'humanist' psychologists and therapists who do not value or support that view that people tend to actualize. The second category error, then, is an error of category: practitioners identify – and are too readily identified – with, in effect, a (one) category, rather than being specific about differences which are ontological, epistemological, methodological and practical.

To give a theoretical example: the person-centred approach is known for being 'non-directive' and, though there are differences within the approach about this (see Levitt, 2005), this principle and its practice are based on a theory of knowledge that the client 'knows' her or his own direction; as such it is a view which represents an anti-positivist epistemology. Theory and practice that privilege what the practitioner knows and, in effect, tell the client what to do are based on positivist epistemology. Thus, when a person-centred therapist tells a client what to do or how to think, they are committing a category error.

To give a practical and professional example: when I was active in the then Humanistic and Integrative Section (HIPS) of the UKCP, and also as a member of the Institute of Transactional Analysis, I remember great debates about the terms and conditions of personal therapy for training psychotherapists. Due to the fact that some trainees had presented for their qualifying examination without having done sufficient personal therapy, and the realization that some trainers were not taking the existing requirements seriously and, perhaps, more importantly, holding the principles and *spirit* of the existing requirements with integrity, there was much discussion about the necessity (or otherwise) of further requirements. In the end, the HIPS asserted its position by clarifying its further condition of 40 hours personal therapy per year (see UKCP HIPS Training Standards Committee, 2003; for further commentary about which, see Tudor, 2008b, 2008c). The HIPS' decision was one clearly based on, in Burrell and Morgan's (1979) terms, a nomothetic or legal methodology. My own view was – and is – that personal therapy is too important to have as a requirement of training, a principle which was embodied in the training philosophy and standards of Temenos, Sheffield (www.temenos.ac.uk), a member organization of the UKCP and its HIP Section/College; and, as such, represents the ideographic end of what might be viewed as a methodological dimension.

If humanistic therapies are claiming, as their fundamental difference with and from the other two forces, that they are based on different philosophical assumptions about various aspects of human nature and our psychology, then it seems more straightforward and honest to claim these as such: as differences of philosophy and not 'force', 'tradition', 'approach', 'school' or 'modality'. By using and claiming the title of a 'force', Humanistic Psychology has – and, more specifically, the humanistic therapies that sit under this umbrella term have, especially with regard to psychoanalysis – confused *philosophy* (as in humanism and, specifically, with regard to ontology and human nature) with *method* (as in psychoanalysis). In other words, the three 'forces' are not the same category of things, and to present them as such is to commit what, in philosophical terms, is a 'category error'. Rather than assuming a vague humanism about our colleagues' or practitioners' practice – and personally, I have found more humanism in certain psychoanalytic colleagues than in some nomothetic, regulatory members of HIPS – we should be asking the question, 'What is "humanistic" about "Humanistic" Psychology?'

Asking this question, I suggest, leads us to be able to resolve the second error of category by analyzing or understanding both genuine differences and genuine similarities between different therapies across all forces, traditions, etc., as a result of which we may draw different conclusions. Gomez, for example, regards (or, at least, in 2004, regarded) herself as a 'humanistic and psychodynamic' practitioner, and I have some sympathy and association with that, in that one may hold broadly humanistic values and work with a psychodynamic or a psychodynamically informed understanding of therapy. Others may be clearer that humanism is fundamentally antithetical to the philosophical traditions on which psychoanalysis and, differently, behaviourism sit. Either way, this clarification, using the kind of paradigm analysis outlined by Burrell and Morgan (1979) (see, for example, Tudor, 1996), and the resulting philosophical congruence between values, theory and practice (see Tudor and Worrall, 2006), is only possible when we are clear about categories (what goes with what) and category errors (i.e. what does not). As Rogers (1957) put it, interestingly in an article he wrote as a comment on a previous article by Walker (1956), comparing Freud's view of the nature of man with his own:

> One cannot engage in psychotherapy without giving operational evidence of an underlying value orientation and view of human nature. It is definitely preferable, in my estimation, that such underlying views be open and explicit, rather than covert and implicit.
>
> (p. 199)

In this sense, it may be helpful for 'humanistic' practitioners or those who identify with this force or tradition of psychology to return to a broader and deeper understanding of humanism, its history from the *umanisti* of the late fifteenth century, based especially in Italy, and its various forms: Renaissance, secular, religious, inclusive and even naturalistic (which meets the criticism that humanism is overly anthropocentric).

Conclusion

Clearly, Humanistic Psychology is an important part of our history, and I am proud to be associated with it and, not least, as an Associate Editor of the journal *Self & Society: International Journal of Humanistic Psychology*. Clearly, Humanistic Psychology as a third force has, and humanistic therapies have had, a crucial role in broadly humanizing psychology and psychotherapy, akin perhaps to an extra parliamentary political party: it has challenged the first two forces of psychology, especially with regard to their (implicit) values and the underlying assumptions of their theories and practices. It has been hugely successful in a number of ways:

- It is a recognized 'force' or tradition with a number of 'schools', 'modalities' or 'approaches', including: bioenergetics and other forms of body psychotherapy; co-counselling; creative and expressive therapies; encounter; experiential therapy; feminist therapy; Gestalt therapy; the person-centred approach; primal integration; psychodrama; psychosynthesis and other transpersonal approaches; transactional analysis; and many others – and, of course, some of these would also identify with, or with aspects of, the other two forces.
- It has well-established training courses and programmes, from the first one established in 1966 in the Psychology Department of Sonoma State College, to others at West Georgia College and the Humanistic Psychology Institute, San Francisco, and many others since (see DeCarvalho, 1990); and, of course, other training courses and programmes in the modalities noted above.

- It has been the subject of a number of publications with regard to Humanistic Psychology and its therapies (see, for example, May, Rogers, Maslow et al., 1986; DeCarvalho, 1991; Moss, 1999; Rowan, 2001; Schneider, Bugental and Pierson, 2001; Cain and Seeman, 2001; Whitton, 2003), as well as of numerous publications about its various modalities; and has given birth to three professional journals: in the USA, the *Journal of Humanistic Psychology* (from 1961) and *The Humanistic Psychologist* (from 1973), and in Britain, *Self & Society* (also from 1973).

- It has a presence in organizations, including, significantly, as a Division (32) in the American Psychology Association, and as a College of the UKCP.

We can – and should – take enormous confidence from this. Four years ago, I and my family emigrated from the UK to Aotearoa New Zealand. As part of settling into our new professional home, both I and my wife, Louise Embleton Tudor, presented papers to colleagues (Tudor, 2009; Embleton Tudor, 2010). Having heard both talks, one colleague came up to me and said: 'You know, one thing that strikes me about you and Louise is that neither of you are apologetic for not being Freudian.' I thought this was an interesting comment, not only about us and, no doubt, him, but also about the dominance, or perceived dominance, of psychoanalytic thinking. My colleague is correct in that I am not apologetic for not being Freudian, although, following Maslow, I would claim to be epi-Freudian!

In so far as Humanistic Psychology arose as a 'third force' in some way to act, one might say (somewhat mischievously) as a corrective *organizational* or *philosophical* experience to its two older 'brothers', it has made its presence felt: 'Humanistic Psychology' or, perhaps, more accurately and robustly, humanistic therapies are here to stay; it is, in many respects, mainstream and institutional, if not institutionalized (see DeCarvalho, 1990). Perhaps now it is established and confident enough to regard itself not simply or merely as a 'third', but as representing, at best, a philosophy (humanism) in clinical practice (see Tudor and Worrall, 2006).

As a third force, 'Humanistic Psychology' is dead; long live humanism!

References

Association of Humanistic Psychology (1963) *Newsletter*, No. 1.
Association of Humanistic Psychology Practitioners (2009) *UKAHPP core beliefs statement;* document available online at: www.ahpp.org/about/core.htm (Original work published in 1998)
Bugental, J.F.T. (1964) 'The third force in psychology', *Journal of Humanistic Psychology*, 4 (1): 19–26.
Bühler, C. (1959) 'Theoretical observations about life's basic tendencies', *American Journal of Psychotherapy*, 13 (3): 501–81.
Bühler, C. (1965) 'Some observations on the psychology of the third force', *Journal of Humanistic Psychology*, 5: 54–5.
Burrell, G. and Morgan, G. (1979) *Sociological Paradigms and Organisational Analysis*, London: Heinemann.

Cain, D.J. (2001) 'Defining characteristics, history, and evolution of humanistic psychotherapies', in D.J. Cain and J. Seeman (eds), *Humanistic Psychotherapies: Handbook of Research and Practice* (pp. 3–54), Washington, DC: American Psychological Association.

Cain, D.J. and Seeman, J. (eds) (2001) *Humanistic Psychotherapies: Handbook of Research and Practice*, Washington, DC: American Psychological Association.

DeCarvalho, R.J. (1990) 'A history of the "third force" in psychology', *Journal of Humanistic Psychology*, 30: 22–44.

DeCarvalho, R.J. (1991) *The Founders of Humanistic Psychology*, New York: Praeger.

Embleton Tudor, L. (2010) 'Dissociation: a fragile process', talk given to the New Zealand Association of Psychotherapists (Northern Branch) meeting, Auckland, Aotearoa New Zealand, 9 September.

Freud, S. (1862) 'The aetiology of hysteria', in *The Standard Edition of the Complete Psychological Works of Sigmund Freud* (Vol. 3, pp. 191–221; J. Strachey, ed. & trans.), London: Hogarth. (Original work published in 1896)

Gomez, L. (2004) 'Humanistic or psychodynamic: what is the difference and do we have to make a choice?', *Self & Society*, 31 (6): 5–19.

Kramer, R. (1995) 'The birth of client-centered therapy: Carl Rogers, Otto Rank, and "The Beyond"', *Journal of Humanistic Psychology*, 35 (4): 54–110.

Levitt, B.E. (2005) *Embracing Non-Directivity: Reassessing Person-Centered Theory and Practice in the 21st Century*, Ross-on-Wye: PCCS Books.

Maslow, A.H. (1962) *Toward a Psychology of Being*, New York: Van Nostrand.

Maslow, A.H. (1968) *Toward a Psychology of Being*, 2nd edn, New York: Van Nostrand Reinhold.

May, A.H., Rogers, C.R., Maslow, A.H. et al. (1986) *Politics and Innocence: A Humanistic Debate*, Dallas, TX: Saybrook Publishers.

McWilliams, N. (2005) 'Preserving our humanity as therapists', *Psychotherapy: Theory, Research, Practice, Training*, 42 (2): 139–51.

Mearns, D. and Thorne, B. (2000) *Person-Centred Therapy Today: New Frontiers in Theory and Practice*, London: Sage.

Moss, D. (1999) *Humanistic and Transpersonal Psychology: A Historical and Biographical Sourcebook*, Westport, CT: Greenwood Press.

Orange, D.M. (2010) *Thinking for Clinicians: Philosophical Resources for Contemporary Psychoanalysis and the Humanistic Psychotherapies*, New York: Routledge.

Rogers, C.R. (1942) *Counseling and Psychotherapy: Newer Concepts in Practice*, Boston: Houghton Mifflin.

Rogers, C.R. (1957) 'A note on "The nature of man"', *Journal of Counseling Psychology*, 4(3): 199–203.

Rowan, J. (2001) *Ordinary Ecstasy: The Dialectics of Humanistic Psychology*, 3rd edn, London: Routledge.

Rowan, J. (2013) 'Early days in humanistic and transpersonal psychology', *Self and Society: International Journal for Humanistic Psychology*, 40 (2): 47–57.

Rowan, J. and Hinshelwood, B. (1987) 'Is psychoanalysis humanistic? A correspondence between John Rowan and Bob Hinshelwood', *British Journal of Psychotherapy*, 4 (2): 14–27.

Schneider, K.J., Bugental, J.F.T. and Pierson, J.F. (2001) *The Handbook of Humanistic Psychology: Leading Edges in Theory, Research and Practice*, Thousand Oaks, CA: Sage.

Sutich, A.J. (1962) *American Association of Humanistic Psychology: Progress Report*, Palo Alto, CA: AAHP, 1 November.

Sutich, A.J. (1968) 'Transpersonal psychology: an emerging force', *Journal of Humanistic Psychology*, 8: 77–8.

Traue, J.E. (2001) 'Ancestors of the mind: a pākehā whakapapa', in R. Brown (ed.),

The Great New Zealand Argument: Ideas about Ourselves (pp. 137–47), Auckland, Aotearoa New Zealand: Activity Press. (Original work published in 1990)

Tudor, K. (1996) 'Transactional analysis *intra*gration: a metatheoretical analysis for practice', *Transactional Analysis Journal*, 26: 329–40.

Tudor, K. (2008a) 'Person-centred therapy, a cognitive behavioural therapy', in R. House and D. Loewenthal (eds), *Against and For CBT: Towards a Constructive Dialogue?* (pp. 118–36), Ross-on-Wye: PCCS Books.

Tudor, K. (2008b) 'To be or not to be in personal therapy, that is the question. Part I', *ITA News*, 35 (1): 3–8.

Tudor, K. (2008c) 'To be or not to be in personal therapy, that is the question. Part II', *ITA News*, 36 (1): 3–7.

Tudor, K. (2009) 'Building bridges across troubled waters: regarding humanistic and psychodynamic psychotherapies', paper presented at the AUT Psychotherapy Forum, Auckland University of Technology, Auckland, Aotearoa New Zealand, 24 September. (Published 2010)

Tudor, K. (2010) 'Building bridges across troubled waters: regarding humanistic and psychodynamic psychotherapies', *Forum* [The Journal of the New Zealand Association of Psychotherapists], 15: 8–25.

Tudor, K., and Worrall, M. (2006) *Person-Centred Therapy: A Clinical Philosophy*, London: Routledge.

United Kingdom Council for Psychotherapy Humanistic and Integrative Psychotherapy Section Training Standards Committee (2003) 'Personal therapy requirements', London: UKCP, May.

Walker, D.E. (1956) 'Carl Rogers and the nature of man', *Journal of Counseling Psychology*, 3(1): 89–92.

Watson, J.B. (1913) 'Psychology as the behaviorist views it', *Psychological Review*, 20: 158–77.

Whitton, E. (2003) *Humanistic Approach to Psychotherapy*, London: Whurr.

20 | Humanistic Psychology and the Evolution of Consciousness

Jill Hall

How are we, at this particular stage in the long, complex journey of unfolding consciousness, to do justice to the full spectrum of human experience? What I most value about Humanistic Psychology is not only its acknowledgement but its active exploration of this spectrum. Commitment to open-minded enquiry follows as an inevitable consequence, all the more salient as preoccupation with either desired or dreaded 'regulation' of 'professionals' in the field of psychotherapy and counselling fuels a contraction of perspective. How did this stealthy slippage towards reductionism come about?

In the 1980s and 1990s I spoke of the effects of what I termed 'Ego Imperialism' (see Hall, 1993). This not only energizes the blossoming of the Victim Archetype, but the concurrent creative urge towards individuation – enabling the taking of personal responsibility for one's choices in life – tends to be waylaid and hijacked into individualism. The last thing acknowledged by ego is the uniqueness of each and every human being, as this makes comparisons between us redundant. An unintegrated ego, being fundamentally insubstantial, can only too easily be drawn beyond its necessary task of delineation which the ability to make comparisons is designed to serve. Comparison then feeds notions which go beyond that of being a differentiated entity: it enables the notion of being 'better' than others which, of course, carries the threat of being 'worse' than others. What was intended to boost a sense of security inadvertently undermines it, and a circularity results. Mechanisms which are necessary for the phenomenon of consciousness can only too easily be subverted and can, when this occurs, carry a heavy price.[1] Is this not mirrored on the socio-political level by the spread of Western capitalism, with its emphasis on competition as prior to that of co-operation? Compelling but increasingly insubstantial as it loses its original grounding, capitalism has to adapt at a radical level or play itself out – just as life itself has eventually to respond to real conditions or else live itself to collapse or

---

1. I ponder on the notion that this is what is meant by the 'forgiveness of sins' revealed by the multi consciousness realized in the person called Jesus.

death. An ego-dominated psyche not only regards fellow human beings as competitors, but Nature as an object of exploitation, a resource from which to extract whatever we want and believe we need – and the more incomplete we experience ourselves to be, the more we feel driven, even justified, to continue in this vein. 'Ultimately neo liberal capitalism is self-destructive', Madeleine Bunting writes in the *Guardian Weekly* (10 October 2008). We could add – yes, and destructive to the individual selves caught up in it.

A parallel surge in ego-level 'takeover' of religion is revealed both in ever-more ardent and reductive forms of fundamentalism or a progressive diminuation of energy – a sense of gradually fading out, as access to wonder and mystery is curtailed. Spiritual energy is often left somewhat rootless (unless still culturally entwined with its ancient timeless Source), and thus moves and unfolds here and there, all over the world, within and through and between individuals.

What is the role of Humanistic Psychology in this 'story'? Not only its underlying philosophical base in a holistic metaphysics, but its insistence on applying this on the experiential level of human exchange is surely of crucial import.

As I see it, Humanistic Psychology evolved as an inspired expression of the creative impulse in those drawn towards self-development and/or involved in psychotherapy. It was about the individual, in commonality with other individuals, taking responsibility for their wellbeing, along with the healing of their woundings rather than being defined by the 'experts', with their rationalizations and theories about 'the other' (i.e. 'patients'). A flurry of fresh ideas and practices were born, developed and offered, tasted and tested, through active participation. A search towards greater consciousness and fulfilment ensued, courageously experimental, flawed and sometimes chaotic, but essentially liberating and life affirming. An experiential and holistic approach established a place in the field of practical psychology, embracing body, mind and spirit with the built-in assumption that those engaging in such exploration would take responsibility for their choice to participate in such explorations. The very idea of regulation would have appeared alien, and would have stifled the green shoots of what so many in the field now take for granted.

What are practitioners in the arena of therapeutic human exchange now bringing on ourselves if, or as, we begin to find ourselves tempted to claim and control, formalize and 'scientize', a relational activity which is closer to an art and cannot help but work differently for different people? Have not many who are drawn to Humanistic Psychology begun to let fear slip in, often dressed up as 'being responsible' or 'realistic', and thus found themselves sliding towards increasing professionalization unaware of those aggregations of collective misplaced ego energy? Clients (or co-workers) fall into the background, as debates ensue about who should be included and who excluded among those who erstwhile were free to focus on them. If clients are seen as victims who need specialized 'protection' or 'direction', rather than sensitive respect, those who deem this necessary will inevitably, even if inadvertently, end up as victims of controlling systems themselves. What a diversion of energy. And who decides? By what criteria? Who judges? On and on and on, while the immediate urgent needs of actual clients recede into oblivion. What an ironic outcome of the rise in risk and safety rhetoric. Safe for whom?

And so I ask again, what is the role of Humanistic Psychology in this 'story'?

I believe it has a vital role to play, as new insecurities emerge in this time of uncertainty and transition to 'we know not what'. Rather than being dragged backwards, drawn by the energy of contraction, giving way to caution and fears of exclusion from controlling bodies which will subsequently be seen as blatantly inadequate and limiting, may we remember our roots. May we continue to embrace, in ourselves and in those with whom we work, all that it means to be a human being.

Only by acknowledging the whole of whom we are – body, heart, mind, soul and spirit – can ego relax into a less dominant role. Only then can ego cease exacerbating our insecurity by over-reaching its necessary contribution of delineation on the three-dimensional plane. Only then can we give fitting attention and weight to the uniqueness and mystery of each human being. And only then can we become resilient enough to be able to respond creatively to the new and unknown challenges that lie ahead. For they are likely to be exacting.

As previously posited, we face the phenomenon of global capitalism fuelled by the essentially insubstantial but inflated energy of 'Ego Imperialism', and thus glorifying highly organized and yet anarchic competition, not just for natural resources, but for what we do not actually need (other than to boost ego). It is not surprising we eventually land up trading fictions – packaged figures with no material base whatsoever, deficit financing (which even the vast US arms industry cannot 'make good') with increasing reliance on elusive future 'growth' fanning active encouragement of more and more people taking on more and more debt.[2] The inherent vulnerability of non-holistic, ego-driven systems is all too evident, and it is fascinating to witness a political culture that so reveres rationality increasingly reduced to blind faith and the manipulation of 'facts' through the game of statistics. And all this relying on a climate of conscious or semi-conscious deception.

Our 'profession' is already tainted with this global pull to rationalize and ignore what it cannot deliver. This is evidenced in the proliferation of training courses for therapists and counsellors (and this includes those with a Humanistic Psychology orientation) in the full knowledge that there are not enough jobs for them all. The pretence that a degree or two will solve the problem has become a means of 'upping the package' – a selling point. The acceptance of students looking for a career and who have never had any therapy themselves, or shown an interest in focused self-development, is another worrying tendency. Clients' needs are easily marginalized if the agenda is dictated by forces outside them. It isn't only the bankers who have been sliding into a loss of integrity. It could be any one of us, including people we value and respect.

---

2. It is telling that Microloan – lending small sums to people to establish small enterprises to sustain themselves – truly does lead to growth. And being 'person-centred', 99 per cent of the loans are repaid.

I believe that we must wake up and stand aside from these defective trends, as we did some decades ago – although at that time the dangers and limitations we hoped to transcend appeared more specific to our field, then dominated by psychiatry, with its labelling and emphasis on pathology (Barnett, 1973). Humanistic Psychology recognized that a fundamental shift was necessary: an expansion in how we see ourselves as human beings.[3] This needs to be affirmed afresh. And the holding of a well-grounded space or context that is inclusive of the spiritual dimension experienced by human beings, and the integration of such experience in the lives of individuals, is one of our greatest contributions to the field in which we work, and one of our most crucial tasks for the future as we move towards an increasingly secularized Western world.

I myself arrived in the experimental and exploratory arena of early Humanistic Psychology days straight from the world of academic philosophy, having just completed an examination in formal logic. A few weeks earlier I had been visited by a most unsought and unwelcome intuition. While gazing at an avenue of trees in South London I suddenly knew I had to give up my studies. They had become an absorbing passion which at that time balanced domestic life and motherhood, and I knew in the same instant that I would fall into a state of depression if I did give them up. However, since early childhood I had always known that I must follow such inner promptings. Sure enough, I dived into a place of internal darkness that my intense 'head' activity had held at bay – thinking about metaphysical matters had eased the pain of my reluctant atheism. I was rescued by a flyer advertising Encounter Groups being dropped through our letter box. A commitment to four evenings was required. I had never heard of such things, but signed up out of curiosity. Although stunned and amazed by this new mode of interaction, after two evenings I found I was 'working' in the centre of the group myself. Within a few weeks I tracked down and joined a one-year 'Intensive' course in Body Work. My whole world changed, and I was no longer depressed.

However, the lack of 'evidence-based data', let alone feasible argument, for the array of assumptions and spiritual notions that others took as truth, astounded and taxed me greatly, in spite of becoming as passionate about bio-energetics as I had been about philosophy. What a liberation when, one day, I relieved myself of the burden of deciding whether someone else's views (or even my own) were either true or false. I decided to suspend this practice, and replace it with discerning if someone felt authentic to me. What mattered was making a real connection with who they happened to be as a unique fellow human being. Gradually, through my own incremental experience, sometimes somewhat startling and inexplicable in purely rational terms and yet undeniable as a lived reality, I could do no other than reclaim the immediacy of the spiritual 'knowings' that had sustained me as a child.

Iain McGilchrist, in his fascinating book *The Master and His Emissary: The Divided Brain and the Making of the Western World* (2009), makes a brilliantly compelling and informed case for the necessity of letting the right brain, with

---

3. Our success is reflected in the 2002 report by The Royal College of Psychiatrists: 'Strict adherence to guidelines, for fear of risk, should not be allowed to stifle responsible innovative practice or the patient's choice of alternative therapeutic solutions to the same problem.'

its all-inclusive intuitive consciousness, lead, while welcoming the necessary service of the left brain as its emissary. This is precisely what Humanistic Psychology stood for and practised in its initiating days. The powerful reign of left-brain dominance which rose to ascendance in the 17th century – what we call the Enlightenment – has served its time. It has both affirmed and encouraged the robust questioning of the independent rational mind, and brought about phenomenal advancement in the mechanical and technological arena; but it cannot handle a holistic appreciation of what it is to be a human being, nor see why the right brain is so essential for this purpose. The job of the left brain is to be selective and blot out anything extraneous to a particular focus. It literally does not see, or take account of, that which lies outside its selected task. It does not aim to know the whole picture, and is not set up to do so. All great scientists rely on flashes of right-brain intuition and creative thought, both to explore and actualize the possible. Mathematicians posit imaginary numbers to further the power of equations, which later result in effective applications on the material plane. The left brain cannot cope with mystery. It is not surprising, therefore, that its dominance gave birth to Literalism, Reductionism and Realism, without even being aware that these were perspectives only – mere 'ways of seeing' the world – enabling the illusion of 'having' the truth. Unfortunately, the clarity afforded by selection, or unacknowledged abstraction, from the intricate ever-mobile complexity of the whole supports this illusion. The left brain can never deal with, let alone apprehend, ontological unity.

Deprived of the means of acknowledging what we don't know, the prominence of this bias invited arrogance, and rendered understanding of our full humanity unavailable or radically diminished. It also left the field clear for the inflation of ego with the costly and dysfunctional repercussions previously described. Given that this can never serve workers in our field, Humanistic Psychology with its right/left brain balance has an important, and urgent, contribution to make at this point in the unfolding of consciousness.

I remember, when working in a residential group setting, the thrill and liberation of experiencing the mystery of the other – both the commonality and inherent mystery. And then discovering the fruitfulness of honouring that mystery which also continually reveals itself, the more you honour it. We can never fully know another (although we know ourselves more fully through the other), and in the respectful wonder and fascination and appreciation of difference, we discover that more and more becomes evident and we dare to find ways to communicate to that other what they reveal of who they are. And yet far from allowing the leadership of the right brain in this way, it seems that training courses in our field give ever more prominence to left-brain preoccupations. Surely we betray all we once stood for if we move away from giving priority to in-the-moment utterly creative and unplanned occurrences of connection with another that no theorizing or writing of papers and getting of further degrees can win for us.

It is essential that we take stock and honour our genesis. The establishment of connection with the other, at whatever level they endeavour to offer of themselves, and responding, if possible, with that level in oneself;

being in the living moment with them, knowing not where it can take us – from the ordinary, the petty, tainted or tragic, obscure or self-evident or perhaps sublime. The bonus is that learning through connection with the other leads to a further unfolding of oneself, and to the discovery of new levels of consciousness.

Reciprocal learning; this is how I see the essence of Humanistic Psychology, and thus the seed for the continual regeneration of its future. All our work experientially based, inspired and structured by creative theorizing, but these hypotheses and theories elucidated in training as much as is possible face to face, and not primarily through the written word, nor the trainee's understanding of them primarily assessed through the written word. I am a great lover of theories, and enjoy exploring them, but had to learn to hold them lightly. (I believe it was Jung who urged us to 'Learn your theories as well as you can, but put them aside when you touch the miracle of the living soul', Jung, 1928: 361. He certainly had quite a lot to drop!)

Theories are like different intellectual 'species' which can illuminate different modes of psychic and energetic structure and expression. My foundational training was with Gerda Boyeson, who founded the Institute of Biodynamic Psychology in London. She embodied what she taught, and thus communicated the reality of unfolding life energy, along with the means of accessing and regulating that life energy, and thus the bio-dynamic nature of being-in-the-world. Gerda herself didn't advocate the practice of mixing different methods and approaches to therapy – what she called 'fruit salad'. However, such an approach could be viewed as exploring different 'fruits' for different people in different circumstances or on different occasions, and seeing if they bring forth illumination and greater wellbeing for that client. This is how I see that vital combination of inclusiveness and particularity expressed in the rich and comprehensive range of therapeutic practices that characterize Humanistic Psychology in its responsiveness to the diversity within our oneness.

It is the unique individual expression of our common nature that Humanistic Psychology endeavours to address. And the creativeness of the different approaches that have evolved under this title could be seen not as 'fruit salad' but as a bunch of flowers, each whole and distinct in itself and 'right' (i.e. therapeutically releasing and revealing) for different individuals in their particularity. It is of vital importance that we stand clear and firm and resist the current pull towards more contained models with set numbers of sessions, while not excluding that such methods have some value for many people. We must be alert to the danger of any creeping resignation with regard to this trend as some sort of inevitable convergent reality.

If Humanistic Psychology is to have a vibrant future, it could do well to sustain the spirit of its vibrant past. It is not a call to mimic the past, but to reconnect with the source that enabled the courageous and innovative growth of the Humanistic Psychology movement. After a period of contraction and control, consciousness at some point will expand once more. After a 'season' of regulation and reduction to the measurable, continued out-of-date left-brain dominance and thus the prestige of numerical outcomes, tick boxes, caution and reductionist notions of experimentation, I feel confident that a fresh thrust of consciousness will surge forth yet again. I believe that Humanistic Psychology, if it holds to being truly humanistic, will then ride on a further tide of courageous innovation, based on the lived appreciation of the pain and wonder of being a human being.

We must endeavour neither to react nor capitulate to the disheartening backsliding which so often occurs within the underlying evolutionary expansion of consciousness, and I find it helpful to view this present state of contraction in our field within this wide-ranging context. Helpful because it allows an uncompromising short-term pessimism while embracing an irrepressible optimism and confidence in the thrust of life itself. It is not surprising that agonizing excursions and countless deviations occur, as we attempt to integrate the complexity of who we are. It appears that all life on earth evolved in this marvellous but hazardous process of becoming, and so we human beings are equally vulnerable – we who have the most complex journey to undertake. For we have many dimensions of being to integrate before we become free enough to enter into fully loving relationship with each other and All That Is.

I believe the time will come when ego relaxes into its necessary function as an instrument of delineation employed by the self, each individual active on a three-dimensional plane, but informed by the multi-dimensional awareness of soul (mediated by the phenomena of imagination, intuition and inspiration) and the promptings of spirit – the 'Whole' emanating as a dynamic all-embracing collective of unique sparks of conscious loving.

Humanistic Psychology has its tiny but significant part to play in all this. However depressing current trends may be, I have a deep confidence in the ultimate realization of humanity. Although shadowed now in somewhat ludicrous individualism resulting in inadequate, misleading and divisive forms of association or 'ego-collectives', do we not have glimpses of true connection between individuating beings, enabling the exchange of love and an empathetic sense of the underlying affinity of all beings in the universe? No matter if the fulfilment of what it means to be a human being takes eons, all the seeds and intimations are discernable, although not yet sustainable. May we hold faith and do our bit.

References

Barnett, M. (1973) *People, Not Psychiatry*, London: Allen & Unwin.
Bunting, M. (2008) *Guardian Weekly*, 10 October.
Hall, J. (1993) *The Reluctant Adult: An Exploration of Choice*, Bridport, Dorset: Prism Press.
Jung, C.G. (1928) 'Analytical Psychology and education', in *Contributions to Analytical Psychology*, trans. H.G. and C.F. Baynes, London: Kegan Paul; quoted in *Self & Society*, 27 (1) (March, 1999): 22.
McGilchrist, I. (2009) *The Master and His Emissary: The Divided Brain and the Making of the Western World*, New Haven, CT: Yale University Press (2nd edn, 2012).

21 | Humanism: The fourth wave

John Heron

The first three waves of humanism

In the history of civilization in the Western world, there have so far been three main waves of humanism. The first wave arose in Greece in the 5th century BC when the Sophists and Socrates 'called philosophy down from heaven to earth', as Cicero put it, by introducing social, political and moral questions.

The second wave, the Renaissance, was well under way in the 15th century in Florence. Through the recovery of the classical culture of Greece and Rome, it affirmed the worth and dignity of human achievement – the unique genius and extraordinary ability of the human mind – over against the Christian pre-occupation with human sin. However, while Renaissance humanists made humanity the centre of interest, they were far from being atheists, for God still remained as creator – though more remote. And the artists of the Renaissance had an important spiritual declaration to make about our relation with our world, as we shall see.

The powerful third wave began with the Enlightenment of the 18th century, and became the rational, scientific, secular and atheistic humanism of modern times.

Humanistic Psychology and the third wave of humanism

Humanistic Psychology, when it emerged in the USA in 1961, had a clear affiliation with this third wave of humanism, as exemplified by two of its primary protagonists. Abraham Maslow insisted that he was an atheist, and as such regarded the peak experiences of his self-actualizing exemplars as simply an expression of the best of their selfhood.

> I want to demonstrate that spiritual values have naturalistic meaning, that they are not the exclusive possession of organized churches, that they do not

need supernatural concepts to validate them, that they are well within the jurisdiction of a suitably enlarged science.

(Maslow, 1964: 3)

Carl Rogers was selected in 1964 as Humanist of the Year by the American Humanist Association, which promotes humanism as 'a progressive philosophy of life that, without theism and other supernatural beliefs, affirms our ability and responsibility to lead ethical lives of personal fulfilment that aspire to the greater good of humanity'.

A full-on humanist declaration from Rogers (1961: 23–4) reads as follows:

> It is to experience that I must return again and again; to discover a closer approximation to truth as it is in the process of becoming in me. Neither the Bible nor the prophets – neither Freud nor research – neither the revelations of God nor man – can take precedence over my own direct experience.

A late turn to the spiritual

However, Maslow apparently took a turn toward the non-naturalistic spiritual – 'beyond humanistic' – as he got a bit older. Stan Grof (2004: 2) reports that:

> In spite of the popularity of humanistic psychology, its founders Maslow and Sutich themselves grew dissatisfied with the conceptual framework they had originally created. They became increasingly aware that they had left out an extremely important element – the spiritual dimension of the human psyche.

In 1967 they joined up, says Grof, with him and others to create:

> a new psychology that would honour the entire spectrum of human experience, including various non-ordinary states of consciousness. During these discussions, Maslow and Sutich accepted Grof's suggestion and named the new discipline 'transpersonal psychology'. This term replaced their own original name 'transhumanistic' or 'reaching beyond humanistic concerns'.
>
> (Grof, 2004: 3)

Soon afterwards the Association of Transpersonal Psychology was launched. Maslow died in 1970.

Rogers kept the spiritual out of his psychology for a long time. But finally, in the last decade of his life, he turned toward it in terms of presence, inner spirit and self-transcending relationship:

> I find that when I am closest to my inner intuitive self, when I am somehow in touch with the unknown in me then whatever I do seems full of healing. Then simply my presence is releasing and helpful to the other. When I can relax and be close to the transcendental core of me it seems that my inner spirit has reached out and touched the inner spirit of the other. Our relationship transcends itself and becomes a part of something larger.
>
> (Rogers, 1980: 129)

Rogers died in 1987.

What I find prescient – albeit conjectural – about these two late turns is that they appear to embrace three fundamental spiritual dimensions: Maslow turns to the Beyond (the transpersonal), and Rogers turns to the Within (the intrapersonal) and the Between (the interpersonal), opening to the Beyond (for more on this triad, see Heron, 2006, 2007; and for related notions, see Ferrer, 2011; Shirazi, 2005; Chaudhuri, 1977). And these three are basic *spiritual* elements contributing to, and interdependent with, but not reducible to, the *humanism* of the fourth wave, as I will discuss after a brief look at the issue of separation.

The humanistic–transhumanistic separation

The existence of two Associations, one humanistic and the other, in Maslow's choice of a title, transhumanistic – the first dealing with the personal, and the second dealing with what is beyond the personal – tends to condone a separation between the spiritual and that which is distinctively human. Their co-existence also implies that neither of them is giving an integrated account of the full range of human experience.

Lajoie and Shapiro (1992) reviewed 40 definitions of transpersonal psychology in the literature between 1969 and 1991. They found five key themes: states of consciousness, higher or ultimate potential, beyond the ego or personal self, transcendence, and the spiritual. This clear emphasis on the higher, the ultimate, the beyond, the transcendent, echoes the historical fact that spiritual traditions, beliefs and practices for the past 3,000 years have been predominantly transcendent in their orientation. And as several commentators have pointed out (e.g. Walsh and Vaughan, 1993), this has led to definitions and declarations of transpersonal psychology being invaded by the ontological assumptions, belief systems and practices of the traditions.

Some of these early definitions, declarations and demarcations have been modified in recent years, but the whole movement is still dogged by the implicit transcendental focus of the 'trans', the beyond, in its title. This can be confirmed by scanning through the titles of all the articles published in the *Journal of Transpersonal Psychology* over the 43 years between 1969 and 2012. They are listed on the journal's website.

John Rowan (2005: 6) says that Humanistic Psychology 'has a place for the spiritual', but then he also makes it plain that those who are really interested in the spiritual aspects of Humanistic Psychology work under the aegis of 'a separate *Journal of Transpersonal Psychology*'.

On its website, the Association for Humanistic Psychology in the USA makes a brief mention of 'the interaction of body, mind and spirit', but otherwise focuses on a third-wave humanist account of Humanistic Psychology as 'a value orientation that holds a hopeful, constructive view of human beings and of their substantial capacity to be self-determining'. It ends with a problematic statement to the effect that because Humanistic Psychology has spread into many other areas of society, it is no longer Humanistic Psychology, and that, although it is still represented by the AHP, it is also represented in transpersonal psychology and in many other movements.

Wilber has long since adroitly stepped away from the humanistic–transpersonal divide and commandeered 'integral' to name his attempt to present an all-inclusive psychology (Wilber, 2000). But it too has suffered invasion, in his case by the non-dual traditions, and it has no adequate model of spiritual inquiry, only consensus within a school or tradition (Heron, 1998).

I myself thought for a while, in the context of writing about the Institute for the Development of Human Potential, that it would be wise to re-unite Humanistic Psychology and transpersonal psychology under the name Holistic Psychology (Heron, 2001). However, I now rescind that view, while putting some of the ideas advanced in that paper to better use. Rather than a simple name change, today I think it is more fundamental and fruitful radically to reconstruct the meaning of 'humanism', and thus, by its extension, the meaning of 'humanistic'. My reconstruction is both radical and tentative in its first expression. In later sections of the chapter I sketch out some of the recent background to the fourth wave, and the possible role of collegiality in its future.

The fourth wave of humanism

1. Inaugural statement

The fourth-wave paradigm, as I conceive it, is fully committed to the self-determining capacity of humans, and believes that the development of this capacity presupposes a dynamic context of spiritual animation/inspiration in which persons can actively participate. This animation has three interdependent immediate dimensions – intrapersonal, interpersonal and transpersonal. It can move deep *within* the psyche in the case of autonomous decision-making; centrally and crucially in the energetic relation *between* collaborating persons; and in the potent field of universal mind *beyond* and including personal mind. The paradigm proposes that humans become more fully human when exercising their self-determination in a co-creative relation with these three kinds of spiritual animation in ongoing dynamic interaction with each other.

In truth, I think it is Carl Rogers who implicitly launches the fourth-wave paradigm in the 1980 quotation cited above, which, in my reading of it, gives a deeply *human* account of his helping relationship in terms of the spirit *within* reaching out to the spirit *between*, which in turn opens to the spirit *beyond* – 'becomes a part of something larger' (p.129).

2. Some primary features

Here are some of the initial working assumptions underlying the inaugural statement:

1. The 'personal' in each of the three dimensions always refers to a person in their local and wider eco-system, including all other forms of life.

2. The dimensions are *sui generis* with respect to their shared ontological status as spiritual. They engage fully with the naturalistic, but are not reducible to it.
3. They are mutually supportive in their interactions with each other and in co-creative relations with humans, in whom they may elicit self-determining capacity, collaborative capacity including eco-effective capacity, and multi-dimensional awareness capacity.
4. They provide a dynamic context for ongoing human action research into the greater emergence of the breadth, depth and height of intrinsically human flourishing, within flourishing eco-systems, and as such:
5. They are part and parcel of the practice of Humanistic Psychology.

What is culturally unusual about this strange declaration – which I elaborate further in sub-section 6 below – is that it makes human action research and essential human flourishing central to the measure of all things spiritual. For reasons of space, I will look at only three areas of my personal experiential inquiry which have a bearing on this thesis.

3. Co-counselling experience

I first encountered – experientially and phenomenologically – what I now realize is the fourth wave of humanism when I was fully engaged with applied Humanistic Psychology in the 1970s and 1980s. In my own co-counselling sessions, there were three quite distinct and interrelated phenomena. I will describe these in terms of 'animation', by which I mean a spiritual stimulation of a co-creative human response. So when I write below of an animation eliciting something, I mean that the person is making an instantaneous micro-choice to engage creatively with the eliciting process.

As a self-directing client, when engaging with the free attention of my counsellor, I would feel, (1) an animation of the shared field of awareness *between* us, eliciting a living liberating interest, which in turn released, (2) an animation deep *within* my psyche eliciting an impulse to attend to, and work creatively with, an emerging emotion, image, memory, felt sense to move or breathe in a particular way, or give voice or sound, etc. This in turn, when followed through, would release a whole series of further intrapsychic animations eliciting and sustaining a clearing and healing process. After a pause to re-enter fully the shared field of awareness *between* myself and my counsellor, there would suddenly occur, (3) an animation like a discreet light from *beyond* my mind, eliciting spontaneous insights and realizations, cognitively restructuring the life-experience I had been dealing with.

In my micro-world as client, the developmental series went from an animation *between*, to a series of animations *within*, to a pause in the *between*, to an animation as if from *beyond*. The *beyond* in a session can cover a wide range, from illuminations of cognitive restructuring as above, to the following:

> *I was giving free attention to a self-directing client who was repeating the phrase 'I am a loving person' to contradict a deep-seated self-deprecation*

distress pattern. This brought forth various degrees and kinds of emotional discharge. After a longish pause, she looked up and quietly and simply declaimed 'I am', and between further pauses repeated this with ever greater fullness and radiance. In reporting on this afterwards, she said it was as if the declaration 'I am' brought her to a threshold where personal consciousness is open to consciousness that is anywhere and everywhere. She has long since given me permission to share this story with others.

4. The inquiry group experience

'The inquiry group' is the simple name of a group meeting regularly here in New Zealand, in the early years every three weeks, in recent years every fortnight, since 1994. The description which follows amplifies the account given in Heron and Lahood (2008). The group's original purpose is to celebrate together through charismatic sound and movement our individual and interactive coming into being, and to carry this arousal forward into individual practical behaviour in everyday life and work. The core method is collaborative action inquiry, an innovative variant of Torbert's individual action inquiry (2001). We often start with a check-in round, in which each person is animated from *within* to share anything about their current inner and outer life. There is no comment on, nor interaction with, what each person shares, because the check-in is offered to the presence *between* us. There may then be a period of verbal silence, or this plus someone stroking the rim of a Tibetan bowl with a stick of wood to produce a tone.

At a certain point there is a distinct, spontaneous animation of the energy field *between* us, which elicits a further animation *within* each person, expressed in idiosyncratic improvised posture and gesture, movement, toning, rhythmic sounding of a diversity of instruments. This co-created orchestration is both an enlivenment by the spirit *within* us, and a resonant engagement with the animation *between* all our individual enlivenments. It is also both a heart-felt communion with the living presence *within* and *between* us, and an aware inquiry into its nature and credentials – a dynamic marriage of appreciation and experiential research.

This dynamic, charismatic, inquiring opening goes on for a considerable period – on average about 45 minutes – with series of crescendos and diminuendos which are potently co-created with the rhythmic life *within* us and *between* us.

There is an unmistakable final diminuendo. We become entirely still. We draw together and hold hands, or sit silently apart, and for a long period feast on, and probe with the soul, the extraordinary depths of the spiritual presence *between* us, also aptly named by one of our members as 'the band of golden silence'. This also has a clear ending. It may, or may not, be followed by a sharing, an affirmation, and an inquiring review, of what has been going on. Then we close the meeting, and people depart for their homes.

A very important outcrop of what is generated in the depths of the *between* is that, at varying intervals, we plan a co-operative inquiry into some specific human-spiritual activity undertaken in everyday life between our fortnightly meetings. Then we make space during the session for each person to report on and review the previous two weeks of activity, and, in the light of that, plan the next two weeks.

In summary of the primary process, the check-ins from *within* arouse, and engage with, the build-up of presence *between*, which, in the following period of silence, deepens to the point at which enlivenment *within* each bursts forth, further intensifying the charismatic resonance *between* all. It is also clear that the deeper the presence *between* us, the more intrinsically open it is, out of the intensity of its subtle passion, to the *beyond* – like the deep resonance between trees in a forest participates in the glory of the overarching sky beyond them and including them. The beyond is also always within and between.

5. Daily living experience

It seems to me that these three kinds of animation are also available for co-creating my daily living – if and when *I* am available, and not forgetful and distracted, not caught up in self-perpetuating maladaptive attitude and action. In this context, the interpersonal widens out into the situational, a felt dynamic resonance with the presence *between* myself and the other persons and the place here where I am now. The intrapersonal is the ongoing play of animations deep *within* my psyche, each animation arousing a creative adaptation to, and interaction with, the immediate presenting situation. The transpersonal is an animation from the *beyond*, arousing me from the sleep of limited awareness, and inviting me to open the margins of my mind to an all-embracing awareness, in the light of which everything integrally possible is appropriate.

Animations *within* and *between* are in continual interplay with each other, in the light of the *beyond*. And this is especially so in a close personal relationship, where the *between* is clearly central, enriched by the *within* and the *beyond*.

6. More on primary features

There are several further provisional points I would like to share from my experience of these animations, to elaborate further the five key points presented above:

6. Depending upon the human structure of the situation – session, group or daily life – they come and go in their own rhythms; they both call, and can be called up; and their sequencing can vary, they can interweave and interrelate in diverse ways.

7. They are micro-gifts of living grace and discreet congeniality, three dynamic spiritual dimensions, which, when given human space to interact *together*, supportively enhance the essential humanity of our nature. And it is inherent in each animation that while it calls to be recognized as a spiritual gift, it also honours the liberty of humans to ignore it. Indeed, the animations respectfully allow for agnosticism and atheism, since anyone is free to regard any of them as naturalistic.

8. Most importantly, these gifted animations invite humans to be co-creative with them: they elicit and facilitate autonomous, intentional, innovative

adaptations and initiatives. Intrapersonal animations in particular cultivate the emergence of self-determining capacity in humans. Spirited self-determination is one primary feature of the intrinsically human.

9. I have an overall sense that the *between* and the *within* provide the best conditions for effective and appropriate human co-creation with the *beyond*. I also believe, as a fourth-wave humanist, that spiritual animations between persons, *and between persons and place including other kinds of beings in that place*, are central, and that this centrality is serviced by animations both within and beyond (Heron, 2006).

10. These or any other propositions about the animations can be researched by collaborative phenomenological action research (Heron, 1996, 1998, 2006; Heron and Lahood, 2008). This kind of inquiry can establish the intentional human conditions within which these spiritual animations may occur, and clarify their distinguishing characteristics. Practical wisdom also suggests the benefits, for any such inquiry – whether individual or collective – of times of wise suspension, in which every dimension is abandoned for a period in favour of not-knowing – the paradoxical way of intentional nescience.

7. Sacralization

My impression is that the spiritual deeply values the unique nature of the human, delights in co-creatively enhancing and expanding it, and does this in a way that sacralizes and exalts the embodied realm of individuated persons who are creatively interacting in regenerating their world. The notion of humanism as a sacralizing force is certainly not new, for it was brilliantly foreshadowed in the second wave of humanism.

The Renaissance was an awakening of the senses: its artists rediscovered the lushness, beauty and exuberance of nature. But they did not just reproduce nature in a humdrum manner:

> They brought sanctity to nature. Renaissance landscapes are alive precisely because they are infused with spiritual energy. Beneath the visible currents of the sensuous forms of life, a deep process of re-sacralization is going on.
> (Skolimowski, 1994: 130)

The artists of the Renaissance showed through their own achievements that the human being is an imaginal co-creator of the world. It was not just the person as the measure of all things, but the person as the measure of a sacral reality, of a spiritually co-generated world. However, as Skolimowski points out, the world-transforming potential of this aesthetic achievement was interrupted by the dominance of the mechanistic-materialistic worldview of Bacon, Galileo, Descartes, Newton – and the third wave gradually took over.

There is indeed a sense in which the fourth wave of humanism completes and carries forward the work of the second phase, which is perhaps why I lived for ten years in the triangle between Florence, Pisa and Siena – cities of the Renaissance – where I wrote four books central to my fourth-wave worldview.

The recent background of the fourth wave

Let us start with Carl Rogers, for whom personality was governed by an innate actualizing tendency, the inherent tendency of the organism to develop all its capacities in ways which serve to maintain or enhance the organism. This organismic tendency, he believed, is selective, directional and constructive. It affects both biological and psychological functions. Psychologically, it guides people toward increased autonomy and self-sufficiency, expanding their experiences and fostering personal growth. The connotation of organismic tendency construed self-actualization as a naturalistic drive, and affirmed a grounding element of third-wave humanism in the humanistic approach (Rogers, 1959, 1980).

Eugene Gendlin, following in Rogers' footsteps, developed experiential focusing as a method for making quite explicit, within the body-mind, the selective and directional guidance of the actualizing tendency. You create a relaxed space within the body-mind, take an issue of concern into that space, let it take shape in appropriate symbolic form, and attend to the form, with all its associated affect, within that pregnant space. You focus until there is an emergent resolution of the issue in imagery and/or words, the hallmark of resolution being a subtle liberating release of somatic energy. Once again the action of the actualizing tendency was seen as organismic, i.e. somatic (Gendlin, 1981).

The spiritual animation breakthrough comes with McMahon and Campbell (1991), practitioners of experiential focusing, who re-categorize Gendlin's somatic release as a bio-spiritual event, an experience of grace in the body. Letting go into the body-feeling about an issue, Gendlin's felt shift, is now sensed as a movement of the indwelling life-giving presence and power of the spirit.

Here returns Schelling's *deus implicitus,* not only in this form, but also in several other related versions: the entelechy self, the root self, the ground of one's being, and the seeded coded essence which contains both the patterns and the possibilities of one's life (Houston, 1987); the dynamic ground (libido, psychic energy, numinous power or spirit) of somatic, instinctual, affective and creative-imaginal potentials (Washburn, 1995); Eros as spirit-in-action, the indwelling divine drive at the root of human aspiration (Wilber, 1995). Human motivation is grounded in the spiritual life-potential within. The organismic actualizing tendency becomes reconfigured as, replaced by, a process of spirit-human becoming and co-creation (Bruteau, 1997; Hubbard, 1998; Heron, 1992, 1998, 2006, 2007).

This spiritual animation within people appears to have a basic polarity, a radical and dynamic complementarity: there is the impulse to realize individual distinctness of being, and the impulse to realize interactive unity with wider fields of being (Heron, 1992). The same basic principle is found in Hindu psychology: Bhagavan Das postulates a polarity of the primal Shakti, or divine creative power within the psyche, as a will to live as an individual, and a will to live as the universal (Das, 1953). It is a subtle balance: too much individualism leads to egocentric narcissism; too much universalism leads to spiritual fascism, authoritarianism and subtle oppression.

Collegiality in the fourth wave

I think a guiding principle for balance is that of collegiality – a collegiality of unbound mutuality and *co-inherence* of distinctness of being without separation of being, the flowering of individual diversity in free unity. Berdyaev (1937) gives a good account in terms of *sobornost*: the creative process of spirit manifest through the self-determining subjectivity of human personhood engaged in the realization of value and achieved in true community. The co-inherence of persons in such a community is an interpersonal true unity-in-diversity, a dynamic, developing social form of diune awareness (Heron, 1998: 99; Heron and Lahood, 2008; compare and contrast with the nondual in Wilber, 2000: 181).

Translated into my conceptual system, Berdyaev's account means that living spirit manifests as a dynamic interplay between, and animation of, autonomy, hierarchy and co-operation. It emerges through co-creation within and between autonomous people, each of whom can identify their own idiosyncratic true needs and interests; each of whom can also think hierarchically in terms of what values promote the true needs and interests of the whole community; and each of whom can co-operate with – that is, listen to, engage with, and negotiate agreed decisions with – their peers, celebrating diversity and difference as integral to genuine unity.

Hierarchy here is the creative leadership which seeks to promote the values of autonomy and co-operation in a peer-to-peer association. Such leadership is exercised in two ways: first, by the one or more people who take initiatives to set up such an association; and second, once the association is up and running, as spontaneous rotating leadership among the peers, when anyone takes initiatives that further enhance the autonomy and co-operation of other participating members.

The autonomy of participants is not that of the old Cartesian ego, isolated and cut off from the world. Descartes sat inside a big stove to get at his *cogito, ergo sum* – I think, therefore I am; and while his exclusively subjective self provided a necessary leverage against traditional dogmatisms to help found the modern worldview, it left the modern self alienated from the separated world it commands. The autonomy of those who flourish within *sobornost*, by contrast, is an autonomy that is rounded and enriched by a profound kind of inner animation that develops and flourishes only in felt interconnectedness, participative engagement, with other persons, and with the biodiversity and integral ecology of our planet (Spretnak, 1995).

This is the participatory worldview, which I see as the foreground of the emerging fourth wave of humanism. It is also expressed in an extended epistemology: our conceptual knowing of the world is grounded in our experiential knowing – a felt resonance with the world and imaginal participation in it. This epistemic participation is the ground for political participation in social processes that integrate autonomy, hierarchy and co-operation. What we are now about is a whole collaborative regeneration of our world through co-creative engagement with the spirit that animates it and us. For just a few of the many contributors to the early dawn of the participatory worldview, see: Abram, 1996; Bateson, 1979; Berman, 1981; Ferrer, 2002; Heron, 1992, 1996, 1998, 2006; Merleau-Ponty, 1962; Reason, 1994; Reason and Rowan 1981; Skolimowski, 1994; Spretnak, 1991; Tarnas, 1991; and Varela, Thompson and Rosch, 1991.

A humanism-4 account of Humanistic Psychology

What would Humanistic Psychology look like if it were an expression of this account of fourth-wave humanism? Primarily, it would take spirituality out of the 'transhumanistic' realm, and put it back where it belongs, in an enhanced, more rounded and grounded form at the very core of the human realm. It then manifests as collegiality, a collaborative regeneration of what it is to be a human being.

On this overall view, spirituality is located in the interpersonal heart of the human condition, where people co-operate to explore meaning, build relationship and manifest creativity through collaborative action inquiry into the integration and consummation of many areas of human development. One possible model of such collegial-applied spirituality has at least eight distinguishing characteristics:

1. It is *developmentally holistic*, involving diverse major areas of human development; and the holism is both within each, and between them. Prime value is put on relational areas, such as gender, psychosexuality, emotional and interpersonal skills, communicative competence, peer communion, morality, human ecology, supported by the individualistic, such as contemplative competence, physical fitness.

2. It is *psychosomatically holistic*, embracing a fully embodied and vitalized co-creative expression with spirit. Spirituality is found not just at the top end of a developmental line, but is explored co-creatively with spiritual animations in the living root of its embodied form, in the relational heart of its current level of unfolding, and in the transcendent awareness embracing it.

3. It is *epistemologically holistic*, including many ways of knowing: knowing by presence with, by intuiting significant form and process, by conceptualizing, by practising. Such holistic knowing is intrinsically dialogic, action- and inquiry-oriented. It is fulfilled in peer-to-peer participative inquiry, and the participation is both epistemic and political.

4. It is *ontologically holistic*, open to the manifest as nature, culture and the subtle, and to spirit as immanent life, the situational present, and transcendent mind. It sees our relational, social process in this *present human situation* as the immediate locus of unfolding human co-creative integration with immanent life and transcendent mind (Heron, 1998, 2006, 2007).

5. It is focused on worthwhile practical purposes that promote a flourishing humanity-cum-ecosystem; that is, it is rooted in an extended doctrine of rights with regard to social and ecological liberation.

6. It embraces peer-to-peer relations and participatory forms of decision-making. The latter in particular can be seen as a radical discipline in relational spirituality, burning up a lot of the privatized ego.

7. It honours the gradual emergence and development of peer-to-peer forms of association and practice.

8. It affirms the role of both initiating hierarchy, and spontaneously surfacing and rotating hierarchy among the peers, in such emergence.

In a sentence: it encourages us to inquire together, imaginatively and creatively, about how to act together in a spirited way to flourish on and with our planet.

References

Abram, D. (1996) *The Spell of the Sensuous*, New York: Vintage Books.
Bateson, G. (1979) *Mind and Nature: A Necessary Unity*, New York: Dutton.
Berdyaev, N. (1937) *The Destiny of Man*, London: Ayer.
Berman, M. (1981) *The Reenchantment of the World*, Ithaca, NY: Cornell University Press.
Bruteau, B. (1997) *God's Ecstasy: The Creation of a Self-Creating World*, New York: The Crossroad Publishing Company.
Chaudhuri, H. (1977) *The Evolution of Integral Consciousness*, Wheaton, IL: The Theosophical Publishing House.
Das, B. (1953) *The Science of Emotions*, Madras: Theosophical Publishing House.
Ferrer, J. (2002) *Revisioning Transpersonal Theory: A Participatory Vision of Human Spirituality*, Albany, NY: State University of New York Press.
Ferrer, J. (2011) 'Participatory spirituality and transpersonal theory: a ten-year retrospective', *Journal of Transpersonal Psychology*, 43 (1): 1–34.
Gendlin, E. (1981) *Focusing*, London: Bantam Press.
Grof, S. (c. 2004) *A Brief History of Transpersonal Psychology*, www.stanislavgrof.com; also published in the *International Journal of Transpersonal Studies*, (2008), 27: 46–54.
Heron, J. (1992) *Feeling and Personhood: Psychology in Another Key*, London: Sage.
Heron, J. (1996) *Co-operative Inquiry: Research into the Human Condition*, London: Sage.
Heron, J. (1998) *Sacred Science: Person-Centred Inquiry into the Spiritual and the Subtle*, Ross-on-Wye: PCCS Books.
Heron, J. (2001) 'Holism and collegiality', *Self & Society*, 29 (2): 17–19.
Heron, J. (2006) *Participatory Spirituality: A Farewell to Authoritarian Religion*, Morrisville, NC: Lulu Press.
Heron, J. (2007) 'Participatory fruits of spiritual inquiry', *ReVision: A Journal of Consciousness and Transformation*, 29 (3): 7–17.
Heron, J. and Lahood, G. (2008) 'Charismatic inquiry in concert: action research in the realm of the between', in P. Reason and H. Bradbury (eds), *Handbook of Action Research: Participative Inquiry and Practice*, 2nd edn (pp. 439–49), London: Sage.
Houston, J. (1987) *The Search for the Beloved*, Los Angeles: Tarcher.
Hubbard, B.M. (1998) *Conscious Evolution: Awakening the Power of our Social Potential*, Novato, CA: New World Library.
Lajoie, D.H. and Shapiro, S.I. (1992) 'Definitions of transpersonal psychology: the first twenty-three years', *Journal of Transpersonal Psychology*, 24 (1): 79–98.

Maslow, A. (1964) *Religions, Values, and Peak-Experiences*, New York: Penguin Press.
McMahon, E. and Campbell, P. (1991) *The Focusing Steps*, Kansas City, MO: Sheed and Ward.
Merleau-Ponty, M. (1962) *Phenomenology of Perception*, London: Routledge & Kegan Paul.
Reason, P. (ed.) (1994) *Participation in Human Inquiry*, London: Sage.
Reason, P. and Rowan, J. (eds) (1981) *Human Inquiry: A Sourcebook of New Paradigm Research*, Chichester: Wiley.
Rogers, C.R. (1959) 'A theory of therapy, personality, and interpersonal relationships, as developed in the client-centered framework', in S. Koch (ed.), *Psychology: A Study of a Science, Vol. 3, Formulations of the Person and the Social Context* (pp. 184–256), New York: Penguin.
Rogers, C.R. (1961) *On Becoming a Person: A Therapist's View of Psychotherapy*, London: Constable.
Rogers, C.R. (1980) *A Way of Being*, Boston: Houghton Mifflin.
Rowan, J. (2005) *A Guide to Humanistic Psychology*, 3rd edn, London: UKAHPP.
Shirazi, B.A.K. (2005) 'Integral psychology: Psychology of the whole human being', in M. Schlitz, T. Amorok and M.S. Micozzi (eds), *Consciousness and Healing: Integral Approaches to Mind–Body Medicine* (pp. 233–47), St. Louis, MO: Elsevier Churchill Livingston.
Skolimowski, H. (1994) *The Participatory Mind*, London: Arkana.
Spretnak, C. (1991) *States of Grace: The Recovery of Meaning in the Postmodern Age*, San Francisco: Harper-Collins.
Spretnak, C. (1995) 'Embodied, embedded philosophy', *Open Eye* (California Institute for Integral Studies), 12 (1): 4–5.
Tarnas, R. (1991) *The Passion of the Western Mind: Understanding the Ideas that Have Shaped Our World View*, New York: Ballantine.
Torbert, W.R. (2001) 'The practice of action inquiry' in P. Reason and H. Bradbury (eds), *Handbook of Action Research* (pp. 207–18), London: Sage Publications.
Varela, F.J., Thompson, E. and Rosch, E. (1991) *The Embodied Mind: Cognitive Science and Human Experience*, Cambridge, MA: MIT Press.
Walsh, R. and Vaughan, F. (1993) 'On transpersonal definitions', *Journal of Transpersonal Psychology*, 25 (2): 199–207.
Washburn, M. (1995) *The Ego and the Dynamic Ground: A Transpersonal Theory of Human Development*, Albany, NY: State University of New York Press.
Wilber, K. (1995) *Sex, Ecology, Spirituality: The Spirit of Evolution*, Boston: Shambhala.
Wilber, K. (2000) *Integral Psychology*, Boston: Shambhala.

Editorial Conclusion

Richard House, David Kalisch and Jennifer Maidman

It was some half a century ago when Humanistic Psychology first burst on to the scene in the USA, and then a little later in Britain, being widely hailed at the time as a 'third force' that would humanize what was seen as an increasingly *de*humanizing psychology, helping to counterbalance the perceived shortcomings of behaviourism and psychoanalysis. In this book we have deliberately presented readers with a broad spectrum of views from right across the humanistic field; and as you'll have seen, while there is some degree of consensus around core, defining humanistic values and practices, there is also a great deal of diversity, even disagreement – witness, for example, the very different takes on the place of spirituality and 'the transpersonal' in Humanistic Psychology from Gaie Houston (in Chapter 18), on the one hand, and from John Heron and John Rowan (Chapters 21 and 12 respectively), on the other.

It is certainly difficult to dispute the contention that Humanistic Psychology has had a significant impact on modern Western culture. In Chapter 19, for example, Keith Tudor highlights just some of the ways in which Humanistic Psychology has been a big success story – namely, that it is 'a recognized "force" or tradition with a number of "schools", "modalities" or "approaches"'; that it has well-established training courses and programmes; that it has generated a considerable literature, including three professional journals, the *Journal of Humanistic Psychology*, *The Humanistic Psychologist* and *Self & Society*; and that it has a presence in mainstream organizations, including the American Psychological Association and as a College of the UK Council for Psychotherapy (UKCP).

One key question that arises from this is that of how important it is that Humanistic Psychology works harder to provide a clear and unambiguous definition of its subject matter, values and practices. Such a move (as suggested by Windy Dryden in Chapter 16) can appear attractive and pragmatic. However, Humanistic Psychology has historically stood for counter-cultural values that challenge head-on the taken-for-granted assumptions of a modern technocratic society; and so for many of its adherents, it would be in grave danger of abandoning its key cultural role of 'ideology critique', if it were to collude with 'audit culture' values and practices (King and Moutsou, 2010). So when Dryden urges us to really 'get our act together', sharpen up our theory and self-publicity, publish some key texts, and in the process, earn legitimacy and recognition within the mainstream, some will likely think long and hard before going down this path. Thus, in Chapter 15, we find Nick Totton writing that:

> Humanistic therapy ... has paid less attention than other therapy modalities to clarifying and defining its unique positions in terms recognizable to administrators. This is *in itself* a reason to defend the independence of humanistic work, as a terrain where freedom is recognized as an inherent value – a powerful position worth defending ....

However Keith Tudor argues in this book that Humanistic Psychology 'is, in many respects, mainstream and institutional, if not institutionalized' already. So clearly, even within Humanistic Psychology itself, there are very different views on the extent to which the approach has already become part of 'the mainstream'.

If it *is* the case that a poorly defined and inherently 'undefinable' humanistic approach is floundering amidst the current audit-obsessed *Zeitgeist*, is this an acceptable – indeed, unavoidable – price to pay for retaining Humanistic Psychology's integrity and counter-cultural edge? For if Humanistic Psychology and its advocates were to embrace and merely 'fit in with' current cultural toxicities, who would be left to hold the counter-cultural space (see below) that many believe to be necessary for any healthy and growthful society? As postmodern theorist David Harvey poignantly shows, fitting in with the status quo can only ever generate what he terms 'status quo theory' (Harvey, 1973) – surely the very antithesis of what Humanistic Psychology represents and stands for.

So we certainly don't see any pat solutions or easy answers emerging from this book. Indeed, those of us with some postmodern (Hansen's Chapter 10) and phenomenological and/or existential sympathies might well argue that it is actually vitally important *not* to close down what Humanistic Psychology might be or become, or to fetishize the quest for clarity of identity and definition. From this perspective, an intrinsically indissoluble aspect of Humanistic Psychology is precisely that it *is* counter-cultural, difficult to pin down and codify, with a fluid and ever-evolving identity whose very mutability is part of what the approach is all about. And if being marginalized relative to mainstream culture is the price we have to pay for staying true to these values, then, perhaps, some would say, so be it. Richard Mowbray wrote eloquently about this issue nearly two decades ago in his seminal text *The Case Against Psychotherapy Registration*. Referring to what he calls 'Preserving the Fringe' (the title of his Chapter 27) – or a kind of 'counter-cultural space' – Mowbray wrote that Humanistic Psychology and the human potential movement:

> ... must stay on the margin and not be 'absorbed', not be tempted by the carrots of recognition, respectability and financial security into reverting to the mainstream but rather remain – on the 'fringe' – as a source that stimulates, challenges convention and 'draws out' the unrealized potential for 'being' in the members of that society.
>
> (1995: 198–9)

And he continued, 'A society needs a healthy fringe ... *it must not be absorbed into the mainstream* – which would stultify it with 'establishment' thinking and respectability' (p. 199, our italics).

A caveat here is that of course the 'fringe' does not remain fixed. The 'cultural margins' are themselves always moving, and that which may have once seemed incontrovertibly radical and 'counter-cultural' may be experienced as conservative and stuck-in-the-past by a younger generation. We can't help wondering whether some aspect of this dynamic might account for the increasing average age of the humanistic community. If so, it is even more crucial that humanistic practitioners and academics be ruthlessly honest with themselves regarding taken-for-granted assumptions and potential blind spots. We hope this book might, amongst other things, facilitate reflection on such issues, because it is by no means unthinkable, in an age of increasing personal autonomy and 'service user' involvement, that Humanistic Psychology, at least in some of its more overtly professionalized and status-obsessed manifestations, could come to be perceived as *itself* part of an unhealthy and even redundant 'expert-driven' status quo, rather than the empowering, counter-cultural force which its traditional adherents would wish and believe it to be.

Editing this book has helped to remind us that there are also quite different humanistic *identities*, as between American, British and (no doubt) other Humanistic Psycholog*ies*; and that in a culturally relative world, it seems wholly apt that different cultures should indeed generate different manifestations of the humanistic impulse, and that therefore there never can be one, universal definition of Humanistic Psychology. Thus, John Heron (Chapter 21) reminds us that the founding fathers of Humanistic Psychology in the USA were self-proclaimed atheists; whereas in the UK, both of the Johns who are very much the respected Elders of British Humanistic Psychology, John Heron and John Rowan, see transpersonal and spiritual concerns as being central to the humanistic impulse (Chapters 21 and 12, respectively). So the cultural struggle between secular and transpersonal humanism is one that is also playing itself out within Humanistic Psychology itself; and far from this being a problem or an unwelcome contradiction, one might ask, why should Humanistic Psychology itself not faithfully reflect the cultural and evolutionary struggles and arguments that are preoccupying humankind at this juncture in the evolution of human consciousness? (e.g. see Hansen, 2012; Rowan, 2012).

Might Humanistic Psychology, then, help to build a philosophical bridge between the transpersonal/spiritual and the secular? Certainly, at this time there appears to be a dire need for a counterbalance to the extreme and fundamentalist visions of both science and religion which increasingly predominate, and Humanistic Psychology, with its emphasis on mutual respect and diversity, appears well placed to facilitate some common ground. What sometimes seems to be absent amidst the sound and fury of clashing ideologies is something which humanistic approaches have historically been very good at: fostering a sense of the significance and value of relationships and, crucially, the necessity for authentic, human *encounter* as a fundamental foundation for understanding, movement and creativity.

Another tension within Humanistic Psychology is that between modernity and postmodernity – that is, whether or not to embrace, or at least forge some kind of relationship with, the postmodern, post-structuralist and social constructionist thinking represented by theorists like Nietzsche, Derrida, Foucault, Lacan, and others? Again, there are very different viewpoints on this *within* Humanistic Psychology, with writers like Jim Hansen (Chapter 10) strongly supporting an engagement with postmodern thought, while others, such as John Rowan (2000), are sceptical of the value and the relevance of such engagements. Certainly, some hallowed Humanistic Psychology notions, like that of the unitary, actualizing 'self', *are* fundamentally problematized by postmodern thinking (as Hansen argues); yet our hunch is that many, if not most critical humanists are actually instinctively drawn to such deconstuctionist ideas, and are also open to having the 'shadow' side of our humanist ontologies and epistemologies subjected to a critical deconstructionist 'gaze'. Indeed, it might well be that – to coin a phrase – 'scratch a humanist and you'll likely find an incipient post-structuralist underneath'! – and also, perhaps, vice versa! Certainly, at the very least we should perhaps be open to building bridges with adjacent cosmologies such as these, just as Humanistic Psychology has historically found, and is currently finding, a great deal of common ground with the existential and phenomenological thinking of the likes of Heidegger, Husserl, Merleau-Ponty, Buber and Levinas (e.g. Loewenthal and Snell, 2003; Orange, 2009).

Another key theme with which Humanistic Psychology today has to grapple is that of identity and (dare we use the term!) 'branding'. In an age where – rightly or wrongly – clear and unambiguous 'branding' increasingly seems to be a taken-for-granted requirement, can Humanistic Psychology (and the therapeutic practices that have historically aligned themselves with it) effectively 'sell itself' without compromising its core values? Fundamentally, should Humanistic Psychology seek ways to establish its own place at the mainstream 'high table', or does *intrinsically* counter-cultural humanistic praxis still 'hold' something crucially important which is absent from other therapeutic and cultural discourses – something which desperately needs preserving from the dead hand of bureaucracy, fear-driven regulation, and the professional 'status wars' that have characterized the therapy world for decades?

In her Chapter 17, Dina Glouberman writes that 'if we look closely at some of the areas where we [Humanistic Psychology] have been pioneers, we will see that the ideas may have been adopted, but the application has narrowed so that they no longer represent the original vision'. For us this is a crucial point, for it is commonly argued that there is a very real sense in which 'we are all humanists now', and that most core humanistic ideas have long since been assimilated into the mainstream. Glouberman rightly cautions us to be aware that it can often *look* as if mainstream culture has been humanized, when in reality this is far from being the case. As J.-F. Lyotard might have said (Sim, 2001), the march of 'the inhuman' is always something that we have to be vigilant about.

In Chapter 20, Jill Hall, in offering an Iain McGilchrist-informed evolution-of-consciousness perspective, also emphasizes the contemporary relevance of Humanistic Psychology. She writes that 'Humanistic Psychology recognized that a fundamental shift was necessary: an expansion in how we see ourselves as human beings. *This needs to be affirmed afresh*' (our italics). Hall goes on to highlight the importance of the 'holding of a well-grounded space or context that is inclusive of the spiritual dimension', with 'the integration of such experience in the lives of individuals [being] one of our ... most crucial tasks'; and of a 'reconnect[ion] with the source that enabled the courageous and innovative growth of the Humanistic Psychology movement'. For Hall, if it can stay true to its core values, Humanistic Psychology 'will ... ride on a further tide of courageous innovation'.

Notwithstanding these passionately held positions, with which we have much sympathy, in our view Humanistic Psychology should also strive to be a broad-enough 'church' to encompass a range of principled positions – e.g. those who wish to reconnect with core values (*à la* Jill Hall), those who really believe that we need to sharpen up our theoretical act (e.g. Dryden and Totton, Chapters 16 and 15 respectively), and those who sincerely believe that it *is* possible to 'professionalize', codify and make Humanistic Psychology 'respectable' (Chalfont, Chapter 13), without *necessarily* selling our soul (Edwards, 1992). Here, perhaps, is where Andrew Samuels' perspective on pluralism becomes crucial (Samuels, 1997); for rather than seeing these as contradictory positions that somehow need to be resolved and extinguished, these ongoing dynamic tensions and conflicts are actually (healthily) *constitutive of* what Humanistic Psychology always has been and will be – indeed, they are arguably its very lifeblood. On this view, then, perhaps we need to let the 'contraries' continue to generate 'progression' (to misquote that quintessentially humanistic visionary William Blake), and even to *welcome* The Other who disagrees with us, as they both help us to define our own position, and also help us to imagine how it – and we – might conceivably be different. It can be challenging at times to hold open a space in which to honour diverse subjectivities and divergent opinions, to resist the temptation to either retreat into entrenched positions or expediently subsume our differences into an incongruent and false unity; yet what ultimately could be a more humanistic undertaking? That has been our driving ethos and overarching intent throughout the selection and editing process for this book; we hope that, at least to some extent, we may have succeeded.

Attempting to summarise a book such as this is a hazardous, even impossible exercise. Some may say that Humanistic Psychology has 'had its day', others that it has been successfully assimilated into society. Whatever the case, it seems to us that a humanistic perspective remains, in its essence, a progressive and potentially emancipatory force. Without the existence of the 'healthy fringe' mentioned earlier, it is difficult to imagine how such promising counter-cultural innovations as the UK Independent Practitioners Network (or IPN; e.g. House, 2004; Totton, 2011), or Denis Postle's recent important work on what he terms the 'PsyCommons' (Postle, 2012, 2013) could have taken root and begun to flourish. These are just two of a number of important humanistic initiatives that certainly warranted greater coverage in this book. We do believe that we live in a time when humanistic values are urgently needed and under threat, and that therefore their explicit re-affirmation is essential.

Humanistic Psychology, at its best, provides us with some of the theoretical tools, the ideological commitment, and the practical means with which to challenge the dominance of the scientistic-technocratic, 'evidence-based', over-professionalized, expertise-fixated, pathologizing, instrumentalist, inauthentic and eco-abusive mentalities that are so prevalent in late-modern culture. And notwithstanding its arguable flakiness, its sometimes infuriating definitional fluidity, and its occasional lapses into self-satisfied moral superiority, Humanistic Psychology offers an explicit privileging of authenticity, creativity and imagination, uniqueness, phenomenological experiencing, curiosity, irony and paradox, human potential, spontaneity, and the power of empathy and love – an extraordinary list of attributes, whose very existence, with all its richness and attendant contradictions, provides a rich source of encouragement for our belief in a fruitful and exciting future for Humanistic Psychology. For if Humanistic Psychology didn't already exist, there is surely no doubt whatsoever that we would urgently be needing to invent it.

References

Edwards, G. (1992) 'Does psychotherapy need a soul?', in W. Dryden and C. Feltham (eds), *Psychotherapy and Its Discontents* (pp. 194–224), Buckingham: Open University Press.

Hansen, J.T. (2012) 'The future of humanism: cultivating the humanities' impulse in mental health culture', *Self & Society: International Journal for Humanistic Psychology*, 40 (1): 21–5.

Harvey, D. (1973) *Social Justice and the City*, London: Edward Arnold; (revised edn, 2009).

House, R. (2004) 'An unqualified good: the IPN as a path through and beyond professionalization', *Self & Society: International Journal for Humanistic Psychology*, 32 (4): 14–22.

King, L. and Moutsou, C. (eds) (2010) *Rethinking Audit Cultures: A Critical Look at Evidence-based Practice in Psychotherapy and Beyond*, Ross-on-Wye: PCCS Books.

Loewenthal, D. and Snell, R. (2003) *Post-modernism for Psychotherapists: A Critical Reader*, Hove: Brunner-Routledge.

Mowbray, R. (1995) *The Case Against Psychotherapy Registration: A Conservation Issue for the Human Potential Movement*, London: Trans Marginal Press; downloadable as a pdf file free of charge at: www.transmarginalpress.co.uk

Orange, D.M. (2009) *Thinking for Clinicians: Philosophical Resources for Contemporary Psychoanalysis and the Humanistic Therapies*, London: Routledge.

Postle, D. (2012) *Therapy Futures: Obstacles and Opportunities (Introducing the Psycommons)*, London: Wentworth Learning Resources (available from Lulu.com).

Postle, D. (2013) 'Beyond market and state – the Commons and Commoning'; report on the Economics and the Common(s) Conference, 'From Seed Form to Core Paradigm', Berlin, 22–4 May 2013; see http://psycommons.wordpress.com/2013/06/03/beyond-market-and-state-the-commons-and-commoning/ (accessed 10 August 2013).

Rowan, J. (2000) 'Humanistic Psychology and the social construction of reality', *British Psychological Society Psychotherapy Section Newsletter*, 29 (December): 1–8.

Rowan, J. (2012) Letter to the editors, *Self & Society: International Journal for Humanistic Psychology*, 40 (2): 64.

Samuels, A. (1997) 'Pluralism and psychotherapy: what is good training?', in R. House and N. Totton (eds), *Implausible Professions: Arguments for Pluralism and Autonomy in Psychotherapy and Counselling* (pp. 199–214), Ross-on-Wye: PCCS Books (2nd edn, 2011, pp. 221–37).

Sim, S. (2001) *Lyotard and the Inhuman*, Cambridge: Icon Books.

Totton, N. (2011) 'The Independent Practitioners Network: a new model of accountability', in R. House and N. Totton (eds), *Implausible Professions: Arguments for Pluralism and Autonomy in Psychotherapy and Counselling* (pp. 315–22), Ross-on-Wye: PCCS Books (1st edn, 1997).

Afterword

Maureen O'Hara

The humanistic voice was introduced into psychology as a challenge not only to the methods of psychotherapy and research promoted by behaviorists, biomedicalists and psychoanalysts, but as an antidote to the dehumanization, alienation and anomie of modernity. The founders rejected the idea that human beings are just like any other animal – reducible to stimulus–response cycles or driven by unalterable predispositions. They held up a vision of ourselves as more than that and insisted on respect for the dignity of personhood and for the right to realize one's unique potential. For this they were seen – often dismissively – as 'counter-cultural' and held responsible for the narcissistic excesses of the so-called 'me generation'. These days, when so much of our mental health policy is based on a round of diagnostic abstractions that is propelled by rampant bio-reductionism, their warnings about the loss of reverence for what is deeply human – our capacity to love, imagine, sacrifice, build relationships and communities based in justice and mutual respect – appear more prophetic than contrarian.

Humanistic Psychology was both a response to and driver of intense cultural upheaval in the 1960s. Maslow, who was sometimes messianic, wanted to bring about a humanistic utopia, a 'psychology for the peace table'. The more understated Rogers sought the conditions that would enable people to actualize their inherent potential. A generation of young and not so young people carried dog-eared books by Rollo May, Erich Fromm, Fritz Perls, Abe Maslow and Carl Rogers into their bold experimentations with freer forms of expression and new ways of being. Oppressed people of color, women, sexual minorities, people with disabilities also found in these ideas a powerful antidote to reductionist behaviorist and Freudian concepts that often rationalized abuse and blamed the victims. Humanistic ideas changed the way people thought of themselves. In humanistic psychotherapy sessions, growth centers, schools and universities, churches, community groups, workplace training, mental health facilities and even the military and police forces – in fact anywhere where people asked existential questions about what it means to be a person and how we should live with other persons – a more expansive, emotionally rich view of human potential formed in the public mind.

The 21st century is also a time of cultural upheaval, and human freedom and dignity are once more under siege. The modernist consensus is fracturing, provoking widespread uncertainty and mental distress. There are huge external threats looming that will require urgent and coordinated action among people who know how to love, collaborate and offer each other mutual respect to get things done. Leaders in modernist bureaucracies – the same people who accused humanistic psychologists of encouraging narcissism and self-interest – hang on to a neurotic belief that there is a technological fix to these problems, but it is clear from the endless political deadlock and turmoil on the streets, that there is no such solution. The key to making the changes necessary to avoid global catastrophe and build a just and peaceful global society will be more psychological than technical.

Humanistic Psychology was offered as a more hopeful and authentic view of human potential and as an antidote to an alienated view driven by hyper-rational, reductionist and individualist thinking of modernity. As lives are increasingly defined by systems run by computers and impersonal algorithms that bet on us behaving like self-interested automatons driven by 'selfish genes', a humanistic alternative is far more than counter-cultural. It actually provides the intellectual framework for an emerging new culture. The chapters in this book offer concrete examples of ways in which a deeply Humanistic Psychology contributes to rehumanization in our sense of who we are as persons and what kind of civilization we must build if we are to have a future worth living in. It is a welcome contribution.

Contributors

CAROLINE BRAZIER is course leader of the Tariki Psychotherapy Training Programme in the Other-Centred Approach and the Ten Directions Programme in Ecotherapy. Author of six books on Buddhism and psychotherapy, including *Buddhist Psychology* (Constable and Robinson, 2003) and *Other-Centred Therapy* (O-Books, 2009), and many articles and papers, Caroline travels internationally, teaching and running workshops. She practises as a psychotherapist and supervisor from her base in the Tariki Buddhist community, which is situated in Narborough, Leicestershire (www.buddhistpsychology.info). Caroline has three adult children and two brand new grandchildren.

ALEXANDRA CHALFONT is a UKCP-registered psychotherapist, a trainer, supervisor and executive coach. She works integrally–relationally in private practice with individuals and couples in West London. Recent specialisms have been mixed-culture relationships and intergenerational trauma. Over the years, cross-cultural and intercultural understanding, literature and philosophy have been continuing core interests and themes as an educator, translator and communications consultant in Europe. Alexandra is an associate editor of *Self & Society*, was its managing editor for six years, and is on the International Advisory Board of the *International Journal of Psychotherapy*. She currently serves as co-chair of the Association of Humanistic Psychology, and as chair of the Book Editorial Board of the UKCP.

WINDY DRYDEN is Professor of Psychotherapeutic Studies, Goldsmiths University of London, and a Fellow of the British Psychological Society and the British Association for Counselling and Psychotherapy. Windy has authored or edited nearly 200 books, including *Counselling in a Nutshell* (2nd edn, Sage, 2011) and *Rational Emotive Behaviour Therapy* (Routledge, 2009). He edits 20 book series, including the 'Distinctive Features in CBT' series (Routledge) and the 'Counselling in a Nutshell' series (Sage). Major interests are in Rational

Emotive Behaviour Therapy and CBT; the counselling–coaching interface; pluralism; and writing short, accessible self-help books for the general public. Correspondence: w.dryden@gold.ac.uk

COLIN FELTHAM is Emeritus Professor of Critical Counselling Studies, Sheffield Hallam University. His most recent publications are *Failure* (Acumen, 2012), *The Sage Handbook of Counselling and Psychotherapy*, 3rd edn (ed. with Ian Horton, Sage, 2012) and *Counselling and Counselling Psychology: A Critical Examination* (PCCS Books, 2013). Colin lives and teaches in Denmark, and is an external examiner for training courses and doctoral projects in the UK. He has a regular 'interview' feature in *Therapy Today* magazine and is on the boards of the *British Journal of Guidance and Counselling*, the *Irish Journal of Psychology*, and *Self & Society: International Journal for Humanistic Psychology*.

HARRIS L. FRIEDMAN, Ph.D., is Research Professor of Psychology (Retired) at the University of Florida and Professor Emeritus at Saybrook University, as well as a Florida-licensed psychologist. He received his Ph.D. in Clinical Psychology at Georgia State University, holds the Diploma in Clinical Psychology, as well as in Organizational and Business Consulting Psychology, from the American Board of Professional Psychology, and is a Fellow of the American Psychological Association. Harris is past president of the International Transpersonal Association, and serves as senior editor of the *International Journal of Transpersonal Studies* and associate editor of *The Humanistic Psychologist*. He has published over 200 professional books, book chapters and articles. Currently he is co-editing *The Wiley-Blackwell Handbook of Transpersonal Psychology*, *The Praeger Handbook of Applied Transpersonal Psychology* (2 vols), *The Praeger Handbook on Social Justice and Psychology* (2 vols), and *Advances in Parapsychological Research* (Volumes 9 & 10).

DINA GLOUBERMAN, Ph.D., is the visionary co-founder and director, since 1979, of Skyros Holidays, world leader in holistic holidays and trainings. She is also the author of the classic books *Life Choices, Life Changes* and *Joy of Burnout*. Formerly Senior Lecturer in Psychology and a consultant editor, she leads Imagework training courses internationally, is Honorary President of the International Imagework Association and a psychotherapist. Her focus now is on understanding and guiding people through turning points and new beginnings, and she is writing a book series entitled *You Are What You Imagine*, the first book of which is *From Difficult Times to New Beginnings*. Contact: www.dinaglouberman.com; www.skyros.com

JILL HALL was born in South Africa into an environment of extreme inequality and oppression, and cannot remember a time when she was not disturbed, puzzled and fascinated about what it means to be a human being. She moved to London in her late teens, working as an actress until becoming a mother and philosophy student. Attracted to the arena of self-development in the early days of Humanistic Psychology, she later became a tutor at the Institute of Biodynamic Psychology. She now runs weekend residential groups and has been a guest lecturer for various professional bodies and universities. She is the author of *The Reluctant Adult: An Exploration of Choice* (Prism Press, 1993).

JAMES T. HANSEN is a professor at Oakland University in the Department of Counseling. His primary scholarly interests are philosophical and theoretical issues in counseling and critical examination of contemporary mental health culture. Dr Hansen has published about 50 refereed articles in leading counseling journals. He is co-editor of an award-winning book on humanism, and his new book on philosophical issues in counseling will be published in early 2014. Dr Hansen has over 25 years of experience as a practitioner, supervisor and consultant.

JOHN HERON is a co-director the South Pacific Centre for Human Inquiry in New Zealand. He was founder and director of the Human Potential Research Project, University of Surrey; assistant director, British Postgraduate Medical Federation, University of London; director, International Centre for Co-operative Inquiry, Volterra, Italy. John was also a co-founder in the UK of the Association of Humanistic Psychology Practitioners (AHPP), Co-counselling International, the Institute for the Development of Human Potential, the New Paradigm Research Group, the Research Council for Complementary Medicine. He is a researcher, author, facilitator and trainer in co-counselling, co-operative inquiry, educational development, group facilitation, management development, personal and transpersonal development, and professional development in the helping professions. His books include *Feeling and Personhood*, 1992; *Group Facilitation*, 1993; *Co-operative Inquiry*, 1996; *Sacred Science*, 1998; *The Complete Facilitator's Handbook*, 1999; *Helping the Client*, 2001; and *Participatory Spirituality*, 2006.

LOUIS HOFFMAN, Ph.D., is an executive faculty member and director of the Existential, Humanistic, and Transpersonal Psychology Specialization at Saybrook University. He served as president of the Society for Humanistic Psychology (Division 32 of the American Psychological Association) from 2012 to 2013 and serves on editorial boards of the *Journal of Humanistic Psychology*, *The Humanistic Psychologist*, *Janus Head*, and *PsycCRITIQUES*. Dr Hoffman has five books to his credit, including *Existential Psychology East-West* and *Brilliant Sanity: Buddhist Approaches to Psychotherapy*. Additionally, Dr Hoffman is active in promoting international dialogues on existential psychology, particularly in China and Southeast Asia.

LOIS HOLZMAN, Ph.D., is an advocate for conceptual tools and practices that empower people to transform the alienation and passivity of our culture. A developmental psychologist and activist scholar, she promotes postmodern, culture-change approaches to human growth and learning. Lois is director of the East Side Institute (www.EastSideInstitute.org), an international training and research center for new approaches to therapeutics, education and community building; and a founder of the biennial 'Performing the World' conference, which brings together hundreds of practitioners, scholars and researchers, for whom theatrical performance and the creative arts are essential for personal and social–political transformation. With colleague Fred Newman, the late public philosopher and founder of social therapy, she has advanced social therapeutics, a 'psychology of becoming' that incorporates play, performance and practical philosophy to inspire life-long human development through group creativity. Lois' 2009 *Vygotsky at Work and Play* and Newman and Holzman's *Lev Vygotsky Revolutionary Scientist* (2013 Classic Text Edition) have introduced psychologists, educators and helping professionals the world over to an activist-take on the methodological writings of psychologist Lev Vygotsky.

RICHARD HOUSE, Ph.D., C.Psychol., lectures in Early Childhood, University of Winchester, formerly lecturing in psychotherapy at Roehampton. Co-editor of *Self & Society* and associate editor of *Psychotherapy and Politics International,* Richard is founder-member of the Independent Practitioners Network and the Alliance for Counselling and Psychotherapy. His books include *In, Against and Beyond Therapy* (PCCS, 2010), *Therapy Beyond Modernity* (Karnac, 2003), and *Against and For CBT* (PCCS Books, 2008, co-edited with Del Loewenthal). A campaigner for childhood, a trained Steiner teacher and founder-member of the renowned Open EYE Campaign, in 2006, 2007 and 2011 Richard organized the three *Daily Telegraph* Open Letters on the state of modern childhood. He loves John McLaughlin's Mahavishnu Orchestra, and trying (and failing) to work less hard. Email: richard.house@winchester.ac.uk

GAIE HOUSTON used to be a playwright, has worked on the management board of a large psychiatric hospital, been a local councillor, worked as a television presenter and in other roles in the BBC, is a senior lecturer at The Gestalt Centre London, teaches and supervises in the UK and in many other countries, and has just published her tenth book on aspects of psychotherapy and group behaviour. Gaie is also the author of *Gestalt Counselling in a Nutshell* (Sage, 2013). She is specially interested in using Humanistic Psychology in education and organizations. You can contact Gaie via her website, www.gaiehouston.co.uk

DAVID KALISCH, M.A.(Cantab), UKCP-registered psychotherapist, UKAHPP (Aff.Member), AHP(B). After working initially in social work and education, David trained in Gestalt therapy and then in core process psychotherapy, and subsequently established The Centre for Humanistic Psychology and Counselling (CHPC) in Exeter, Devon, where he and his colleagues have run courses in Humanistic Psychology, Humanistic counselling, Gestalt psychotherapy, Gestalt groupwork and personal development for over 20 years. David also has private practices in Exeter and Taunton and has written a number of articles for *Self & Society* journal, which he now co-edits, having formerly served on the editorial board for many years. He lives with his long-term partner, Christine, in Devon, and has a grown-up son and daughter, three grown-up stepchildren and seven grandchildren.

Contributors

STANLEY KRIPPNER, Ph.D., is Professor of Psychology at Saybrook University in San Francisco. He has been president of both the Association for Humanistic Psychology and the Society for Humanistic Psychology, and has received the Pathfinder Award for his contributions to this field, as well as the Ashley Montagu Peace Award and the Lifetime Achievement Award from the International Association for the Study of Dreams. In 2002, Stanley received the American Psychological Association Award for Distinguished Contributions to the International Advancement of Psychology. His books include *Personal Mythology*; *Demystifying Shamans and Their World*; *Haunted by Combat*; and *The Voice of Rolling Thunder*.

DEREK LAWTON works as a person-centred psychotherapist, and after 37 years of service he retired from his NHS practice and UKCP registration at the beginning of 2013. Derek was honoured to be awarded UKAHPP Honorary Life Membership in 2011. Between 2007 and 2012 he was a UKAHPP delegate to the UKCP: HIP College, where he also held the office of College treasurer and was thus a member of the College Executive. Derek continues to sit on the UKAHPP Board as vice-chair. As treasurer, he is a co-ordinating group member of the British Association for the Person-Centred Approach. He grew up in Newcastle upon Tyne, and now lives with his wife Anne and son Jack in Yorkshire. In other circles Derek is known for producing the complete music cues CD box set to the classic 1960s TV series 'The Prisoner'.

JENNIFER MAIDMAN, MBACP, Dip.Couns., has made music for over 40 years, performing with Joan Armatrading, Gerry Rafferty, David Sylvian, Robert Wyatt, The Proclaimers, Bonnie Raitt and Van Morrison, amongst others. She has written for Boy George and Sam Brown, and produced albums for Paul Brady, Murray Head, Linda McCartney, and her partner, trombonist Annie Whitehead. She played extensively with the original Penguin Café Orchestra, and recently formed 'The Orchestra that Fell to Earth' with other original PCO members. Jennifer has been involved with human potential work since the 1970s and has written for *Therapy Today* magazine and *Self & Society* journal, which she also co-edits. She trained as a humanistic counsellor with Noreen Emmans and Jimmy McGhee, and is a member of the British Association for Counselling and Psychotherapy and the 'Leonard Piper' group of the Independent Practitioners Network. Jennifer lives with her partner, by the sea, in East Kent.

SEAMUS NASH is a UKCP-registered psychotherapist working within a hospice in West Yorkshire. He was a UKAHPP delegate to the UKCP: HIP College, 2008–12. Seamus is passionate about the person-centred approach, remains optimistic about people, the planet and life. He is currently a doctoral student researching practitioner's meaning of person-centredness at the University of Huddersfield. Seamus believes that his practice is informed by being a father, and his children have taught him much about living and 'being' person-centred. He is equally passionate about music, guitars and spirituality.

Contributors

MAUREEN O'HARA is Professor of Psychology, National University, La Jolla, California; President Emerita, Saybrook University, founding member International Futures Forum (Scotland and USA), a 'learning, thinking and action group' working with individuals and groups trying to undertake wise action in a world we don't understand and can't control. She practiced for two decades as a humanistic psychotherapist and worked closely with Carl Rogers for over 18 years, training counselors and therapists in many countries, including several years in Brazil. Maureen's current preoccupations include the impact on psychological coherence and emotional wellbeing of 21st century cultural shifts. A prolific writer: most recently *Dancing at the Edge: Competence, Culture and Organization in the 21st Century* (2012, Triarchy Press) with Graham Leicester, and co-editor with M. Cooper, P.F. Schmid and A.C. Bohart of *The Handbook of Person-Centred Psychotherapy and Counselling* (2013, Palgrave Macmillan). More about Maureen can be found at www.maureen. ohara.net

DANIEL B. PITCHFORD, Ph.D., is on the faculty at Saybrook University, and co-developed and co-leads the University's trauma certificate and specialization programs. He also developed and led the Trauma Specialization within University's former Psy.D. program. Dr Pitchford is an award-winning researcher of his work with traumatic stress (Rollo May Award for his research in traumatic stress and combat trauma) with interests in trauma psychology, suicidology, culture, meaning making, death studies, loss, and existential and transpersonal psychology. He has authored and co-authored several research articles on various interests, including his latest publication, *Post-traumatic Stress Disorder* (Greenwood Press, 2012).

STEVEN PRITZKER is director of the M.A. and Ph.D. Creativity Studies Specialization and The Creativity Studies Certificate at Saybrook University. He is co-editor-in-chief of *The Encyclopedia of Creativity* published by Academic Press. Steven is a Fellow of the American Psychological Association and president-elect of Division 10 (Psychology of Aesthetics, Creativity and the Arts). His research has examined creativity and film, collaborative creativity in writing and business; creativity and spirituality; audience flow; comedians and longevity and the creative process in high-achieving writers. Dr Pritzker is a writer and creativity coach who has written and produced over 200 episodes of network television.

RUTH RICHARDS, Ph.D. (Education) and M.D. (Harvard Medical School), is a licensed psychologist (Massachusetts) and Board Certified Psychiatrist, working as educational psychologist and research psychiatrist. Professor of Psychology at Saybrook Graduate School, Ruth won the Arnheim Award from Division 10 of the American Psychological Association for Outstanding Lifetime Achievement in Psychology and the Arts. She has written numerous papers and chapters, and edited two books – most recently, *Everyday Creativity and New Views of Human Nature* (APA Books, 2007).

ANDY ROGERS has worked in the therapy field since the late 1990s. He trained at the University of East Anglia's Centre for Counselling Studies and now coordinates a counselling service in a large college of further and higher education. He has published numerous articles, reviews and columns in a variety of therapy journals, and been an active participant in the Alliance for Counselling and Psychotherapy. Andy is also a father, contemporary music obsessive and half-decent home cook.

JOHN ROWAN is well known as a humanistic therapist and writer, and has also done a good deal of work in the transpersonal area. His more recent efforts in the area of the Dialogical Self have borne fruit both in his work and in his writing. John is a Fellow of the British Psychological Society, and also of the British Association for Counselling and Psychotherapy and the UK Council for Psychotherapy. He has consistently pushed for more attention to the Primal and to the Transpersonal, which he has dubbed 'the Terrible Twins of Therapy'. His most recent book is *Personification: Using the Dialogical Self in Psychotherapy and Counselling*.

ANDREW SAMUELS is Professor of Analytical Psychology at the University of Essex, and holds visiting chairs at New York, Roehampton and Goldsmiths College, London. A Jungian training analyst, he also works internationally as a political consultant. Andrew is a member of the Association for Humanistic Psychology and has been a long-standing member of the editorial board of *Self & Society* journal. He is the former chair of the UK Council for Psychotherapy (UKCP), and former honorary secretary of the International Association for Analytical Psychology. Andrew is also co-founder of Psychotherapists and Counsellors for Social Responsibility (CPSR) and of the Alliance for Counselling and Psychotherapy, and a founder board member of the International Association for Relational Psychoanalysis. His many books have been translated into 19 languages. Contact: www.andrewsamuels.com

KIRK J. SCHNEIDER, Ph.D., is a leading spokesperson for contemporary existential-humanistic psychology. Dr Schneider is the recent past editor of the *Journal of Humanistic Psychology* (2005–2012), vice-president of the Existential-Humanistic Institute (EHI), and adjunct faculty at Saybrook University, Teachers College, Columbia University, and the California Institute of Integral Studies. A Fellow of the American Psychological Association (APA), Dr Schneider has published over 100 articles and chapters and has authored or edited ten books. His most recent books are *The Polarized Mind: Why It's Killing Us and What We Can Do About It; Awakening to Awe;* and *Existential-Humanistic Therapy*.

ROBIN SHOHET is co-author of *Supervision in the Helping Professions* (Open University Press, 4th edn, 2012) and editor of *Passionate Supervision* and *Supervision as Transformation* (both published by Jessica Kingsley). Robin has been teaching supervision through the Centre for Supervision and Team Development (www.cstdlondon.co.uk) for over 30 years. He has been researching forgiveness and its place in therapy since 1999, when he focalized an international conference on that topic at the Findhorn Foundation.

NICK TOTTON is a therapist and trainer with 30 years' experience. Originally a Reichian body therapist, his approach has become broad based and open to the spontaneous and unexpected. Nick holds an MA in Psychoanalytic Studies, and has worked extensively with process-oriented psychology and trained as a craniosacral therapist; he is currently involved with ecopsychology and addressing climate change. He has a grown-up daughter. Nick has written several books, including *Psychotherapy and Politics*; *Press When Illuminated: New and Selected Poems*; *Wild Therapy*; and most recently, *Not a Tame Lion*, published by PCCS Books. See www.nicktotton.net. He lives in Cornwall with his partner and grows vegetables.

KEITH TUDOR is a Certified Transactional Analyst (psychotherapy) and a Teaching and Supervising Transactional Analyst (psychotherapy). He is an associate professor and Head of the Department of Psychotherapy and Counselling at AUT University, Auckland, Aotearoa New Zealand. Keith retains his voluntary professional registration with the UK Council for Psychotherapy, which he has held since 1994, for ten years of which (1999–2008) he was, additionally, a registered group psychotherapist and facilitator through full membership of the Association of Humanistic Psychology Practitioners (UKAHPP). Keith is the author/editor of eleven books, is editor of *Psychotherapy and Politics International*, the co-editor of *Ata: Journal of Psychotherapy Aotearoa New Zealand*, and an associate editor of *Self & Society*.

HEWARD WILKINSON, D.Psych., UKCP Honorary Fellow, chair of the UKCP Humanistic and Integrative Psychotherapy College, is based in London. Author of *The Muse as Therapist: A New Poetic Paradigm for Psychotherapy*, he focuses on the interface between religion, philosophy, the arts, and psychotherapy. Heward edited the *International Journal of Psychotherapy*, the journal of the European Association for Psychotherapy, from 1994 to 2004. He loves people, also the natural world, butterflies, the sea, moors and mountains – as well as music, soccer and cricket.
Contact: hewardwilkinson@gmail.com; http://hewardwilkinson.co.uk

Index

A

acceptance and commitment therapy (ACT), 99
ACT: *see* acceptance and commitment therapy
action research: *see* human action research
activist psychology (Holzman), 29–42
activity (theory)
    and postmodernism, 35–6, 38
    vs truth, 37
actualization: *see* actualizing tendency, self-actualization
actualizing tendency, 164
Advaita Vedanta, 108
adversity-activated development, xii
aggression, xii
AHP: *see* Association for Humanistic Psychology
AHPP: *see* UK Association for Humanistic Psychology Practitioners
All Stars Project, 30, 38n, 39–40
Alliance for Counselling and Psychotherapy, 50
Allport, Gordon, 11
Alternative Professional Accountability, 50
American Association for Humanistic Psychology, 101, 138
    third-wave humanism of the, 158
American Board of Examiners in Professional Psychology (1947), 58
American Psychiatric Association, 32
American Psychological Association (APA), 18, 20, 31, 32, 62
    Division 32, 146

Analytic Psychology, Psychoanalytic and Psychodynamic section (UKCP), 141
Anderson, Walter, 101
anti-capitalist protests, 6
    see also capitalism
anti-psychoanalytic dogmatism, 78
'anxiety', ix
APA: *see* American Psychological Association
APPP: *see* Analytic Psychology, Psychoanalytic and Psychodynamic section
'Are We All Humanistic Psychotherapists Now?' (UKCP HIPC), 56
Arons, Mike, 9
art, 102
    expressive arts, xii, 12
    of not-knowing, 66
Association of Black Psychologists, 32
Association for Humanistic Psychology in Britain (AHP), xiii, xxi, 59
Association for Humanistic Psychology Practitioners: *see* UK Association for Humanistic Psychology Practitioners
Association of Transpersonal Psychology, 157
Association for Women in Psychology (AWP), 32
Assured Voluntary Register scheme (AVR), 56
audit culture, 170
audit-mindedness, xix

Index

Augustine, 81
Austin, Stephanie, 31
authenticity, xvii
autonomy, 117
    inflated/false sense of, 135
AVR: *see* Assured Voluntary Register scheme
awe, 18
    awe-based psychology (Schneider), 75

B

BACP: *see* British Association for Counselling and Psychotherapy
Bakhtin, Mikhail, 34
Bandler, R., 128
BAPCA: *see* British Association for the Person-Centred Approach
Barrett-Lennard, G.T., 103
Barron, Frank, 9
Barth, Karl, 81
becoming, 155
    psychology of (Holzman), 29, 35
    spirit-human (Heron), 164
behaviourism, 138, 142, 144
    behavioural model, 73
    as 'second force', 136
Berdyaev, N., 165
Berguno, George, 103, 105
Berne, Eric, xvi, 102
Better Angels of Our Nature, The (Pinker), 6
Bhagavan Das, 164
bio-energetics, 152
bioethics, 23
Bion, Wilfred, 134
bio-reductionism, 177
birth trauma, 5
Blanton, Brad, 5
Bohm, David, 5
Boyeson, Gerda, 154
brain: divided (McGilchrist), 152–3
Brandeis University, 125
Brazier, Caroline, xxi, **93–7,** 179
British Association for Counselling and Psychotherapy (BACP), 56
British Association for the Person-Centred Approach (BAPCA), 48
Buddha (the), 5
    see also Buddhism, Buddhist psychology
Buddhism, xxi, 108
Buddhist psychology, 95–6
Bugental, J.F.T. (James), 98, 141
Bühler, C., 141, 142

Bunting, Madeleine, 150
bureaucracies: modernist, 178
    see also audit culture
burnout, 129
Burrell, G., 143

C

Cain, D.J., 140
Campbell, Joseph, 101
Campbell, P., 164
capitalism, 149–50
    anti-capitalist ideologies, 33
    anti-capitalist protests, 6
    capitalist realism, 5
    Ego Imperialism and, 151
    neo-liberal, 150
Cartesian ego, 165
Case Against Psychotherapy Registration, The (Mowbray), 170
Casement, Patrick, 115
Castillo Theatre, 30
category error, 144
    defined, 142
CBT: *see* cognitive behaviour(al) therapy
Centaur, the (Wilber), 99
'certified charlatans' (Rogers), 58, 67
Chalfont, Alexandra, xxi–xxii, **101–6,** 173, 179
change: *see* therapeutic change
character: Reichian theory of, 113
charisma, 113
CHAT: *see* cultural-historical activity theory
China, 13
Chomsky, Noam, xvi
CHRE: *see* Council for Healthcare Regulatory Excellence
Civilisation and Its Discontents (Freud), 82
Clarkson, Petruska, 4
Cleare-Hoffman, H.P., 14
client-centred psychotherapy: *see* person-centred therapy/approach
coaching: 'Mind, Heart and Soul' (Glouberman), 128
co-counselling
    experience of, 160–1
    see also re-evaluation co-counselling
co-creation, 160, 165
Cognitive Behaviour Therapies (Dryden), 119n
cognitive behaviour(al) therapy (CBT), ix, 4, 119

bolt-on courses in, 117
current dominance of, 66
'Distinctive Features' series (Dryden), 121, 121n
growth in use of, 95
privileging of, 117
territorialism of, 140
see also Rational Emotive Behaviour Therapy
cognitive science, 73
collaboration, 160
vs competition, 133
see also co-operative enquiry
common factors, 47, 48
community, 129
competition: vs collaboration, 133
Conrad, Joseph, 79–82
consciousness
anthropopathology-free, 5
contraction/control of, 151, 154
different states of, 10
evolution of human, xxiii, 149–55
holistic, 20
in humanistic therapy, 114
and relationship to the world, 127
contact disturbances, 113
see also Gestalt therapy
Cooper, Mick, 98, 99, 122
co-operative enquiry, 67
group experience, 161–3
spontaneous animations in, 161–3 *passim*
core conditions, xix, 116, 123
see also empathic understanding, unconditional positive regard
Council for Healthcare Regulatory Excellence (CHRE), 56
counselling and psychotherapy
ambivalence regarding, ix
present moment in (Stern), xix, 77, 128
'relational turn' in, xi
as self-discovery, xv
'state therapy' (Samuels), x
see also acceptance and commitment therapy, cognitive behaviour(al) therapy, expressive arts therapies, Gestalt therapy, humanistic therapy, narrative therapy, other-centred therapy, person-centred therapy, psychoanalysis, solution-focused therapy, transactional analysis

counter-culture, 171, 172, 174, 177, 178
countertransference, 113, 141
Courage to Create, The (May), 11
creative visualization, 129
creativity, 135
capacity for, 140
in Humanistic Psychology, 8–16
protective effect of, 10
psychology and, 10
relational, 13
self-actualizing (Maslow), 9, 10
critical psychology, 31–5
epistemology-based, 33–5
identity-based, 31–2
ideology-based, 32–3
Critical Psychology: An Introduction (Fox and Prilleltensky), 31
critical thinking, 4
cultural-historical activity theory (CHAT), 31, 34

D

daily living experience (Heron), 162
Darwin, Charles: the overlooked, 11
DeCarvalho, R.J., 138–9
defences: Rogers' concepts of, 140
denial, 140
'depression', ix
Descartes, R., 165
development
adversity-activated, xii
developmental holism (Heron), 166
through performance and play, 29
source of (Holzman), 36, 37
development community, the (Holzman), 29–42
diagnosis 113
Diagnostic and Statistical Manual of Mental Disorders
DSM-5, x
homosexuality as 'mental disorder', 32
dialectical methodology, 35
dialogue (Bohm), 5
dignity of personhood, 177
Dilthey, W., 17
distortion, 140
diversity, xi–xii, 173
engagement with, 14
see also pluralism
Divided Self, The (Laing), 102
Doors of Perception (The), and *Heaven and Hell* (Huxley), 102

Index

'dreaming up' (Mindell), 113
drive model, 73
Dryden, Windy, xxii, **119–24**, 169, 173, 179–80
DSM: *see Diagnostic and Statistical Manual of Mental Disorders*
duality: *see* non-duality

E
East-Side Institute for Group and Short Term Psychotherapy (NYC), 30, 38n
eclecticism: technical, 48
ecopsychology, xii–xiii
eco-therapy, 96
ecstasy: *see* MDMA
education/schools, 133, 134
  competitive mass, 5
'Ego Imperialism' (Hall), 149, 151
ego-dominated psyche, 150, 151
  see also Cartesian ego
Eliot, T.S., 83
Elkins, David, 12, 87
Elliott, Professor Robert, 49
Embleton Tudor, Louise, 146
embodied presence, xix
emotional distress: 'war' regarding, ix
empathic understanding, 89
  and mirror neurons, 132
Emperor's New Drugs (The): Exploding the Anti-depressant Myth (Kirsch), x
empirically supported treatments, 90
Enabling Excellence (2011), 56
encounter, 172
entropic forces, 5
epistemology
  anti-positivist, 143
  -based critical psychology, 33–5
  epistemological holism (Heron), 166
  pluralism, 20
Erasmus, 81
Erhard, Werner, 102
Esalen (Calif.), 101
Ethics and Lao Tzu: Intimations of Character (Mendelowitz), 12–13
Eupsychian Network (Maslow), 138
European Association for Humanistic Psychology (EAHP) Congress (1981), xvi
EUROTAS, 98
Everyday Creativity and New Views of Human Nature (Richards), 9

'evidence-based regime'/culture/treatment, xix, 66, 67
  oversimplified, 117
evil, 80
  existence of, 84
  Kafka on, 104
evolution of consciousness, 149–55
  see also consciousness
existence: groundlessness of, 74
existential psychology, 13, 14
  existential crises, 25
  existential-humanistic base, 73–6
  see also existential-integrative approach, existentialism
existential-integrative approach (Schneider), 12
existentialism, 103, 138, 172
  see also existential psychology
experiential dimension, 150, 154
expertise
  absence of, 64
  dependency on, 94
expressive arts therapies, xii, 12

F
Failure (Feltham), 4
Feltham, Colin, xx, **3–7**, 180
Ferrer, Jorge, 100
Ferrucci, Piero, 102
financial crisis, 151
flourishing, 160
Fonagy, Peter, 47, 78
forgiveness, 107
Foster, Jeff, 108
fourth wave (of humanism) (Heron)
  collegiality in the, 165–6
  inaugural statement, 159
  preliminary features, 159–60
Fox, Dennis, 31
Freud, Sigmund, 10, 82, 140, 145
Friedman, Harris L., xx, **17–22**, 180
Friedrich, Kaspar David, 102–3
Fromm, Erich, 177
fully functioning person (Rogers), 96
  attributes of the, 103
Furedi, F., 94
Future in Your Hands, The (UKCP HIPS), 50

G
Gadamer, H.-G., 33
Games People Play (Berne), xvi, 102

Index

gay liberation movement (USA), 32
Gendlin, Eugene, 164
Gergen, Ken, 34
Gestalt therapy, 114, 129
    theory and, 116
Gestalt Therapy (Perls et al.), 128
Girard, René, 81–2
Glouberman, Dina, xxii, **125–30**, 172–3, 180
Goldfried, M.R., 47–8
Gomez, L., 141, 144
government/political systems: learning more about, 134
Gramsci, Antonio, 50
Grinder, J., 128
Grof, Stan, 157
groundlessness of existence, 74
group activity, 38, 39
    group work, 125–6, 133
    small groups, 134
    social therapy, 39
growth, 139
    vs cure, 112, 113
    inherent tendency to, 117
Guide to Humanistic Psychology, A (Rowan), 99

H

Hall, Jill, xxiii, **149–55**, 173, 180–1
Handbook of Humanistic Psychology (Schneider et al.), 98, 121
Hansen, James T., xxi, **86–92**, 170, 172, 181
happiness, 95
Harvey, David, 170
healing, 25
health
    ancient Greek idea of, 127
    holistic notion of, 127
Health Professions Council (UK), 44, 55, 67
healthy fringe (Mowbray), 171, 174
helping professions: hierarchical model of, 90
Henderson Hospital, 126, 127
hermeneutic psychology: *see* phenomenological/hermeneutic psychology
Heron, John, xxiii, **156–68**, 169, 171, 181
hierarchy: in fourth-wave humanism, 165
    initiating, 167
Hinshelwood, B., 140, 141
Hippocrates, 127

HIPS section (UKCP), 44–57 *passim*, 141, 144, 146
    HIPS political group, 46–52 *passim*
    Integrity group, 52
Hoffman, Louis, xx, **8–16**, 181
holistic approaches, 129–30, 134, 140
    appreciation of the human being, 153
    Holistic Psychology (Heron), 159, 166
Holzman, Lois, xx, **29–42**, 181–2
homosexuality
    depathologizing of, 32
    as DSM 'mental disorder', 32
honesty: radical (Blanton), 5
hope, 132
Horney, Karen, 32
House, Richard, xv–xxiv, 123, **169–74**, 182
Houston, Gaie, xxii, **131–5**, 169, 182
Houston, Jean, xvi
'How green is your mind?' (Shohet), 108
human action research (Heron), 160, 163
human nature
    differences about, 142
    humanistic theory of, 139
    Rogerian vs Freudian view of, 145
human potential (movement), 7, 81, 101, 170–1
    demise of, xvii
    see also potential
humanism, xix, xxi, 77–85 *passim*, 86–92, 142, 146
    brief history of, 86–7, 156
    Carl Rogers on, 157
    existential versions of, 80
    fall of, 87
    'fourth-wave' (Heron), xxiii, 156–68
    of the human (Wilkinson), 84
    and Humanistic Psychology, 7
    and humour, 83–4
    as integrative, 84
    and irony, 83
    modernist assumptions of, 89
    as a movement, 81
    and postmodernism, 89
    psychological, 88, 89
    reconstruction of, 159
    Renaissance, 156, 163
    as a sacralizing force, 163
    secular vs transpersonal, 171
    suppression in mental-health culture, 87
    theoretical updating of, 89–90

Index

third wave of, 156–7
waves of, 156
Humanistic and Integrative Section (UKCP): see HIPS section
Humanistic Psychologist, The, 20, 146
Humanistic Psychology, 3–7 *passim*, 144
  aggression and, xii
  alignment with pluralism, 122–3
  alleged demise of, 17, 20
  as alternative to behaviourism/psychoanalysis, 138–9
  as antidote to modernity, 177, 178
  'branding of', 172
  brief history of, 138–9
  clinical ethos, xi
  coaching and, 128
  comparison with psychoanalytic tradition, 141
  contribution to rehumanization, 178
  as counter-cultural force, 171, 172
  courageous innovation in/of, 155
  creativity in, 8–16
  critical, 31–5
  and cultural upheaval, 177
  definition of, 142, 169–70
  different approach to life and, 129
  difficult emotions and, xii
  diverse identities of, 171
  diversity and equalities, xi–xii
  early oppositional identity, 139
  ecopsychology and, xii–xiii
  education/schools and, 133, 134
  encounter and, 172
  engaging with reality, 123
  and the evolution of consciousness, 149–55
  experiential aspect of, 150, 154
  fear and, 150
  as 'flaky', 77
  framework for a new culture, 178
  gratitude to, 125
  groups and, 133, 134
  'healthy fringe' and (Mowbray), 171, 174
  as holistic, 134, 150
  humanism and, 7
  humanism-4 account of (Heron), 166–7
  humanistic–transhumanistic separation, 158–9
  humanizing role of, 145
  imagery and, 128–9
  integration with neuroscience, 132
  as a label, 6
  marginalization of, 20
  mindfulness and, 128
  need for a manifesto, 7
  open-minded enquiry in, 149
  and Positive Psychology, 17–22
  as quasi-belief system, 78
  as reciprocal learning, 154
  resemblance to Jungian psychology, xiii
  revisioning community, 129
  role of 'ideology critique', 170
  schools within, 145
  secular vs transpersonal in, 78
  spirituality and, xiii
  strengths/successes of, 120–1, 145–6, 169, 177
  theory of human nature, 139
  as 'third force', xv, xxii, 11, 19, 47–9 *passim*, 131, 137–46 *passim*, 169
  and third-wave humanism, 156–7
  trauma and, xii, 23–8
  up-to-date texts on, 119, 121–2
  urgent need for, 174
  use of our theory, 133
  values of (Sutich), 139
  visibility problem of, xv
  weaknesses of, 3, 119–21 *passim*
  working with parents/families, 133
  see also American Association for Humanistic Psychology, Association for Humanistic Psychology, humanism, *Humanistic Psychologist*, humanistic therapy, *Journal of Humanistic Psychology*, *Self & Society*, 'third force', UK Association for Humanistic Psychology Practitioners
Humanistic Psychology: A Clinical Manifesto (Elkins), 12, 87
Humanistic Psychology Institute (San Francisco), 11, 12, 145
humanistic therapy, xxii, 77–85 *passim*, 137
  aims of, 139
  autonomous status of, 112
  bridges to other modalities, 112–13
  clinical improvements in, 114–15
  differences between schools of, 114
  distrust of theory in, 113

humanizing role of, 145
inclusiveness/wooliness of, 114
Integrative Humanistic Psychotherapy, 47, 59
leaning forward/back and, 115
learning more restraint, 113
over-involvement with clients in, 113
PTSD and, 26–8
reliance on charisma in, 113
theoretical improvements, 115–16
theory in, 115
see also Humanistic Psychology
Humanistic Vision (Wilkinson), 79–83 *passim*
humanistic voice (O'Hara), 177
humanistic–transhumanistic separation, 158–9
humanities impulse, 86–92
humility, 135
humour: humanism and, 83–4
Huxley, Aldous, 102

I

IAPT: *see* Increasing Access to Psychological Therapies
'ideology critique', 170
imagery, 125, 128–9
Imagework (Glouberman), 125
imagination, xii
Increasing Access to Psychological Therapies (IAPT), 123
Independent Practitioners Network (UK), 174
individualism, 155
  excess of, 164
  growth of, 94
  vs individuation, 149
individuation, 149
Institute of Biodynamic Psychology (London), 154
Institute of Psychosynthesis, 50
integral psychology (Wilber), 159
integration, xi, xix, 114
  Integrative Humanistic Psychotherapy, 47, 59
  'integrative' identity, 43
  the integrative question, 43–9, 56–7
  meaning of, 47
  movement towards, 112
Integrity group (HIPS, UKCP), 52
intentionality, 142
internal supervisor, 115

intersubjectivity, xi
IPN: *see* Independent Practitioners Network
irony: humanism and, 83

J

Jackins, H., 4
James, William, 74
Janov, Arthur, xvi, xvii, 4, 6
Jesus, 149n
Joines, V., 116
Jones, Maxwell, 126, 127
Journal of Existential Analysis, 98
Journal of Humanistic Psychology, 98, 138, 146
Joy of Burnout, The (Glouberman), 126
Jung, C.G., xiii, 10, 154
Jungian psychology
  active imagination, 128
  resemblance to Humanistic Psychology, xiii
Junkanoo (Bahamian festival), 14

K

Kafka, Franz, 104
Kalisch, David, xv–xxiv, **169–74**, 182
Katie, Byron, 108
Kimble, G., 17
Kirsch, Irving, x
Klein, Melanie, 82
knowledge: nature of, 34
  see also epistemology, not-knowing
Krippner, Stanley, xx, 12, **23–8**, 183
Kris, Ernst, 10
Krishnamurti, Jiddu, 4, 6
Krishnamurti, U.G., 6

L

Laing, R.D. (Ronnie), xvi, 102
Lajoie, D.H., 158
language
  as meaning making, 34
  role in acculturation, 34–5
Laws of Manifestation (Spangler), 128
Lawton, Derek, xxi, **43–61**, 183
learning: reciprocal, in Humanistic Psychology, 154
  see also social learning
Leavis, F.R., 78
Lennon, John, xvi
  shooting of, xvii
Levinas, E., 33

Index

Linden, Roger, 108
Lock, A., 34
Loewenthal, D., 123
loss of reverence, 177
Love Song of J. Alfred Prufrock, The (Eliot), 83
Lowen, Alexander, 101
Loye, D., 11
Luther, Martin, 81
Lyotard, J.-F., 173

M
Maharishi, Ramana, 108
Maidman, Jennifer, xv–xxiv, 169–74, 183
Maltz, Maxwell, 102
Maps of Meaning (Peterson), 103
Marcuse, Herbert, xvi
Marx, Karl, 35
    absence of, 33
Maslow, Abraham, 11, 78, 87, 98, 99, 115, 138, 141, 156–7, 177
    late turn to the spiritual, 157–8
    self-actualizing creativity, 9, 10
Master and His Emissary (The): The Divided Brain and the Making of the Western World (McGilchrist), 152–3
May, Rollo, 10, 11, 98, 177
McGilchrist, Iain, 152–3, 173
McLeod, J., 122
McMahon, E., 164
MDMA, 25n
meaning, 140
    co-constructed nature of, 34
    -making, 34
    meaningfulness, 9
    systems, 88, 91
    trauma and, 23
medical model, 86, 90
meditation, 6
Mendelowitz, E., 12–13
Merleau-Ponty, M., 33, 127
methodology
    dialectical, 35
    qualitative and quantitative, 19
    randomized controlled trials, x
methodolotry, 19
Microloan, 151n
Milroy, Vivian, 131
Mindell, Amy, 116
mindfulness, xix, 4, 95, 128
    see also acceptance and commitment therapy, Buddhism, Buddhist psychology

Mines, Stephanie, 107
mirror neurons, 132
Mitchell, Stephen, xi
mixed-methods research, 19
Moats, M., 14
modernism:
    assumptions of humanism, 88, 89
    fractured consensus of, 178
    modernist bureaucracies, 178
    tension with postmodernism, 171
    see also modernity, postmodernism
modernity: antidote, to, 177, 178
    see also modernism
Monk-Steel, J., 53–4
morality: and tragedy, 82
Moreno, Jacob, 135
Morgan, G., 143
Mowbray, Richard, 170, 171
Murray, Henry, 11
mystery of the other (Hall), 153

N
Naikan (Japanese therapy), 96
narcissistic excess, 177
narrative therapy, 88
Nash, Seamus, xxi, 43–61, 183
National Health Service (UK), x, 66, 113
National Institute for Health and Care Excellence (NICE), x, 99, 123
    guidelines, 66
Neimeyer, R.A., 37
neurobiology, 20
neuro-linguistic programming, 128
neuroscience, 73
    integration with Humanistic Psychology, 132
Newman, Fred, 29–30
NHS: *see* National Health Service (UK)
NICE: *see* National Institute for Health and Care Excellence
Nietzsche, Friedrich, 81–2
NLP: *see* neuro-linguistic programming
non-duality, 105, 108, 159, 165
non-human world, xiii
Norcross, J.C., 47–8
Nostromo (Conrad), 79–82
not-knowing, 67
    art of, 66

O
Obama, Barack, xviii
objectivity: presuming, in psychology, 34
occupational standards, 45

National (2010), 49
Professional Occupational Standards for Psychotherapists (UKCP), 49
O'Hara, Maureen, 177–8, 184
O'Keeffe, Jac, 108
Old Saybrook, CT conference (1964), 11, 138
ontological holism (Heron), 166
optimism, 113
Ordinary Ecstasy (Rowan), 121
originality, 9
other-centred therapy (Brazier), xxi, 95–7
outcomes-based approaches, 77
over-involvement with clients, 113

P
paradigm war(s), xxi, 17, 67
Parker, Ian, 33
participatory worldview, 165–6, 167
pathologization of the ordinary, x
pathology-based model, xvi, 152
patriarchy: damage of, 5
peer-to-peer relations, 167
Pelagius, 81
perennial philosophy, 100
performance activism, 29
performance and play, 36
  development through, 29
  see also play
Performing the World conferences, 30
Perls, Fritz, 78, 80, 101, 125, 126, 128, 129, 177
person-centred therapy/approach, 6–7, 48–9, 57, 62–9 *passim*, 116, 119n
  epistemology of, 143–4
  see also British Association for the Person-Centred Approach, Rogers (Carl)
Peterson, Jordan B., 103
phenomenological/hermeneutic psychology, 33, 172
philosophy, 152
  branches of, 142
  confusion with method, 144
Pinker, Steven, 6
Pitchford, Daniel B., xx, **23–8,** 184
placebo, x
planetary future, 108
play
  capacity to, 36
  Vygotsky on, 36
  see also performance and play

pluralism, xi
  epistemological/methodological, 20
  humanistic alignment with, 122–3
  Samuels on, 173
  see also diversity
poetic shaping of experience, 78–9
Politics of Experience and The Bird of Paradise, The (Laing), xvi
Positive Psychology, 4
  Humanistic Psychology and, 17–22
  rigidity of, 19
positive/negative balance, 18
Postle, Denis, 174
postmodern turn, 31
postmodernism, 5, 88
  activity (theory) and, 35–6, 38
  humanism and, 89
  tension with modernity, 171
  see also postmodern turn
'post-professional' perspective, 67
post-traumatic growth, xii
post-traumatic stress disorder, 23–8 *passim*
potential, 177
  realization of, 178
  see also human potential movement
presence: embodied, xix
present moment, the (Stern), xix, 77, 128
Prilleltensky, Isaac, 31, 33
Primal Scream, The (Janov), xvi
primal therapy, 4
principled non-compliance, 50
Pritzker, Steven, xx, 12, **8–16,** 184
Problem with the Humanistic Therapies, The (Totton), 111, 120
process: vs product in psychology, 36, 104
Professional Liaison Group, 44–5
Professional Occupational Standards for Psychotherapists (UKCP), 49
Professional Standards Authority (PSA), 56
professionalization (of therapy), 57–8, 62
  Jungians and the, xiii
  as misplaced ego energy, 150
  'post-professional' perspective, 67
  Rogers on, xvi
  see also statutory regulation
projection, 141
PSA: *see* Professional Standards Authority
psychiatry, 152
psychoanalysis, 73, 83, 138, 140–4 *passim*
  anti-psychoanalytic dogmatism, 78
  comparison with humanistic tradition, 141

Index

as 'first force', 136
relational, xi
Psycho-Cybernetics (Maltz), 102
'Psychodrama of death' (Weiner), 126
psychologization of society, 94
psychology, 30–1, 93–4
  academic, 3
  activist (Holzman), 29–42
  alienation in mainstream, 36
  Biodynamic, 154
  coalition of branches of, 131
  creativity and, 10
  dehumanizing, 169
  existential-integrative (Schneider), 12
  forces of, 142
  as a hard science, 18
  isolated individual in, 38
  'for the peace table' (Maslow), 177
  phenomenological/hermeneutic, 33
  as philosophically based, 73
  postmodern, 34
  presumption of objectivity/truth, 34
  process vs product in, 36
  scientific, 33
  whole-person, 127
  see also activist psychology, awe-based psychology, Buddhist psychology, critical psychology, ecopsychology, existential psychology, Holistic Psychology, Humanistic Psychology, integral psychology, Jungian psychology, Positive Psychology, psychology of becoming, transpersonal psychology
'Psychology constructs the female' (Weisstein), 32
Psychology of Women division (APA), 32
psychosomatic holism (Heron), 166
psychotherapy: *see* counselling and psychotherapy
PsyCommons, The (Postle), 174
PTSD: *see* post-traumatic stress disorder

Q

qualitative (research) approaches, 88
  elevation of, 19
quantitative (research) approaches, 19

R

'radical honesty' (Blanton), 6
randomized controlled trials (RCTs), x, 99
Rank, Otto, 140
Rational Emotive Behaviour Therapy (REBT), 119
rationalization: pull to, 151
RCTs: *see* randomized controlled trials
realism, 153
  capitalist-, 5
Reality Game, The (Rowan), 108, 121
reciprocal learning, 154
reductionism, 149, 153
  bio-, 177
re-evaluation co-counselling, 4
regulation
  as an alien idea, 150, 154–5
  of counselling/psychotherapy, 117
  see also Mowbray (Richard), statutory regulation
Reich, W., 6
  theory of character, 113
relational approach, 99
  see also relational psychoanalysis
relational creativity, 13
relational depth, 114
relational psychoanalysis, xi, 115
Ren, Z., 13
Renaissance humanism, 156, 163
research: challenge to methods of, 177
  see also co-operative enquiry, human action research, methodology, mixed-methods research, qualitative (research) approaches, quantitative (research) approaches, randomized controlled trials
responsibility-taking, 150
revolutionary practice, 35
Richards, Ruth, xx, **8–16**, 184
Ricoeur, P., 33
Rieff, Philip, xviii
Robbins, Brent, 20
Rogers, Andy, xxi, **62–9**, 185
Rogers, Carl, xv–xvi, xxi, 11, 49, 57, 58, 78, 80, 87, 140, 141, 145
  in 2013, 62–9
  on 'certified charlatans', 58, 67
  core conditions of, xix
  and fourth-wave humanism, 160, 164
  on the fully functioning person, 96
  and/on humanism, 157–8
  late turn to the spiritual, 157–8
  theory for, 64
  see also core conditions, person-centred therapy

196

Index

Rogers, Natalie, xii, 12
Rolf, Ida, 101
Rosie the Riveter (film), 94n
Rowan, John, x, xvi, xxi, **98–100**, 104, 108, 121, 137, 140, 141, 169, 171, 172, 185
Ryle, Gilbert, 48

S

sacralization, 163
Samuels, Andrew, **ix–xiv**, 50–2 *passim*, 54, 173, 185
Sanders, Pete, 116
Sandler, Joe, 126
Sartre, Jean-Paul, xvi
Saybrook (University), 11, 12
    see also Old Saybrook, CT conference
Schelling, S.W.J., 164
Schneider, Kirk, xxi, 12, **73–6**, 185
schools: *see* education/schools
Schutz, Will, 101
scientific method: antipathy to, 105
scientism, 19
script theory (Steiner), 113
self, 88
    as a defence structure, 95
    of traditional humanism, 89
Self & Society journal, 11, 104–5, 127, 145, 146
    early days of, 131, 132
self-actualization (Maslow), xii, 11, 99, 156–7
    and consumerism, xvii
    see also actualizing tendency, self-actualizing creativity
self-actualizing creativity (Maslow), 9, 10
self-discovery: therapy as, xv
Seligman, M., 18
separate 'I', 108
sexual behaviour, xii
Shapiro, S.I., 158
shock, 107
Shohet, Robin, xxii, **107–8**, 185–6
Skills for Health initiative (UK), 43–9 *passim*
    Expert Reference Group, 49
Skolimowski, H., 163
Skyros (Holidays), 126, 126n, 127, 129
Snow, C.P., 17
sobornost (Berdyaev), 165
social constructionism, 34
social learning, 133

social science: nature of, 143
'social spirituality' (Samuels), xiii
social therapy, 31, 37, 39
Social Therapy Group (NYC), 30
sociality: performing, 37–40 *passim*
Society for the Psychological Study of Ethnic Minority Issues (APA), 32
Society for the Psychological Study of Lesbian and Gay Issues (APA, 1985), 32
Society for the Psychological Study of Lesbian, Gay, Bisexual and Transgender Issues (APA), 32
solution-focused therapy, 88
Sonoma State College, 145
Spangler, David, 128
Spinelli, Ernesto, 99
spiritual crises, 25
spiritual energy, 150
spirituality, xiii, xxiii, 99–100, 152, 156–67 *passim*
    differences on, 169
    late turn to, 157–8
    'social' (Samuels), xiii
    unease with, 132
    see also transpersonal (approach)
'state therapy' (Samuels), x
'status quo theory' (Harvey), 170
statutory regulation, 43–9
    scandalous scrabble for, 62
    see also professionalization of therapy
Staunton, Tree, 54
STEM disciplines, 18, 19
Stern, Dan, xix
Stewart, I., 116
Stonewall riots (NYC, 1969), 32
Strategy Reference Group, 47
Strong, T., 34
'substrate': corrupted term, 74
Sullivan, Harry Stack, 134
supervision, 114–15
    internal supervisor, 115
Sutich, A.J., 136, 139
Szasz, Thomas, xvi

T

TA: *see* transactional analysis
technological fix: belief in a, 178
Temenos training, 144
theory
    for Carl Rogers, 64, 116
    distrust of, 113

as 'dogma of truth', 63
and Gestalt therapy, 116
in humanistic therapy, 115
putting aside of (Jung), 154
'status quo theory' (Harvey), 170
and TA, 116
theory-mindedness, 65
uses of, 113
therapeutic change: conditions for, 116
therapeutic relationship, xi, 87, 89, 139
therapy: *see* counselling and psychotherapy
therapy culture: influences of, 94
Thich Nhat Hanh, 128
'thingification', 36
'third force', xv, xxii, 11, 19, 47–9 *passim*, 131, 169
as a category error, 137–46 *passim*
Thorne, Brian, xiii
Tolle, Eckhart, 6, 108
Torbert, W.R., 161
Totton, Nick, xxii, **111–18**, 120, 121, 122, 170, 173, 186
tragedy, 77–85 *passim*
morality and, 82
tragic dimension, xxi
training
courses, 145
excessive amount of, 151
left-brain preoccupied, 153
-therapy, 144
transactional analysis (TA), 4, 114, 140
Institute of, 144
theory and, 116
transference, 113
transpersonal (approach), 99
Association of Transpersonal Psychology, 157
increased interest in, 98
Journal of Transpersonal Psychology, 158
psychotherapy, 140
see also transpersonal psychology
transpersonal psychology, xiii
definitional themes in, 158
transcendental focus in, 158
Traue, J.E., 140
trauma
epidemic of, 25–7
Humanistic Psychology and, 23–8
see also birth trauma, post-traumatic stress disorder
Trilling, Lionel, 82
Triumph of the Therapeutic, The (Rieff), xviii

Trust, Assurance and Safety (2007), 44
truth, 88
vs activity, 37
illusion of 'having' the, 153
presumption of, in psychology, 3
theory as dogma of, 63
Tudor, Keith, xxii, **136–48**, 169, 170, 186
'turf wars', 137

U

UK Association for Humanistic Psychology Practitioners (AHPP), 43, 50, 56, 137
UKCP: *see* United Kingdom Council for Psychotherapy
unconditional positive regard, xi
United Kingdom Council for Psychotherapy (UKCP), 43–59 *passim*, 137
Chair election, 2009, 50–2
college elections, 53–6
colleges of the, 52–6
Constitution (2009), 52–3
transpersonal psychotheray sub-section, 98
see also HIPS section
universalism: excess of, 164
university-style development school ('UX'), NYC, 30
Upanishads (The), 108
US military, 25–6
UX: *see* university-style development school

V

Varieties of Religious Experience, The (James), 74
Victim Archetype (Hall), 149, 150
violence: decline of, 6
visualization: creative, 129
Vygotskian theory, 31
tool-and-result, 35–6
Vygotsky, Lev, 34–6 *passim*,
see also Vygotskian theory

W

Wampold, B.E., 12, 90
We Are All in Shock (Mines), 107
Weiner, Hannah, 126
Weisstein, N., 32

Weisz, Janet, 54
West Georgia College, 145
What We May Be (Ferrucci), 102
What's Wrong with Us? (Feltham), 4
Whitton, Eric, 114, 121
Wilber, Ken, 5, 99
 integral psychology of, 159
Wilkinson, Heward, xxi, 54, **77–85**, 186
working/therapeutic alliance, xi, 141
Wundt, Wilhelm, 73

Z
Zerzan, John, 5

Self & Society

An International Journal for Humanistic Psychology

Only £40 standard annual subscription

Self & Society, the quarterly journal of the Association for Humanistic Psychology in Britain, is now in its 41st year of continuous publication, offering a vibrant and leading-edge vista into the world of Humanistic Psychology and the associated psychological therapies, and featuring leading humanistic writers from across the globe.

Edited by Richard House, David Kalisch and Jennifer Maidman (the editors of this book), the journal was recently re-designed to mark its 40th birthday year. Regular features include, peer-reviewed papers, general and 'opinion' articles, regular series on 'The Roots and History of Humanistic Psychology' and 'The Future of Humanistic Psychology', and an Ethical Dilemmas section, penetrating book reviews (including a regular 'Retro review' of a humanistic classic), letters, a topical 'news interchange' section, and poetry.

Recent theme issues have looked at Critical Psychiatry and Ecotherapy, and themes for future planned issues include 'Carl Rogers 40 Years On', Merleau-Ponty, and Ecopsychology.

At **just £40** standard annual subscription rate for four packed 84-page issues, *Self & Society* is arguably by far the best-value English-language psychology and therapy publication on the market today.

Subscription inquiries to: the AHP Administrator, Beverley Crouch, at admin@ahpb.org, or AHPB, BM Box 3582, London WC1N 3XX, UK

www.ahpb.org

AHP *new vistas*